AF905075

Oxford Studies in Private Law Theory: Volume 1

OXFORD STUDIES IN PRIVATE LAW THEORY

Oxford Studies in Private Law Theory is a biennial forum for some of the best new work in private law theory by scholars from around the world. The essays range widely over issues in general private law theory as well as specific fields, including the theoretical analysis of tort law, property law, contract law, fiduciary law, trust law, remedies and restitution, and the law of equity. OSPLT will be essential reading for academic lawyers, philosophers, political scientists, economists, and historians who wish to keep up with the latest developments in the flourishing field of private law theory.

Editors

Paul B. Miller, University of Notre Dame

John Oberdiek, Rutgers University

Advisory Board

Lisa Austin, University of Toronto

Molly Brady, Harvard University

Hanoch Dagan, Tel Aviv University

John Goldberg, Harvard University

Matthew Harding, University of Melbourne

Irit Samet-Porat, King's College London

Seana Shiffrin, University of California, Los Angeles

Oxford Studies in Private Law Theory: Volume 1

Edited by
PAUL B. MILLER
University of Notre Dame

JOHN OBERDIEK
Rutgers University

OXFORD
UNIVERSITY PRESS

OXFORD
UNIVERSITY PRESS

Great Clarendon Street, Oxford, OX2 6DP,
United Kingdom

Oxford University Press is a department of the University of Oxford.
It furthers the University's objective of excellence in research, scholarship,
and education by publishing worldwide. Oxford is a registered trade mark of
Oxford University Press in the UK and in certain other countries

© The Several Contributors 2020

The moral rights of the authors have been asserted

First Edition published in 2020

Impression: 1

All rights reserved. No part of this publication may be reproduced, stored in
a retrieval system, or transmitted, in any form or by any means, without the
prior permission in writing of Oxford University Press, or as expressly permitted
by law, by licence or under terms agreed with the appropriate reprographics
rights organization. Enquiries concerning reproduction outside the scope of the
above should be sent to the Rights Department, Oxford University Press, at the
address above

You must not circulate this work in any other form
and you must impose this same condition on any acquirer

Crown copyright material is reproduced under Class Licence
Number C01P0000148 with the permission of OPSI
and the Queen's Printer for Scotland

Published in the United States of America by Oxford University Press
198 Madison Avenue, New York, NY 10016, United States of America

British Library Cataloguing in Publication Data

Data available

Library of Congress Control Number: 2020940066

ISBN 978–0–19–885135–6

DOI: 10.1093/oso/9780198851356.001.0001

Printed and bound by
CPI Group (UK) Ltd, Croydon, CR0 4YY

Links to third party websites are provided by Oxford in good faith and
for information only. Oxford disclaims any responsibility for the materials
contained in any third party website referenced in this work.

For my children, Serena and Kieran, with endless love and pride.
—PBM

For Sophie, Lucas, and Greta.
—JO

Acknowledgments

We gratefully acknowledge generous financial assistance provided to this volume and series by the Notre Dame Program on Private Law and Rutgers Institute for Law and Philosophy. We are appreciative of logistical and administrative support provided by Bridget Keating and Alicia Sachau. We are also grateful to Jamie Berezin and his team at Oxford University Press for their support of us and of this series. Papers collected in this volume were presented at a workshop hosted by the London Law Program at the University of Notre Dame's London Global Gateway in August 2019. The London Law Program Director, Prof. Michael Addo, lent us his inexhaustible stores of energy and goodwill. We remain ever grateful to him, as well.

Contents

About the Editors

Paul B. Miller is Professor, Associate Dean for International and Graduate Programs, and Director of the Notre Dame Program on Private Law at Notre Dame Law School. He is also a member of the Global Faculty at the Peking University Law School in Beijing. Miller previously held a permanent appointment at McGill University and has had visiting appointments at the University of Melbourne and Tel Aviv University. His books include *Philosophical Foundations of Fiduciary Law* (2014), *Contract, Status, and Fiduciary Law* (2016), *The Oxford Handbook of Fiduciary Law* (2019), and *Civil Wrongs and Justice in Private Law* (2020). With John Oberdiek, he also edits *Oxford Private Law Theory*, the book series within which the present set of volumes is published.

John Oberdiek is Distinguished Professor at Rutgers Law School and Co-Director of the Rutgers Institute for Law and Philosophy. He has been a Visiting Professor at the University of Graz, Austria, and a Laurance S. Rockefeller Visiting Fellow at the University Center for Human Values at Princeton University. In addition to authoring numerous articles in legal philosophy, he is the author of *Imposing Risk: A Normative Framework* (Oxford 2017), editor of *Philosophical Foundations of the Law of Torts* (Oxford 2014), co-editor with Paul Miller of *Civil Wrongs and Justice in Private Law* (Oxford 2020), and series co-editor with Paul Miller of *Oxford Private Law Theory*.

List of Contributors

Shyamkrishna Balganesh, Professor of Law, University of Pennsylvania

Mindy Chen-Wishart, Professor of the Law of Contract, Dean of the Faculty of Law, University of Oxford

Victoria Dixon, D.Phil. Candidate in Law, University of Oxford

Larissa Katz, Professor of Law and Canada Research Chair in Private Law Theory, University of Toronto

Leslie Kendrick, Vice Dean and David H. Ibbeken Professor of Law, University of Virginia

Ben McFarlane, Professor of English Law, University of Oxford and Fellow of St. John's College

Kenneth W. Simons, Chancellor's Professor of Law and Philosophy, University of California, Irvine

Andreas Televantos, Associate Professor of Law, University of Oxford and Hanbury Fellow and Tutor in Law, Lincoln College

Charlie Webb, Professor of Law, London School of Economics and Political Science

Katrina M. Wyman, Sarah Herring Sorin Professor of Law, New York University

1
Duties and Damages

Charlie Webb

I. Duty and Sanction

The common law is notoriously reluctant to make us do what it says we are duty bound to do. If I contract to sell you my shoes but refuse to hand them over, it's not likely that you will get a court to compel me to give them to you. If I take yours, the likelihood once more is that a court will not order that I give them back. Instead all a court will do is order that I pay you damages, aimed at making good the losses I have thereby caused you. Some think this reveals something important about the content of our duties. Though we may say that I owe a duty to perform my contracts and to refrain from interfering with your assets, what courts in fact do tells a different story. When it matters, a court will not make me perform my contracts or refrain from interfering with your assets but will only require me to compensate you for the losses I cause if I do not. And if this, in the end, is all I will be required to do, we would do better to recognize that the law leaves me free to break my promise and free to take your things, my duty, at most, to make good your losses.

This view of what duties we owe reflects a particular understanding of what it means to owe a duty in law. On this understanding, to owe a legal duty is to face a legal sanction and, if we want to know what duties I owe, we need to know what sanctions I will face. So the conclusion that I owe no duty to perform my contract follows from the fact that no court will order me to do this. If the law will not compel it, I am free not to do it. The most notable proponent of this view, or something like it, was Holmes.[1] Holmes' motivation was to keep a clear division between law and morality. One way to maintain such a divide was to show how law mattered even to those who cared nothing for morality. When I am making decisions, moral considerations carry only such weight as I give to them. If I choose to give them no weight at all, there is nothing stopping me. Not so with law. For law cannot simply be ignored or wished away,

[1] Oliver Wendell Holmes, "The Path of the Law" (1897) 10 Harv. LR 457.

Charlie Webb, *Duties and Damages* In: *Oxford Studies in Private Law Theory: Volume 1*. Edited by: Paul B. Miller and John Oberdiek, Oxford University Press (2020). © The Several Contributors. DOI: 10.1093/oso/9780198851356.003.0001

but will forcibly intrude into our lives. If the law is going to take my liberty or possessions if I act in a given way, that is a reality to which I cannot but attend when deciding what action to take. And so, when the law says that I owe a duty to φ, the one unavoidable, undeniable reality of this duty is the sanction which I will face if I do not.

This view proposes not so much a revision of the idea of a legal duty as its rejection.[2] When the law recognizes a duty, it is not simply foreshadowing the imposition of some penalty or other coercive measure on those who fail so to act; it is telling us that this is something we must do, marking out the relevant conduct as non-optional. So the intended message of the "no parking" sign across the road is not "parking here will cost you," let alone "you can park here but you'll have to pay for it," but "don't park here." If I choose to park and to pay the fine, I have not cut through to the law's true, bottom-line message; I have ignored it. Now, given that some will not heed this message, and given that the law's objective in imposing duties is ordinarily to prompt us to do as the duty directs, sanctions serve a useful purpose. The law wants me not to park here; indeed in making this obligatory, it is saying not just that I should choose not to park here but that the option of parking here is not open to me, so that there is, in a sense, no choice to be made. If, nonetheless, I remain open to the idea, the law's threat to visit unwanted consequences on me is there to motivate me to choose differently. But, as this brings out, while sanctions are often necessary and often decisive, they remain a secondary means of the law securing conformity, practically significant only for those who do not accept, or are insufficiently motivated to act on, the obligation the law identifies.[3]

To think our duties are determined by the sanction the law imposes is to assume the law's only language is coercion. But while this may be all some people hear, it is not the only language the law speaks. There are no doubt some who take nothing from the "no parking" sign save that they will have to pay some money if they do, who more broadly see the law's penalties as simply prices. But this perspective offers not a clearer, sharper view of the law but one which is radically incomplete. What makes it incomplete is precisely its failure to account for the way the law purports to bind us, which is to say, its failure to accommodate, or even make sense of, the idea of a legal duty. So the proper implication of the approach Holmes proposed is not that my contractual duty is disjunctive—to perform *or* to pay damages—or conditional—to pay damages

[2] See too H. L. A. Hart, *The Concept of Law* (3rd ed., OUP 2012) 38–42, 82–91, John Finnis, *Natural Law and Natural Rights* (2nd ed., OUP 2011) 320–30.

[3] See too Leslie Green, "Introduction" in Hart (n 2) xxx: "Sanctions are the law's Plan B."

if I do not perform—but that I owe no duty (as the law understands it) at all. True, a court will order me to pay damages if I do not perform. But so what? If I have the option of breaking my contract, do I not also have the option of not paying?[4] Of course, the law says I must pay, but then it also said I must perform. If I do not pay, the court will order my employer to deduct the sum I owe from my wages or authorize a bailiff to seize and sell such of my assets as needed to generate that sum. But as all this happens, I just stand by. In this race to the bottom, duty is redundant, the only reality to law is the brute application of state power.

II. Actionability, Enforceability

So Holmes' account tells us nothing at all about legal duties. Now, the understanding of, for instance, contractual duties attributed to Holmes—that my duty is not to perform but only to pay damages—may yet be true. But if it is true, it is not by virtue of the sanctions attached to those who do not perform. Rather we need to look to what the law tells me I must do: does it tell me that I must do as I undertook (with damages then payable as the sanction for breach) or does it tell me that I am at liberty not to, so long as I compensate you for any losses I thereby cause? This is a distinction we just cannot see if we look only to sanctions. In answering this question, it is significant that the law, through the language and reasoning of legal officials and the broader structure of legal doctrine, presents performance of one's contractual undertakings not as an option but as a duty, with failure to perform a breach of duty and damages its remedy.

Still, one might ask, if it is true that the law sees performance of contractual undertakings as not optional but obligatory, why is it so rarely prepared to take action to see that this happens? No doubt, there is often nothing that can now be done to secure performance. A court cannot compel timely performance when it is already late, some defects and harms cannot be undone. But even when performance remains possible and desired by the recipient, courts will typically limit a claimant to damages. Does this not undermine the suggestion that the law does indeed recognize a duty to perform? No, or at least not without more. The message "you must φ, but we won't make you" is not equivocal. On the question of whether φ-ing is obligatory or optional, it is clear: it is obligatory. Nonetheless, while rejecting Holmes' view that our legal duties

[4] See too Finnis (n 2) 324.

are to be found in the sanctions the law attaches to us, we might yet think that these duties and sanctions should, where possible, match up. If the law's position is that I must φ, then it should, at least all else equal, follow that through by taking what action it can to see that I φ. So, for many, the law's failure to back up its duties with corresponding sanctions involves if not a contradiction then a sort of inconsistency: the law saying one thing and doing another. And, on this basis, we can see how the law's failure to compel performance of its duties might be thought to call into question whether it really means what it says.

This view is not wholly wrong but it is too quick. To see why we need to recognize that our duties and the sanctions which attach to their breach answer different questions. What I should do (or what the law should tell me that I should do) is not the same question as what a court should compel me to do and we should not think that these different questions should receive the same answer. So for contracting parties the question is "must I do as I promised?" For judges charged with resolving claims for breach of contract, however, the question is "should I, as a state official and backed by its coercive machinery, now compel that defendant to perform?" There will sometimes be good reason for the state to tell us to do things which it would be unreasonable for it to compel us to do, and so it may be reasonable for the law to tell us we must perform our contracts even where it would not be reasonable to enforce that duty by compelling performance.[5] To put the point the other way around: that it would, for example, be oppressive and costly to compel me to perform my employment contract are not reasons for the law to tell me that turning up for work is optional.

It is a mistake to think that our legal duties extend only so far as what the law compels. But, as we can now see, it is no less a mistake to think that the law should compel us to do whatever it says is our legal duty. Often, by the time the opportunity for the law to apply a sanction arises, circumstances have changed and performance of the original duty is not possible or, though possible, it may no longer be desirable or indeed reasonable. And where the defendant's performance of that duty remains possible and reasonable, it may yet be unreasonable for the law to compel that performance. Indeed there are occasions where the proper response for the law to a breach of duty is to take no action whatsoever. Some breaches of duty are inconsequential. In such cases, there may be no need for the law to intervene, nothing for it to do if it did. The common law

[5] See too Stephen A. Smith, "The Law of Damages: Rules for Citizens or Rules for Courts?" in Ralph Cunnington and Djakhongir Saidov (eds.), *Contract Damages: Domestic and International Perspectives* (Hart Publishing 2008).

sometimes resists this conclusion, preferring to allow a claim but to award only nominal damages, thereby giving some token expression to the wrong that has been done. But it is not the award of nominal damages which makes the conduct wrongful and where the law holds wrongs to be actionable only on proof of loss or some other consequence, it is not thereby saying that there was no wrong, no breach of duty unless loss results. Just as there is nothing contradictory or equivocal in the law saying "you must φ, but we won't make you," so there need be nothing contradictory, equivocal, or even inconsistent in it saying "you were wrong (i.e. in breach of duty) not to φ, but no action now lies against you."

A good example of courts saying just this comes in cases of harmless negligence. The tort of negligence imposes duties of care, duties breached where reasonable care is not taken. Unless, however, the breach of duty leads to recognized injury, no claim arises. This rule of actionability is taken by some to reflect back on the content of the duty: the fact that liability arises only if and when injury occurs shows my duty is not to take care; rather it is a duty not to injure carelessly—a duty of non-injury rather than non-injuriousness—breached only if and when my carelessness results in your injury.[6] But there is, to repeat, no reason at all to think that the fact the law provides no claim suggests, let alone entails, that there was in truth no breach of duty. Indeed the law's position here—that there has been a breach of duty, but no claim lies—is not only clear but readily explicable. There is good reason for the law to tell me to take care when, say, driving: it is bad if people get hurt, driving is dangerous, I am more likely to hurt someone if I do not take care. Now, sometimes my careless driving will do harm, sometimes it will not. If it does, besides any penalty I may face, it is right that the law should provide my victim with a means of obtaining compensation from me. But what if no harm results? While it may still be reasonable to penalize me, there is no harm to undo or loss to make good. The law reasonably concludes, therefore, that no claim lies: my careless driving cannot itself be undone, there are no consequences to that carelessness which the law might demand I correct or offset.

[6] See, e.g., Donal Nolan, "Deconstructing the Duty of Care" (2013) 129 LQR 559, 561–62; James Plunkett, *The Duty of Care in Negligence* (Hart Publishing 2018) 94–95; cf. John Gardner, "Obligations and Outcomes in the Law of Torts" in Peter Cane and John Gardner (eds.), *Relating to Responsibility: Essays in Honour of Tony Honoré on his 80th Birthday* (Hart Publishing 2001) 122; Arthur Ripstein and Benjamin C. Zipursky, "Corrective Justice in an Age of Mass Torts" in Gerald J. Postema (ed.), *Philosophy and the Law of Torts* (CUP 2001) 218–21; John C. P. Goldberg and Benjamin C. Zipursky, "Unrealized Torts" (2002) 88 Virginia LR 1625, 1652; Robert Stevens, "Rights and Other Things" in Donal Nolan and Andrew Robertson (eds.), *Rights and Private Law* (Hart Publishing 2011) 118.

The argument that duties of care are duties of non-injury sometimes channels a deeper misunderstanding. Thus far I have talked about breaches of duty without further qualification. But, as some are keen to stress, the duties private law deals in are specifically relational duties. My duties not to stamp on your toes or to trespass on your land are duties I owe to you. Accordingly, if I do these things, I do not just commit a wrong; I wrong you. These duties I owe to you correspond to rights you have against me and my breach of such a duty is simultaneously a violation of your rights. This may appear to tell against the view that duties of care are duties of non-injuriousness. For, so the argument goes, while there is no doubt a violation of your rights when my carelessness injures you, what right of yours is violated when I merely put you at risk? Do we have, in addition to our rights to our person and our property, a right not to be subjected to unreasonable risks? And, if we do, must we also then say that, when my carelessness does cause you injury, I commit not one wrong but two: one when I expose you to the risk of injury, another when that risk materializes? This looks a lot like double counting.

The trouble here comes from an indiscriminate use of the language of rights.[7] Sometimes rights describe a sort of practical conclusion, identifying how others must act in their dealings with us. It is when understood in this way that rights correlate with and are equivalent to duties.[8] Our contract puts me under a duty to you to hand over the shoes and this duty corresponds to a right you have that I hand them over. "I owe you a duty to φ" and "you have a right that I φ" are just different ways of saying the same thing. Accordingly, if I owe you a duty of care when driving, you necessarily have a right that I drive carefully. The right does not help us make the case for or against me owing that duty; it just gives us an alternative way of asking the question and expressing our conclusion. At other times, however, we see rights used to capture a different idea. Here rights do not provide an alternative expression of the duties we owe each other, rather they identify a reason we might owe these duties, telling us not, or not just, what duties we owe but why we owe them. So, on one popular view, for you to have a right is for some aspect of your well-being, some interest of yours, to be sufficiently important that its protection or advancement justifies imposing duties on others.[9] Call these respectively rights_1 and rights_2.

We can see why some doubt that we have rights_2 not to be subjected to unreasonable risks. Someone who simply endangers me does not appear to set

[7] See further Charlie Webb, "Three Concepts of Rights, Two of Property" (2018) 38 OJLS 246.
[8] See, e.g., Wesley Newcomb Hohfeld, *Fundamental Legal Conceptions as Applied in Judicial Reasoning* (Walter Wheeler Cook (ed.), YUP 1919) 39.
[9] See, e.g., Joseph Raz, *The Morality of Freedom* (OUP 1986) 180.

back any interest of mine, does not compromise my well-being. Risk matters only because harm matters, an unrealized risk is a harm to no-one. If this is correct, we cannot justify duties of care on the basis that we have rights_2 not to be subjected to unreasonable risks.[10] But the truth is that they do not need this justification. For your interest in, and so your right_2 to, your bodily safety is more than enough to justify the conclusion that I must avoid acting in ways which unjustifiably threaten to injure you. Moreover, this duty to take care is a duty I owe *to you*, whatever view we take on what this means: the duty serves and is grounded in your interests; it is one you are empowered to waive or, where possible, enforce. Accordingly, the duty I owe you to take care, say when driving, corresponds to a right_1 of yours that I drive carefully. In short, you do not need to have a right_2 not to be exposed to unreasonable risks to have a right_1 that I not expose you to unreasonable risks (e.g., when driving); your right_2 to your bodily safety is itself sufficient to ground this right_1 and my corresponding duty of care.

As this brings out, we need to take care when thinking about the law of torts, and private law more generally, in terms of rights. Take the following three propositions:

1. The duties recognized in the law of torts are enforced by claimants bringing private actions, seeking private remedies, against defaulting defendants.
2. These private duties and rights of action advance or protect important interests of these claimants.
3. There can be no breach of such a duty, no such wrong, unless and until some interest of the claimant's is affected or set back.

These three propositions are not equivalent, nor do they follow from one another. 1 can be true without 2 or 3 also being true. 1 and 2 can, as we have seen, be true without 3. But framing them each in terms of "rights" invites their elision or at least suggests, wrongly, that they come as a package deal: torts are breaches of duties owed to others, as is evident from the basic form of tort litigation, *therefore* torts are rights-violations (since a breach of duty just is the violation of a right), *therefore* there can be no tort unless and until some right of the claimant's is violated and injury is caused. The consequence is that "rights-based" accounts of private law often move far too quickly from accurate

[10] Is it correct? For an argument that it is not, see John Oberdiek, *Imposing Risk: A Normative Framework* (OUP 2017) 93–130.

observation of the form and structure of private law actions to claims about private law's proper content. The truth, I think, is that the basic form of private law litigation places few, if any, constraints on the sorts of reasons (principles, policies) which might bear on the range of practical questions private law addresses and so on the content of the duties private law recognizes.[11]

III. Performance Damages

We have seen that for me to owe a legal duty to φ entails neither than the law will take further action to see that I φ nor that it should. The conclusion that I was in breach of duty is a determination of how I should have conducted myself at some earlier point in time. But the central practical question for a court charged with resolving a claim founded on that breach of duty is not what I should have done then but what it should do now. These questions may receive different answers either because circumstances have now changed, so that what was reasonable to expect of me then is not reasonable now, or because there are considerations which bear on the reasonableness of the court compelling me to φ which do not bear, or bear differently, on the reasonableness of me φ-ing.

Sometimes it is too late to see that I φ as φ-ing is no longer possible. Here, necessarily, any action the law takes must be directed toward achieving some other result. Even if it remains possible for me to φ, it may be that the passage of time and the changed circumstances in which we now find ourselves mean that the balance of reasons no longer supports this and so the law should not take action to see that I φ, even if it could do so cost-free. Say we contract for me to give you a lift to the airport tomorrow. You have a flight to catch, taking you to a friend's wedding overseas. (I may know this, I may not.) I don't show up. Should a court order me to take you to the airport at the next available opportunity? You have missed your flight and missed the wedding, you have no interest in going to the airport for any other reason. Whether this is because the reasons that supported my initial obligation to take you to the airport no longer apply or because other reasons—you no longer want that performance, indeed you would now be an unwilling party to its performance—override

[11] For a fuller argument to a similar conclusion, see John Gardner, "Backwards and Forwards with Tort Law" in Joseph Keim-Campbell, Michael O'Rourke, and David Shier (eds.), *Law and Social Justice* (MIT Press 2005).

those reasons, the upshot is that it would be unreasonable now for a court to order me to do this.

Even where it remains possible for me to φ and unreasonable for me not to, the law may still reasonably decline to take action to see that I do on account of the costs of taking such action. Here we see the standard reasons the courts give for refusing specific relief: compelling performance would be too great an infringement of the defendant's liberty, would be too costly to police, would invite further acrimony and litigation, and so on. In such instances, the courts are not saying that it is reasonable for me not to perform, only that it would be unreasonable for them to take further action to see that I provide that performance. On occasion, the denial of specific relief may be based on a blend of both sorts of consideration. I covenant with you not to build on the vacant plot of land I own adjoining yours. Nonetheless I do. By the time the case comes to court, the work is already complete; an apartment block sits on the once-vacant plot. It is not too late to return the land to its prior undeveloped state, the block could be demolished, performance of the covenant could, to this extent, still be secured. But doing this would mean the destruction of good housing at a time when housing is in short supply. The fact that I cannot now perform my covenant without significant social cost is a consideration which rightly bears on whether such performance should now be considered obligatory, even reasonable. (Some influential accounts of private law disagree. Their wilful blindness to the relevance of such considerations testifies to their inadequacy.) And, even if these costs are not sufficient to defeat any obligation to return my land to its prior state, such that this remains, all considered, what I really ought to do, we might still conclude that it would be unreasonable for a court now to take action to secure this, intervening to order that these homes be destroyed.[12]

Nonetheless, when it comes to deciding how the law should respond to breaches of duty, the law's determination that, on the balance of reasons at the time, I was under a duty to φ counts for something. Though what I should do will sometimes change by the time the law has the chance to respond, often it will not. The reasons which make it unreasonable for me to play my music loud late into the night do not diminish if I have now been doing this for weeks. It is unreasonable to drive my car onto your foot and it remains just as unreasonable to keep it there once I have. And while there are always costs involved in the law intervening, there are also benefits to be had, not just in securing my conformity with my duties but also in encouraging others' conformity with theirs. So, it is not surprising that, where the costs of compelling performance

[12] Cf. *Wrotham Park Estate Co. Ltd. v. Parkside Homes Ltd.* [1974] 1 WLR 798 (Ch.).

are low, and certainly no higher than any other meaningful remedy, the courts will tend to do so. We see this in their routine enforcement of duties to pay money, which do not raise the same concerns about supervision and forced labor which attend many other forms of specific relief.

It may be that the law is sometimes too cautious here, too ready to cede to worries about the costs of compelling performance, too slow to see its benefits. The common law's default approach outside duties to pay money is to consider specific relief only where damages would be inadequate, rather than to look beyond specific relief only where it would be too costly. Much depends on how good a substitute for specific relief damages provide. As typically formulated, the standard aim of damages is to put the claimant in as good a position as she would have occupied but for the breach. But this formulation is ambiguous.[13] One way to put a claimant in a position as good as had there been no breach is through compensation. Even if the specific injuries and disadvantages the claimant has incurred cannot or will not be reversed, they may yet be offset or counterbalanced by providing the claimant with alternative benefits—benefits distinct from and additional to those which the defendant's performance of her duty would have secured—which advance her interests, considered in the round, to the equivalent extent as the defendant's breach set them back. (This assumes the possibility of a sort of netting of our diverse interests.) So the pain and suffering my breach caused you cannot be undone, the assets I damaged cannot be repaired or replaced, but by paying you damages I provide you with funds which then enable you to purchase other items you value, satisfying other interests of yours. The upshot is that by adding such advantages to the disadvantages caused by the breach, you can be placed in a position which, though different, is no worse than the position you would have been in had I performed my duty.

But there is another, and in some ways more straightforward, way of putting the claimant in as good a position as she would have occupied but for the breach: namely to ensure that she obtains the very advantages which the defendant's performance of her duty would have given her. This is, of course, the effect of granting specific relief: my duty is to hand over the shoes and an order of specific performance sees that you get those shoes from me. But much the

[13] See further Charlie Webb, "Justifying Damages" in Jason W. Neyers, Richard Bronaugh, and Stephen G. A. Pitel (eds.), *Exploring Contract Law* (Hart Publishing 2009). The distinction, drawn there and here, between different ways a claimant can be put in as good a position as had the defendant performed her duty largely mirrors the distinction identified in Adam Slavny, "Negating and Counterbalancing: A Fundamental Distinction in the Concept of a Corrective Duty" (2014) 33 Law and Philosophy 143, though see n 32 and surrounding text for discussion of examples where negation of the claimant's harms is possible though performance of the defendant's primary duty is not.

same result can also, on occasion, be achieved through an award of damages. You contract to buy 1,000 widgets from me. The widgets I supply are defective. You sue. The remedy you will be awarded is damages assessed at the difference in market value between the widgets I supplied and those you contracted for. These damages may appear straightforwardly compensatory. I have not supplied you with the promised widgets, so the law orders me to pay you a sum of money which can apply to acquire other benefits which will offset the losses this has caused you. But the award can also be viewed in a different light. You still want the correct widgets. You can still get them by going back into the market and buying some from another supplier. The damages award is premised on you doing just this.[14] If you sell the defective widgets I supplied, you get some of the money you need to buy replacements; the damages ensure that the additional money you have to provide to make up the difference is recovered from me. In so doing the award covers the expenses you incurred as a result of my breach. But, more than that, it sees that, at the end of the day, you obtain—or would have obtained had you taken the steps the law expected you to take—the (or such) widgets as I undertook to supply and that it is me who funds this. The end result is not simply that I compensate you for the losses you suffer as a result of my breach, but that I supply you with some part of the performance you were, and remain, due.

Here these two functions of damages awards run together: an award aimed at compensating you for your losses, quantified by reference to the difference in value between the widgets you contracted for and those I in fact provided, also enables you to obtain the widgets you wanted from another source. But we get a clearer sense of the true distinctiveness and significance of damages aimed at securing partial performance where the two come apart. I contract to install a new kitchen in your home. You go away while I do the work. When you return you see that the units I have installed are not the color you had asked for. The cost of removing these units and putting in the right ones is substantial. The difference in market value between the two sets of units may well be nothing, however, and, while you have a preference for the color you chose, the difference in value to you—as reflected in how much less you would have paid for units I in fact installed—falls well short of the sum it would take to replace them.

My breach here, though it leaves you no poorer in balance-sheet terms, does indeed put you in a worse position than had I performed, your interest in

[14] This aspect of these awards is brought out in Andrew Dyson and Adam Kramer, "There is No 'Breach Date Rule': Mitigation, Difference in Value and Date of Assessment" (2014) 130 LQR 259.

having a kitchen which meets your esthetic preferences set back. But to compensate you for this loss, we need only to provide you with a sum of money which reflects this difference in the value you place on the kitchen as promised compared to the kitchen as delivered, a sum which then allows you to purchase other benefits, advancing other interests of yours, sufficient to offset the setback I have caused. Such an award would see that you are left in no worse/as good a position as had I performed. What it would not do is to provide you with the kitchen you contracted for. This end result remains possible, however, and, if the court is not prepared to compel me to do this work myself, it could still see that I put you in the position to get the kitchen you wanted by funding someone else to come in and complete the job. This is what a cost of cure damages award would achieve.

It is, therefore, a mistake to see cost of cure as, or as simply, one possible measure of or formula for calculating a claimant's losses and hence the compensation she is due. True, the award of cost of cure damages is premised not only on the claimant's continuing right to the defendant's performance but also on this money then being used to secure that performance. The effect of the award is therefore to cover the out-of-pocket expenses which the claimant has incurred or is expected to incur. But to see such awards as compensation for these expenses sets us off on the wrong foot. We can see this from the English cases.[15] Cost of cure damages are awarded only where the court concludes that this is the true measure of the losses suffered by the claimant.[16] This will be the case where the cost of cure is equal to or lower than the difference in value between the performance promised and the defective performance in fact provided. Where, however, the cost of cure exceeds the difference in value, it will be seen as the proper measure of the claimant's losses only where the court considers that it would be reasonable for the claimant to incur such costs. This is effectively an application of the mitigation principle: claimants are expected to take reasonable steps to mitigate their losses; if they do not, their damages will not extend to the losses they would have avoided if they had. By the same token, when determining whether a claimant who has yet to get the defective performance put right should recover as damages the sum it would take for her to do so, the court must consider whether incurring such costs would be reasonable. Accordingly, cost of cure damages will be refused where the court

[15] For a fuller version of the argument made in this section and further analysis of these cases, see Charlie Webb, "Performance Damages" in Graham Virgo and Sarah Worthington (eds.), *Commercial Remedies: Resolving Controversies* (CUP 2017).

[16] *Ruxley Electronics and Construction Ltd. v. Forsyth* [1996] AC 344 (HL).

considers that these costs are disproportionate to the benefits that would be derived from having this work done.

But the mitigation principle only kicks in if what you are seeking is compensation for your losses. When we are dealing with a claim for compensation, we are in the business of determining what losses you have suffered, or are likely to suffer, and who should bear them. Where there are losses which you could reasonably have avoided or could yet avoid, the law might reasonably conclude that they should be borne by you and not shifted onto me. But the case for awarding you cost of cure damages set out here is not premised on this being the proper measure of the losses you have suffered as a result of not receiving the performance you were promised. On the contrary, the award is designed to see that you obtain (the better part of) that performance. Here the question for the court is not who should bear what losses but whether I should be ordered to provide you with means to secure the performance you were, and are still, due. Your right to performance, and my duty to perform, is not conditional on this being the most cost-effective way I might advance your interests. That the cost to me of performing the contract exceeds the benefits you take from its performance does not make it any less my duty to do as I undertook. And since, or so long as, this performance remains my duty and given the enforcement costs, in terms of administration and supervision, are no higher here than those which attend other damages awards, the courts should not channel you toward compensation simply because this is the cheaper option for me.

It does not follow that the fact that compensation is the cheaper option is irrelevant. The burden placed on defendants required to meet the costs of funding repairs and replacements is a consideration which bears on the reasonableness of compelling them to do so and there will be times where not only is the extent of this burden disproportionate to any benefit that comes from having this work done but it is also unfair to the defendant to make her bear it.[17] By framing the question as one of mitigation, the courts misidentify the relevant question here, which is not whether the claimant is acting reasonably so as to limit her own losses but rather whether it would be unreasonable to require the defendant to meet the costs of performing her duty. The consequence is that the courts move too quickly from the position that damages are a preferable form of remedy to specific relief to the conclusion that any remedy is properly directed to, and so should be limited by reference to, compensation of the claimant's losses. As a result, the law is doing not only less than it could but less than it should to secure performance of these duties.

[17] *Jacob & Youngs, Inc. v. Kent* 230 NY 239 (1921) may be such a case, though this is not the only way we might support the decision.

IV. Continuity

Of course, however creative the courts are in finding ways to see that I perform my duties, there will be cases where performance is now impossible. In such instances, any action the law takes against me must have some other aim. Where I can no longer perform, or where a court is now unwilling to take action to secure that performance, I might yet be able to undo or offset some of the consequences of my breach, most clearly by compensating you for the losses I have thereby caused. But, just as my contractual duty is not the disjunctive duty often associated with Holmes—to perform or to pay damages—so the court's order that I compensate you for the losses caused by my failure to perform is not an alternative means of securing that performance. Rather, the effect, if successful, is that my duty remains unfulfilled but you are left no worse off for it.

Of course, even on this view, these duties are not independent. It is my breach of my initial (primary) duty which triggers and grounds the (secondary) duty to compensate you for the losses caused by that breach.[18] On occasion, the relationship between the primary duty I breached and my secondary duty to pay compensation is closer still. Imagine that our contract for the installation of the kitchen provides expressly not only for the work I must do but also for the compensation I must pay if I do not. My duty to install the kitchen and my duty to compensate you for your losses if I do not install it remain distinct duties, detailing different actions and bringing about different results. And, as before, my failure to do the work to the specifications we have agreed is, without more, a breach of contract, and it is this breach which then triggers my duty to compensate you for the losses this causes. Here, however, the payment of compensation is provided for in the contract, my duty to pay that compensation is what performance of our contract now requires, your right to performance now a right to that compensation.

Some think that this is the rule rather than the exception: that secondary duties are not simply triggered by the breach of a primary duty but are always versions of that primary duty, remodeled in light of the effects of the breach; or, at least, that the primary duty always continues in some form, always prescribing some sort of secondary, corrective duty. To say this is not simply to say that these secondary duties arise only where and to the extent that the primary duty is unperformed, such that they, in this sense, stand in for the primary duty. This much is true on any view. What is distinctive about the claim that these are remodeled versions or continuations of the primary duty is not what it reveals about the incidence or

[18] Which is not to say that all duties to compensate are triggered by breaches of duty. The fact that I acted wrongfully in causing you loss is not the only reason why it may be just to require me to bear it.

function of secondary duties but what it suggests about their justification. Where our contract expressly provides for me paying you compensation in the event of breach, both my primary duty to do the work and my secondary duty to pay compensation are grounded in the undertakings I made to you; both applications or expressions of my broader duty to do as I undertook.[19] The reasons I came under a duty to do the work are the very same reasons I now owe you a duty to compensate you for your losses.

This gives us what Gardner calls the continuity thesis:[20]

> Once the time for performance of a primary obligation is past, so that it can no longer be performed, one can often nevertheless still contribute to satisfaction of some or all of the reasons that added up to make the action obligatory. [Once we know the rationale of the primary obligation] we also have the rationale, all else being equal, for a secondary obligation, which is an obligation to do the next-best thing. . . . [T]he secondary obligation is a rational echo of the primary obligation, for it exists to serve, so far as may still be done, the reasons for the primary obligation that was not performed when its performance was due.

And so:[21]

> The normal reason why one has an obligation to pay for the losses that one wrongfully occasioned (ie that one occasioned in breach of obligation) is that this constitutes the best still-available conformity with, or satisfaction of, the reasons why one had that [primary] obligation.

Is the continuity thesis sound? No doubt reasons do not disappear simply because they are not acted on and are not conformed to. Again, the reasons not to play music loud late into the night are not extinguished by my doing so. If

[19] This reveals the limitations, or perhaps simply the error, of Gardner's claim that duties are individuated by the actions they make obligatory (John Gardner, "What is Tort Law For? Part 1. The Place of Corrective Justice" (2011) 30 Law and Philosophy 1, 29–30), while supporting his conclusion that, if secondary duties are a continuation of primary duties, the essential continuity is of the reasons which ground these duties (ibid. 30–34).

[20] Ibid. 33. Others who have put forward similar views express the relevant continuity in terms of rights rather than reasons: Ernest J. Weinrib, *Corrective Justice* (OUP 2012) 87–98; Arthur Ripstein, *Private Wrongs* (HUP 2016) 233–54. As noted above (text to nn 7–9), there are different concepts of rights. While these accounts reveal some inconsistency in their use of the term, the claim that my secondary duty to compensate you for the losses caused by my breach is a continuation of your pre-breach right can work only if the "right" here describes a sort of reason. As such rights-continuity is best seen as an example of reasons-continuity.

[21] Gardner (n 19) 33–34.

I have started, I should stop. It is also clear that changes in my circumstances can make a difference to what I have reason to do. If it is raining I have reason to put up my umbrella, if it is dry I (usually) do not. Moreover, what I have reason to do may change without my reasons changing. The same reason can support different actions depending on my circumstances. The fact that it is raining is a reason not only for putting up my umbrella when I am walking to work, but also for choosing to take the bus rather than walking or for delaying my journey. Indeed I think we should say that, while changes in the weather make a difference to whether I should put up my umbrella, this is not because the reasons which count in favor of putting up an umbrella only bear on me on rainy days. What changes is not the applicability of these reasons but rather their application: what, if anything, they actually count in favor of here and now. How, one might object, can the fact that it is raining be a reason (for putting up an umbrella, for anything) when it is not, in fact, raining? But the fact that it is raining does not give a reason (for putting up an umbrella, for anything) in isolation, but only in conjunction with some value which is served by responding to this fact in this, or some such, way. So the reason for putting up an umbrella in the rain is not the bare fact of the rain falling but, say, that it is good to be comfortable and healthy and getting cold and wet is uncomfortable and risks illness.[22] While the rain comes and goes, the value of being comfortable and healthy does not, and the reasons it provides are ever-present even if, right now, there is nothing I need do to conform to them.

So the continuity thesis is, to this extent, true to the way reasons work: a failure to conform to the reasons which apply to us does not make those reasons disappear and changes in our circumstances, such as those brought about by our breaches of duty, may make a difference to what these reasons give us reason to do. Some reason grounds a duty on me to φ at T_1. In breach of that duty, I do not. I cannot now act in accordance with that reason *at* T_1; history cannot be rewritten. But that does not mean I cannot act in accordance with that reason *now*, at T_2. We know that reason continues to apply to me. We also know that I do have reason to compensate you for any losses my breach caused. Still, what we need to know is whether the two marry up: whether it is the reason which grounds my duty to φ at T_1, and which still applies to me, which gives me reason to compensate you at T_2.

Some respond: how could it not? It would be "absurd," Weinrib suggests, were my duty to be discharged, your right destroyed, by its breach.[23] For

[22] Making this point and with this example: John Finnis, "On Hart's Ways: Law as Reason and as Fact" (2007) 52 Am. J. Juris. 25, 44–45.
[23] Weinrib (n 20) 90.

Ripstein, there would be "no sense" in which you have a right, if it could be unilaterally dissolved by its violation.[24] And so, for both of them, it must be that the payment of damages is the performance that duty now requires, the demand your right now supports, for otherwise that right and duty would come to nought. But none of this is true. I kick you on the shin at T_1. I cannot now, at T_2, undo the kick at T_1. The fact that it cannot be undone does not make it any less a breach of duty, any less a violation of your right. *That* would be absurd. Moreover, the reasons which supported my duty not to kick you at T_1 continue to apply to me at T_2, and I remain under a duty not to kick you. Accordingly, before we get to any question of what I might owe you for the harm I have done you and why I owe it, there is no sense in which my duty, your right, or the reasons which ground them have been discharged, destroyed, or dissolved. This way of thinking might seem to have greater purchase where the effect of my breach is that, now at T_2, I can no longer do what I was duty-bound to do at T_1. I snatch your coffee and pour it away. Again, I cannot now undo what I did. But while I could at least avoid kicking you again, here the coffee is gone and there is nothing left of my duty not to interfere with it. Accordingly, we can say that, as a result of my breach, I do not owe you a duty I would otherwise have owed. But this much is true on any view: Weinrib and Ripstein do not think I still owe you a duty not to spill what is already spilled. The relevant duty I owe you now is to compensate you for your losses. Again, however, nobody doubts this. What distinguishes Weinrib and Ripstein's position is their claim that this duty does not just stand in for my duty not to spill the coffee but is the very same duty in revised form. But it is hardly absurd or senseless to question whether this is true.

So what arguments can be made in favor of the view that these are the same duty, grounded in the same reasons? Weinrib and Ripstein proceed by showing how my duty to compensate you can be viewed as an alternative expression or effectuation of the right of yours which grounded the duty I breached. So, for Weinrib, your right can be "restored" not only "qualitatively"—as when the remedy sees that I provide the very performance I was initially duty-bound to provide—but also in "quantitative form," whereby you obtain not that performance but its monetary equivalent as damages.[25] For Ripstein, the rights recognized by private law mark out and protect our "means": things (property) and attributes (our bodily and mental powers) which are ours to employ in the pursuit of our chosen ends.[26] When I wrong you, injuring your person, taking

[24] Ripstein (n 20) 248.
[25] Weinrib (n 20) 94.
[26] Ripstein (n 20) 29–33.

or damaging your assets, I deprive you of some of these means. The payment of damages sees that I restore equivalent means to you.[27]

I doubt this takes us much further. Describing your right to damages as just the quantitative form of your right that I not kick your shin or spill your coffee only begs the question. Similarly, the idea that damages provide you with means equivalent to those I deprived you of is an effective demonstration less of how those damages protect your initial right than of how they are able to offset the losses caused by my violation of that right. Indeed, it is worth repeating the point made at the outset: my primary duty is not that I *either* not kick you *or* pay you damages. Equivalently, your right is that I do not kick you, not that I ensure that you receive full value for any kicks I give or that I preserve the sum of means at your disposal. Of course, Weinrib and Ripstein are not closet Holmesians. The quantitative form of the right and duty comes out only after breach. Till then, there is no qualitative dimension to my duty or your right, no way in which they view your means as fungible. But, once we reject Holmes' reductionism, the stretch to see paying damages as a sort of next-best performance of my primary duty looks unmotivated, unnecessary.

Gardner makes a different case. He starts with an example.[28] I promise my children that I will take them to the beach today. However I forget or some distraction intervenes. What should I now do? Take them tomorrow or, if not tomorrow, then at the next possible opportunity. Why? Not, so Gardner sees it, because I thereby keep some part of my promise. What I promised to do—to take them to the beach today—was one thing, what I am to do instead—taking them to the beach tomorrow—something else. Nonetheless what is required of me now closely resembles what was required of me before. Can it be, Gardner asks, that:[29]

> I [am] bound to take them to the beach tomorrow for reasons that are entirely different from the reasons that I had to take them to the beach today? Surely not. Why me? Why the children? Why the beach? Why tomorrow?

Accordingly my taking them tomorrow amounts not to partial performance of my primary duty but rather to partial conformity to the reasons which ground that duty. This, Gardner believes, then provides a general model for secondary duties: wherever I breach a duty, the reasons which grounded that primary

[27] Ibid. 245–46.
[28] Gardner (n 19) 28–29.
[29] Ibid.

duty continue to bear on me and my secondary duty is the duty those reasons now ground.

I'm not so sure. For one thing, I am less confident that my promise runs out so quickly. No doubt I break my promise simply on failing to take my children to the beach today. Still must we look beyond that promise to find a source for my duty to take them tomorrow? Imagine I tell my children: "I promise to take you to the beach. And I promise to do it today." By not taking them today, I break the second promise. However I can still keep the first. By taking them tomorrow, I do. But do I need to expressly disambiguate my promise(s) in this way for it(/them) to be understood this way or to have this effect? Take another example Gardner uses.[30] I catch the bus. I am to pay the driver as I board, the fare dependent on how far I go. The money I hand over is not enough to take me to my destination but I realize this too late to disembark at an earlier stop. I am now under a duty to pay the rest. For Gardner, this is an example of the continuity thesis in action: the duty I owe now is not the duty I had agreed to—I had agreed to pay the full fare upfront, not some upfront and the rest later—but we can account for this duty by reference to the reasons which grounded my duty to do as I had agreed. Gardner considers the objection that our undertakings should be read as including fallback provisions, obligating us to provide the next best thing if we fail to do what we promised.[31] His conclusion is that this interpretation may be reasonable but only because this is what we would owe in any case. But this way of framing the objection already assumes too much. The question of whether a particular provision may be implied into our agreement arises only where that provision is not expressly agreed; the question of what counts as the next best thing to performance of my undertaking dependent on first establishing what performance I have undertaken. To ask whether an undertaking to pay the shortfall should be read into the contract is already to assume that the duty I expressly undertook was to pay the full fare *only upon boarding.*

No doubt my duty is now to take my children to the beach the next day and to pay the rest of the fare before I get off the bus and that the reasons for this are no different to the reasons I was duty-bound to take them today and to pay the full fare on boarding. But this may simply be because, in each case, I am doing something I undertook to do: my undertaking to take them to the beach one which can effectively be disjoined from my undertaking specifically to take them today, my undertaking to pay the full fare not conditional on that

[30] Gardner (n 19) 31–32.
[31] Ibid. 38–39.

payment being made upon boarding. Even if we reject this interpretation of what I undertook in these cases, the suggestion that it is the reasons which grounded my duty to keep my promise which explain the different duty I owe now looks a lot more plausible where, as here, it remains possible for me to provide a performance which largely replicates the performance I had promised. Whether this provides a model which extends to cases where I can no longer provide any part of, or anything like, the performance which was my initial duty is, I think, more doubtful.

A second concern: consider our earlier example where, in breach of our contract, I fail to give you the lift to the airport. You miss both your flight and the wedding you were to attend. What is my duty now? I could take you to the airport tomorrow, but that would do you no good, indeed would only add insult to injury. If this is not my duty, what accounts for the difference between Gardner's two examples and this one? One answer is to be found in the contents of the respective promises. As I have just proposed, I think it is a reasonable interpretation of the undertakings in Gardner's examples, given their context, that they extend to taking my children to the beach tomorrow if I do not do it today and paying the rest of the fare as I get off the bus if I do not pay it all when getting on. But, at least if I know of your plans, there is no scope for any equivalent interpretation of my undertaking here. If so, the difference between the two cases is that, while in the former cases I am still able to provide some part of the performance I promised, in the latter I cannot. Gardner's examples are not then a template for secondary duties at all.

However, say we reject, as Gardner rejects, this reading of my undertakings in his two examples. How else might we account for my differing duties between his cases and mine? Not by reference to what I promised. In each case I can do later what I promised to do before, in none, *ex hypothesi*, does my promise extend to doing this. Nor is it likely that there is any difference in the reasons which ground my duty to keep these promises. My reasons for making these promises may differ but the reasons for my duty to keep them are, we might think, content- and context-independent. The real difference is to be found in the interests of my promisees and *their* reasons for wanting what I promised. My children have just as much reason for wanting to go to the beach tomorrow as they do today; the bus company wants my money later if it cannot have it now. You, by contrast, have no reason at all to go to the airport tomorrow. So taking my children to the beach tomorrow is indeed a way of putting them in as good a position as they would have been in had I kept my promise, taking you to the airport tomorrow is not.

What does this show? Recall how Gardner used the example of the promise to my children to make the case for the continuity thesis: the duty I now owe them so closely mirrors the duty I undertook, that it would be incredible if the reasons for the duty I owe now were different to the reasons for the duty I owed then. Now, however, we see an alternative explanation of why the contents of these two duties are so close: commonly the best way to leave you in as good as position as you would have occupied but for the breach is to put you in a position as near as possible to that you would have occupied but for the breach. But, as the example of the missed flight shows, this is not always the case. What counts as a position as good as the position you would have occupied but for the breach can be determined only by considering what interests of yours would have been served by, or would otherwise have been implicated in, my performance of that duty. Accordingly, where my secondary duty largely replicates the primary duty I breach, this need not be because that secondary duty shares the primary duty's rationale but because its aim is to see that my breach does not leave your interests set back and the best way to achieve this is to do something for you which directly negates or precludes any such setback. This is what happens when I take my children to the beach the next day and when I pay the rest of the fare before I get off the bus. In other words, I do not need to compensate you for your losses if I can instead ensure that my breach does not cause you loss in the first place.[32]

The fact that my secondary duty tracks your reasons for wanting performance of my primary duty does not establish that the continuity thesis is wrong. It may be that the reasons which support my primary duty require me to attend to your reasons for wanting its performance and the interests that performance will serve. The primary duties we owe one another do not merely serve our obligees' interests, the fact that they do so will, so we might think, typically be key to their justification. Consider, however, the examples we have been discussing. In these cases, my duty arises on account of promises I have made. Some think my duty to keep my promises is grounded not in the interests of my promisees but in my own interests as promisor, for example, in the facility it gives me to shape my own normative relations. Will this understanding of the justification of my promissory duties get us to secondary duties which I have not chosen and which require me instead to attend to your interests? Or are we to assume that different accounts of the justification of promissory obligation

32 And so this would be an example where, though performance of (any part of) my primary duty is no longer possible, I can provide a substitute "performance" which precludes or negates, rather than simply offsets, your losses.

nonetheless support the same sets of secondary duties? If so, this would appear a striking, and rather convenient, coincidence. If not, we might have hoped that proponents of the continuity thesis spent rather more time doing the hard yards, identifying the reasons they take to ground particular primary duties, and showing how these reasons support the specific secondary duties which attend their breach.

This illustrates a broader problem for the continuity thesis. Our secondary duties, or at least a certain class of secondary duties, are said to channel the same reasons as grounded the primary duties to whose breach they respond. Accordingly, if we want to know our secondary duties we need to know the reasons for the corresponding primary duties. But, for the most part, we know our secondary duties already, and we know in particular that they extend at least to making good the losses which result from breach. By contrast, what reasons justify our primary duties is not a question on which we will find any agreement. So the claim is that our reasons to make compensation after breaking promises are the same reasons which support our duty to keep our promises, that our duty to compensate those whose assets we have damaged takes its rationale from the private property interests we thereby infringe and the duties of non-interference these interests entail. But why must we keep our promises? What justifies private property? Here then is the problem: either the validity of the continuity thesis depends on the answer we give to these questions or it suggests that, whatever the reasons we offer in support of a particular primary duty, they make no difference to the content of the secondary duty. If the former, we are being invited to endorse the continuity thesis blind. If the latter, we are left with the implausible view that, while the secondary duty takes its rationale from the primary duty, it does not matter what this rationale is. Indeed, the continuity thesis seems to require us to believe that all the diverse reasons which ground the diverse primary duties we owe nonetheless, following breach, come together, providing parallel justifications for this common compensatory response.

V. Wrongs and Losses

If not the continuity thesis, then what? For the continuity thesis, the reason I now owe you compensation is the same reason I owed you the duty I breached and which resulted in the loss I must now make good. As different primary duties have different rationales, the same goes for our secondary duties. An alternative is that these secondary duties of compensation do not take their rationale from the duty breached and that they do not differ in rationale from one wrong to another. Compare disgorgement. On occasion the law responds to a wrong by stripping the wrongdoer of the gains she made from her breach. Why? Reasons vary. It is sometimes suggested that in so doing the law is giving effect to the defendant's primary duty, as where fiduciaries are said to be under an obligation only to act for and so only for the benefit of their principals.[33] Another suggestion is that these remedies work to deter others from breaching their duties. If so, we might say that they take their rationale from the relevant primary duty but here they work to promote its performance by other defendants on other occasions. But we also see a third justification: wrongdoers just shouldn't profit from their wrongs. On this view, the reasons the defendant must give up her gains do not change from wrong to wrong. What matters is that the gain she made came from a breach of duty, not what duty she breached or what reasons grounded that duty.

I think something similar is true of compensation. There are diverse reasons why I might come under a duty to make good your losses. But one reason is, or is found in, the fact that I caused those losses and that I did so by acting in breach of a duty I owed to you. Here too, what matters is the fact that I wronged you, not how or why my conduct amounts to a wrong or what reasons I failed to conform to in wronging you. This way of thinking offers two initial advantages over the continuity thesis. First: it gives us a ready explanation for why compensation is the appropriate response across a range of duties of very different content and with very different rationales. By the same token, it accounts for why uncertainty as to the justification of these duties is not, at least ordinarily, mirrored in uncertainty as to how we should respond to their breach. Second: the continuity thesis leaves my wrongdoing with no role to play in the justification of my duty to make good your losses.[34] While my duty to compensate you is indeed triggered by my wrong, the reasons I owe you compensation are not found in or connected to that wrong. I owe you compensation for the same reasons I owed you the primary duty I breached, a duty which was not triggered by or grounded in any prior wrongdoing. Instead, my breach is significant only for the change it makes to our factual circumstances and, in turn, to what these reasons now require of me, no different in kind to the way my reasons for delaying my trip when I see it is raining become reasons to put

[33] Lionel Smith, "Deterrence, Prophylaxis and Punishment in Fiduciary Obligations" (2013) 7 J. Eq. 87, Paul B. Miller, "Justifying Fiduciary Remedies" (2013) 63 U. Toronto LJ 570.

[34] Others have made this point before: see Stephen A. Smith, "Duties, Liabilities, and Damages" (2012) 125 Harv. L. Rev. 1727, 1752–53; Victor Tadros, "Secondary Duties" in Paul B. Miller and John Oberdiek (eds.), *Civil Wrongs and Justice in Private Law* (OUP 2020) 188.

up my umbrella if I am now out and the rain starts to fall. On the approach I have proposed, my wrongdoing is central to why I should now compensate you for your losses, for it is precisely my status as someone who has wronged you which makes it appropriate to require me to bear those losses.

There is little mystery to compensatory duties. There may be doubt as to what amounts to full or effective compensation, how we should identify and assess losses, what limits should be put on their recovery, and so on. But all agree that it is appropriate, all else equal, for us to compensate those we have wronged for the losses we thereby caused and that this is the principal function of damages awards. The continuity thesis gets some important things right. Reasons do not disappear when I fail to conform to them. The reasons I failed to act on do not just continue to apply to me but may bear directly on what it is I should do now, in response to my initial failure. I have suggested that the law is often insufficiently attentive to this, failing to do what it could and should to secure the performance I was, and remain, duty-bound to provide. But breach often makes performance impossible and, even where it remains possible, the law may do better to pursue some other objective. In such cases, though the reasons which grounded my primary duty persist and direct me not to repeat my wrongdoing, they may and often do have nothing more to say about the wrong I have done. The continuity thesis is a dead end. In this closing section, I have provided only the briefest sketch of an argument as to how we might better explain our secondary duties of compensation and the duties to pay damages they support. But I hope to have done enough to show why we need some such argument and why this might be thought to mark a more promising way forward.

2

When it is Wrong to Hold On

A Principle of Non-Derogation

Larissa Katz

Private law presumes that people hold on to what they have. This idea animates two well-recognized and pervasive principles. The first is that people are never presumed to make gifts, and the second is that no one is obligated to advance the interests of others in the absence of a special relationship between them.[1] The presumption against gifts is found in the law's response to gratuitous transfers of value in the form of property or services. The originator of value is taken to hold on to it unless the recipient can establish a juridical reason for its transfer, such as a gift, a loan, a contractual or statutory right.[2] The no-duty-to-help principle is evident in the absence of tort liability for failing to rescue a stranger in need.[3] There are other subtler applications of this principle in property law, where it would cost a person very little to help another to acquire a benefit or avoid a burden, and yet the law makes no such demand.[4] In *Jacque v. Steenberg Homes, Inc.*, the plaintiffs, the Jacques, refused to allow the defendant to cross their land to deliver a mobile home to a neighboring customer.[5] Although it would have cost the Jacques little to do so, they had no duty to exercise their property right so as to accommodate the defendant's interest

[1] This is sometimes described as the distinction in private law between misfeasance (to which the law responds) and non-feasance (to which it does not). See Arthur Ripstein, *Private Wrongs* (HUP 2016) 53 ("Tort duties restrict the ways in which each person can use his or her means; they do not require anyone to use his or her means in the way best suited to some other person's ability to use his or her means in a preferred way. You do not need to refrain from building a tower so as to give me access to sunlight.")

[2] See only *Re Vandervell Trustees Ltd.* (No. 2) [1974] EWCA Civ. 7; *Westdeutsche Landesbank Girozentrale v. Islington LBC* [1996] UKHL 12; Peter Birks, *Unjust Enrichment* (2nd ed., OUP 2005) 129; McLachlin J in *Peter v. Beblow* [1993] 1 SCR 980 highlighting the following as one of the questions to assess any claim in unjust enrichment: "Did the plaintiff confer the benefit as a valid gift or in pursuance of a valid common law, equitable or statutory obligation which he or she owed to the defendant?"

[3] Ernest J. Weinrib, "The Case for a Duty to Rescue" (1980) 90 Yale LJ 247.

[4] Cf. *Popov v. Hayashi* WL 31833731 Ca. Sup. Ct. 2002: while there is no general requirement to help anyone acquire a right (e.g., to help Popov make the catch), equity guards against interruptions in the process of acquiring rights. See Larissa Katz, "Equity: Pathways to Rights" in Dennis Klimchuk, Irit Samet, and Henry E. Smith (eds.), *Philosophical Foundations of the Law of Equity* (OUP 2020).

[5] *Jacque v. Steenberg Homes, Inc.* 209 Wis. 2d 605 (1997).

Larissa Katz, *When it is Wrong to Hold On* In: *Oxford Studies in Private Law Theory: Volume 1*. Edited by: Paul B. Miller and John Oberdiek, Oxford University Press (2020). © The Several Contributors. DOI: 10.1093/oso/9780198851356.003.0002

in performing its contract with their neighbors cheaply.[6] Together, these principles set a high threshold for recognizing a change in legal relations: the presumption is that people hold on to what they have.

Against this backdrop is a third principle that provides an important coda to the first two. This is a principle against derogation from a grant: "It is a principle of general application that a grantor must not derogate from his grant; he must not seek to take away with one hand what he has given with the other. This obligation binds not only the grantor himself but persons claiming under him; and the right to enforce it passes to those who claim under the grantee."[7] In the principle of non-derogation, the law seems to take a very different view of how we relate to what we have: rather than presuming grantors to convey *the least* they could in the circumstances, the law presumes that a grantor gives *everything* she has when she makes a grant (*dat quod habet*). It presumes in short that she holds nothing back.

My aim in this paper is to explain this maxim—that a grantor is presumed not to derogate from her grant—and its role in relation to the first two more miserly principles in private law. A principle of non-derogation, I argue, is a regulative principle, aligning grants with the ideal of a grant through a set of presumptions and providing the basis for evaluating and regulating deviations from that ideal.[8] According to the ideal of a grant, a grantor appoints her own successor through a conveyance of full authority, holding nothing back. The ideal of a grant as a conveyance of full, undivided agenda-setting authority reflects the aspirations of property law to establish a system of authoritative decision-making about particular things through the office of ownership.

The ideal of a grant, as the conveyance of full agenda-setting authority with respect to a thing, retains its force even as deviations from the ideal are not only allowed but anticipated. Property law does not enforce the ideal strictly.[9]

[6] In *Jacque v. Steenberg Homes, Inc.*, the defendant mobile home company contracted with the neighbor for the sale of the home *including* the cost of delivery in the purchase price, *after* its employees learned of the steep cost of delivery via the only available road and the Jacques' refusal to bargain with them for the privilege of crossing the Jacques' land.

[7] Stuart Bridge, Elizabeth Cooke, and Martin Dixon, *Megarry & Wade: The Law of Real Property* (9th ed., Sweet & Maxwell 2019) 6. See also *Halsbury's Laws of England* (vol. 32 (2019) para. 258 < https://www.lexisnexis.ca/en-ca/products/halsburys-laws-of-england.page> accessed January 10, 2020.

[8] This ideal is also expressed in the principle of conservation (which tracks and accounts for full ownership authority even in grants of something less), as well as the principle of merger (that reunites the separate parts of ownership authority where the lesser is acquired by the holder of the greater part).

[9] While a system of property always contains the idea of ownership and permissions (personal licenses), property law in some times and places allows for other lesser and included forms of property. The menu of subordinate property rights, limited in number, varies widely across time and jurisdictions. The mortgage for instance emerged later in common law jurisdictions out of the fee simple subject to a condition subsequent. The restrictive covenant is a nineteenth century innovation of equity. In the twentieth century many older forms are no longer available, like the fee tail, or available only in a

A principle of non-derogation aligns actual grants as closely as possible to the ideal of a grant as a conveyance of full authority by regulating the nature and structure of subordinate property rights, like easements, mortgages, leases, profits, and defeasible interests. The principle of non-derogation is also the theoretical underpinning for constraints imposed on grantors in the exercise of the rights and privileges they do retain after a grant. A grantor may be obligated to exercise the rights and powers she has held on to so as not to undermine the integrity of the grant.

I will begin by setting out the ideal of a grant and explaining its robust internal normativity, and then show how the various applications of a principle of non-derogation are best understood as regulating deviations from this ideal. I conclude by explaining how a principle of non-derogation fits together with private law's otherwise miserly view about holding on to what we have.

I. Grant

My explanation of the principle of non-derogation begins with the idea of a grant. [10] A grant is a *conveyance of authority* by someone with authority to convey.[11] Grants are an integral part of a system of property that recognizes derivative modes of acquisition—the acquisition of authority dependent on the exercise of a power by the person in authority now—in addition to

trust, enforced in equity (this is the case in English law following the Law of Property Act 1925 (15 Geo. 5 c. 20)).

[10] The term "grant" has technical connotations in common law. For example, in the case of personal property it refers to a transfer of property for consideration, in contrast to a gift. It is used generally to refer to *inter vivos* transfers, in contrast to a devise in a will. Subordinate property rights, like easements, profits, leases, and intangibles like patents, shares, and options are all objects of grant. Generally, the idea of a grant as a conveyance of authority by someone with the authority to convey is common to all of these ways of transferring property authority, and so too is the idea of non-derogation although it can go by different names, such as the doctrine of patent exhaustion in US patent law. See *Quanta Computer, Inc. v. LG Electronics, Inc.*, 553 US 617 (2008) (license to sell computer components embodying patented method exhausts patent-holder's right later to enforce the patent against a buyer from the licensee, who combines the purchased component with other components, without an express or implied license to practice the patent).

[11] Grant was originally a method of transferring incorporeal hereditaments and only later (after the Statute of Frauds in the reign of Charles II, *Statute of Frauds: An Act for the prevention of frauds and perjuries*, 29 Charles II, c.3 (1677, UK)) became the generic method. See Emory Washburn, *A Treatise on the American Law of Real Property* vol. 3 (6th ed. John Wurts, Boston 1902) para. 1995 at 165 ("Though the word grant was originally made use of, in treating of conveyances of interests in lands, to denote a transfer by deed of that which could not be passed by livery, and, of course, was applied only to incorporeal hereditaments, it has now become a generic term, applicable to the transfers of all classes of real property, and will be used in that broad sense in speaking of the formal transfer of titles to lands."). For modern legislation required the use of deed by grant to transfer interests in land, see, e.g., Ontario's Conveyancing and Law of Property Act, RSO 1990, c. C.34 s.3.

original modes of acquisition, such as creation, possession, accession, where property authority is achieved independently of the current officeholder. A grantor changes legal relations through the exercise of legal power, in contrast to change in legal relations brought about by de facto possession, operation of law, or some natural event that results in the destruction of a thing. The grant itself determines what questions fall within the authority of the grantee (and her successors) to decide and so what if any authority remains with the grantor. A grant serves not only as the foundation of the grantee's authority vis-à -vis the world at large, but also as the shared foundation of the position of the grantor and grantee (and their successors) vis-à-vis each other, in some cases generating bilateral rights and duties not to act so as to undermine that foundation.[12] The normative force of the grant is thus not spent at the moment of granting: a grant is not just something that has happened in the past nor is it just a part of the story of how a person came to be in authority. Rather, a grant is the continuing basis of the grantee and her successor's authority and the rights and duties of both grantor and grantee long after the exercise of the legal power to grant.[13] Any defects in the grant, any limits or conditions that attach to it, as well as any constraints on the grantor, continue as long as the grant does. The grant continues as the foundation of the authority of the grantee and those who succeed her until it is superseded by another, independent basis of authority with respect to that object, such as adverse possession, title by escheat or bona vacantia, legislation, judicial order, etc.

A. The Ideal of a Grant: Conveyance of Full Authority

A principle of non-derogation has to be understood against the backdrop of a system of property already organized around the idea of ownership as an office with full agenda-setting authority. The ideal of a grant reflects property law's aspiration to set up and maintain a network of offices tasked with making decisions that regulate the interactions of people with respect to particular things.[14] In a system like this, for each separate thing, there is someone with

[12] In much the same way as a contract is the shared foundation of rights and duties of the parties to the contract.

[13] The grant serves as the foundation of rights and duties for any whose position is derived from it. Unlike a contract, that can include people other than the original parties. See *The Owners, Strata Plan LMS 3905 v. Crystal Square Parking Corp.*, 2017 BCSC 71; *The Owners, Stata Plan BCS 4006 v. Jameson House Ventures Ltd.* 2017 BCSC 1988 and 2019 BCCA 114.

[14] I defend this view of property law in depth elsewhere. See, e.g., Larissa Katz, "Property's Sovereignty" (2017) 18 Theo. Inq. L. 299; Larissa Katz, "Governing Through Owners" (2012) 160 U. Penn. LR 2029 and more recently in Larissa Katz, "Offices and Horror Vacui" (2020) UTLJ (forthcoming); Larissa

the authority to set the agenda. The separateness of things, real or artificial, is a prerequisite for this idea of ownership. (By the same token the fusion of things or things to land results in a merger of property rights, too, into a single consolidated position of authority.[15]) According to this ideal, the power to grant is not so much the power to transfer rights as the power to appoint one's own successor to a position of authority.[16] *Full* authority is conveyed when the owner appoints a successor to hold the very same office she had.

Because ownership authority is contained in an office, it is held separate and apart from other forms of authority the grantor might have and even other positions of ownership authority. This is why the presumption of *dat quod habet* does not lead to the presumption that the grantor of Blackacre grants everything else she owns—her car, Whiteacre—along with it. We can contrast ownership, and a conveyance of ownership authority, with grants of other forms of authority that stand first to be carved out from a more general position of authority. Where, for instance, the state makes a grant of authority that involves the creation of a new position of authority and not just the appointment to an existing office, for example a public corporation or a new cabinet ministry, the authority has to be carved out from the more general authority of the state to govern in the name of the people. The state cannot be presumed to give all that it has to give when it conveys authority in these contexts—that would be inconsistent with its claim to statehood—but only powers expressly granted and ancillary powers necessarily or fairly implied and whatever further powers are necessary to carry out the purposes for which authority is granted.[17]

Katz, "Philosophy of Property Law, Three Ways" in John Tasioulas (ed.), *The Cambridge Companion to Philosophy of Law* (CUP 2020).

[15] See *Hoppe v. Manners* [1931] OJ No. 29, 66 OLR 587 (Ont. CA) (for the maxim that whatever is attached to the soil becomes part of it); *Royco Homes Ltd. v. Eatonwill Construction Ltd.* [1979] Ch. 276; *Melluish (Inspector of Taxes) v. BMI (No. 3) Ltd.* [1995] 4 All ER 453 (owner of land becomes owner of fixture); *Ilford-Riverton Airways Ltd. v. Aero Trades (Western) Ltd.*

76 DLR 474, [1977] 5 WWR 193 with reference to James Crossley Vaines, *Crossley Vaines on Personal Property*, (5th ed. E. L. G. Tyler and N. E. Palmer (eds.), Butterworth & Co. 1973) at 432 (the owner of the principal chattel becomes the owner of the whole).

[16] *Dat quod habet* ("Everyone gives what she has") is just as basic as *nemo dat quod non habet*, "no one can give what she does not have."

[17] John Dillon famously described the powers of a municipal corporation in this way: "It is a general and undisputed proposition of law that a municipal corporation possesses and can exercise the following powers, and no others: First, those granted in express words; second, those necessarily or fairly implied in or incident to the powers expressly granted; third, those essential to the (accomplishment of the) declared objects and purposes of the corporation,-not simply convenient, but indispensable. Any fair, reasonable (substantial) doubt concerning the existence of power is resolved by the courts against the corporation, and the power is denied." John F. Dillon, *Commentaries on the Law of Municipal Corporations* vol. 1 (5th ed., Little, Brown & Company 1911) § 237 (89), 448–50.

The ideal of a grant has a robust normativity in property law even as it is not strictly enforced: as we will see, property law allows and even anticipates deviations from the ideal. The normative force of the ideal is maintained through the principle of non-derogation. A principle of non-derogation from a grant functions as an "independent rule of law" that tracks the ideal of a grant as conveyance of full authority.[18] It does so, first, by presuming grantors do not deviate from the ideal: grantors are presumed to convey all that they themselves had in the position (*dat quod habet*). The principle of non-derogation aligns a grant as closely as possible to the ideal of a grant by presuming that the grantor has conveyed whatever additional rights and powers that the grantee reasonably requires to enjoy full authority in the circumstances.

Even where the presumption of *dat quod habet* is rebutted (because a grantor clearly did intend to convey less than full authority), the ideal of a grant continues to exert pressure on how property law makes sense of the conveyance.[19] The ideal of full authority with respect to a thing is the theoretical underpinning of three companion principles of property law that regulate the nature and structure of lesser property rights:[20] a principle of conservation (no authority is lost and unaccounted for following a conveyance of less than full authority), a principle of merger (when acquired by the same person, fragments of full authority merge to form a single consolidated position of authority), and a principle of consistency (lesser property rights with respect to a single thing form a consistent set). Finally,[21] a principle of non-derogation maintains the integrity of the grant as the foundation of the grantee's authority by constraining the way that the grantor exercises rights and powers—even non-proprietary rights and powers—that she clearly has retained: grantors have been obligated to forbear

[18] Bridge, Cooke, and Dixon (n 7) 817. *See The Birmingham, Dudley, and District Banking Company Ltd. v. Ross* (1888) 38 Ch. D. 295, 312. There is a very close relationship between non-derogation from a grant in property law and implied terms in contract. As J. F. Burrows, "Contractual Co-Operation and the Implied Term" (1986) 31 MLR 390, has put it, there is a strong convention of rooting every duty between parties to a contract in intention and so to view the intention of the parties as the basis for implying contractual terms. Cf. Peter Benson, *Justice in Transactions: A Theory of Contract Law* (HUP 2019) section I. A. 3. "Implication." Simon Douglas, "Reforming Implied Easements" (2015) 131 LQR 251, 266 has argued that implied easements ought to be understood the same way, as a matter of the actual intention of the grantor. This account offers a defense of a principle of non-derogation as a rule of law that grounds certain presumptions about what a grantor must be taken to have intended, given their role, and that yields only in certain standardized ways to evidence of contrary intentions (even if you may actually have intended to claw back what you have given away, e.g., a court will not give effect to those intentions to deviate from the ideal).

[19] Sometimes referred to as *numerus clausus* principle, the law recognizes a finite number of well-defined forms of lesser property interests.

[20] Discussed in more detail below in Section II(A) et seq.

[21] Ibid.

from exercising their own rights and powers in ways that undermine the purposes for which authority was granted.

The operation of an ideal in law through the articulation of rebuttable presumptions is a familiar one. We see something like this in public law contexts, where rule of law ideals are the basis of presumptions (e.g., the common law presumption that the state intends to compensate for takings), that are rebuttable (e.g., by legislation expressly indicating no intention to compensate). Even as an ideal is not (and could not actually be) strictly enforced in law, it exerts a robust normative force on the view the law takes of the way in which authority can be and has been conveyed.

II. Varieties of Derogation

I have argued that a principle of non-derogation is an "independent rule of law," that makes sense of grant in terms of the ideal of a grant as the conveyance of full authority.[22] Grants are aligned as closely as possible with this ideal through the operation of the principle of non-derogation. There are three aspects of the principle that target different ways that a grantor might derogate from a grant. The first concerns the presumption of *dat quod habet*: a grantor is presumed to hold nothing back—in effect, to appoint her successor to the same position she held. It follows from the presumption of *dat quod habet*, and the idea that in giving everything the grantor appoints her successor, that the grantor has no power to claw-back the authority granted. A coda to the presumption of *dat quod habet* is that a grantor is presumed to have included any additional rights or powers reasonably required for the grantee to operate as her successor—to take up and exercise full authority for the purposes for which it was conferred. It is in this context that we find implied easements. The second aspect of the principle of non-derogation concerns what it implies about grants of partial authority: the presumption of *dat quod habet* can be defeated in circumstances where a grantor clearly has conveyed less. In this context, property law aligns the

[22] Simon Douglas has argued that implied easements are meant to give effect to the actual intentions of the grantors and rejects what he takes to be the only alternative: that implied easements are there to give effect to some other policy goal. See Douglas (n 18) 255 ("are easements implied into deeds in order to achieve some policy goal, or to give effect to the intention of the grantor? In the next section it will be argued that it is the latter, i.e. that implied easements are examples of terms implied in fact.") In this paper, I have set out a third way of understanding a principle of non-derogation as having to do with the ideal of a grant and so neither a free-standing policy goal nor the actual intentions. See also Burrows (n 18) 392 (suggesting that the principle is a rule of law with origins in equity).

grant of partial authority as closely as possible with the ideal of a grant as a conveyance of full authority by regulating the forms that partial authority can take. The third and most controversial aspect of the principle of non-derogation concerns restrictions courts have imposed on the exercise of rights and powers the grantor has retained—even non-proprietary rights and powers. Grantors are constrained to exercise these in ways that do not undermine the grant as the foundation of the grantee's authority. Taken together, my account of these different aspects of non-derogation will reveal just how the principle works in conjunction with the private law's general presumption that we intend to hold on to what we have and its refusal to obligate us to help others. I will argue below that the principle of non-derogation remains consistent with the presumption of an intention to hold on to what one has. Only the clearest intention to convey authority to another displaces the presumption that a person intends to hold on to it. Only when that threshold has been crossed is the presumption of *dat quod habet* triggered, in keeping with the ideal of a grant and the aspirations of property law to set out and maintain offices of agenda-setting authority with respect to things. I will also argue that a principle of non-derogation remains consistent with private law's refusal to recognize a general duty to use one's resources to advance the interests of others: any duties flowing from the principle of non-derogation are contained within the special relationship of grantor and grantee, a *continuing* relationship of privity. These obligations are thus consistent with private law's more general reluctance to impose duties to use one's own resources to suit the needs of others.

A. Non-Derogation and Appointing One's Successor

The first and most basic strand of the principle of non-derogation concerns what a grantor is taken to have granted at the time of the grant. A person, once the law recognizes that she is in "giving or granting mode," is presumed to give away *all* the power, rights, and privileges she has with respect to the object given—*dat quod habet*—except what she has clearly reserved to herself. No one is presumed to be in giving mode. It is only once a person has voluntarily assumed the role of grantor that she is then presumed to hold nothing back. This basic rule of non-derogation, that a grantor gives what she has, is continued in the principle that a grantor cannot claw-back what she has given away.[23] Having made a grant of all that she has to give, the grantor has no further power with respect to the thing. Attempts to claw-back what has already been granted count simply as legal nullities: the owner simply has no authority to regain what she has already granted. [24] This is so even if the grantor was under a duty not to have made the grant in the first place. Take for example a trustee who conveys property to B, in breach of trust to C. The trustee cannot claw back the property in fulfillment of his duty to C, because the principle of non-derogation prevents that. C, by contrast, does not derogate from the grant when he traces the value of the trust *res* into the property in the hands of B—if B has notice or is a donee—because C's right against A and against B is an *in personam* claim, not derogating from B's position as owner but indeed presupposing it in the course of demanding that B exercise that position for C's benefit.

The principle against claw backs, as an extension of the principle of non-derogation from a grant, is more complicated in contexts where the grantor retains some independent source of power with respect to the thing—as is the case when an owner conveys a lesser property right like an easement but retains general agenda-setting authority or when the state grants ownership but retains the general power to create new rights with respect to that thing. In *M'Mahon v. Berton*,[25] the plaintiff was the owner of land granted by the Crown. The defendant claimed a license from the Crown to open a coal mine on the land. The core of the plaintiff's argument was that the Crown could not grant a valid license because that would represent a derogation from the Crown's grant. The Crown must be presumed to convey the full authority of ownership, and so (on the maxim that he who owns the soil owns everything beneath it), the mining rights too. That being so, a later grant to the defendant of mining rights would be a derogation from the plaintiff's grant.

A grant of ownership is presumed to convey the authority to set the agenda for a particular thing and all of the incidental rights that have acceded to that office: the easements, fixtures, airspace, etc.[26] This has been codified in most

[23] This is the basis for distinguishing mere licenses, privileges to perform some action otherwise prohibited, from grants, through which the grantee succeeds to the position of authority the grantor had previously enjoyed. The traditional view of licenses in law, as opposed to grants, is that "a licence is in its nature revocable" although in exceptional cases, the licensor is limited in her power to revoke. See, e.g., *Wood v. Leadbitter*, 13 M. & W. 838.

[24] After a grantor has given all that he has, holding nothing back, any later attempt to exercise control inconsistent with the grant is repugnant and void. See, e.g., *Re Walker* (1925), 56 OLR 517.

[25] (1851) 2 Allens Rep. 321.

[26] *Ewart, et al. v. Cochrane, et al.* (1861) 4 Macq 117 (lessor taken to have those rights usually enjoyed in relation to the premises). See *Babine Investments Ltd. v. Prince George Shopping Centre Ltd.*, 2002 BCCA 289, 2002 Carswell BC 984 (noting that the implied transfer of all rights enjoyed by the grantor is based upon the principle that one may not derogate from a grant). In that case, the Court of Appeal

jurisdictions, as in this legislative provision: "every conveyance of land, unless it is otherwise specified, includes all physical aspects of the land as well as all intangible aspects including easements."[27] The presumption that nothing is reserved or held back in a grant of ownership amounts in effect to a presumption that the grantor is appointing a successor to the very position she herself holds. In conveying authority to another, the grantor does not change the constitution of the position but just the identity of its holder.

The basic presumption that animates the principle of non-derogation, that the grantor holds nothing back, has a simple coda. This is the presumption that the grantor also conveys whatever *additional* rights are required for the grantee to assume full authority in the circumstances. That may sometimes require the grantor to create and convey all those additional rights incidentally required for the grantee to have the authority for the purposes for which it was granted—rights that the grantor herself did not have or require in the circumstances in which she held the office.[28] Take for instance a situation where the grantor has subdivided Blackacre into Greyacre and Pinkacre in such a way that Greyacre is landlocked. If the grantor then conveys ownership of Greyacre to the grantee, holding nothing back, the grantee may yet find herself with less than she requires to take up and exercise the authority for the purposes for which it is given: without access to Greyacre, she cannot operate as an independent agenda-setter for her own separate thing. The owner of Pinkacre would wield the power to resolve the question of whether to permit or deny movement to and from Greyacre—a power that compromises the owner of Greyacre's capacity to set the agenda for it. In the case of landlocked Greyacre, the principle of non-derogation would require the implication of a right of way over Pinkacre.[29] The easement must be implied because a grant of inaccessible Greyacre would be defective as a grant: to appoint a new owner with full authority to set the agenda for Greyacre requires also a minimum of de facto authority and so access to the land itself. The implication of an easement

seemed to treat rights flowing from the doctrine of non-derogation as equitable rights in the context of that jurisdiction's land titles system: enforceable without registration except against a bona fide purchaser for value without notice (but always against the original grantor).

[27] e.g., Ontario's Conveyancing and Law of Property Act, RSO 1990, c. C.34 s. 15.

[28] *Platt v. London Underground Ltd.* [2001] 2 EGLR 121 (*cuicunque aliquis quid concedit concedere videtur et id sine quo res ipsa esse non potuit*).

[29] Necessity: *McClatchie v. Rideau Lake (Township)*, 2015 ONCA 233, [2015] O.J. No. 1737; *Clark v. Cogge* (1607) Cro.Jac. 171 (implied right of way where grantee would otherwise not have any profit in the land); *Nickerson v. Barraclough* [1981] Ch. 426, 440 seq. (Brightman LJ), 446 seq. (Eveleigh LJ) (denying that rights of way originate in public policy concerns, but are implied in the initial grant. Also continuous and apparent use before implied easement in order not to end up giving grantee less than grantor enjoyed as an incident of ownership of the land, see *Wheeldon v. Burrows* (1879) LR 12 Ch. D. 3.

in that context aligns the grant much more closely with the ideal of a grant as the appointment of a successor with full agenda-setting authority. The grantor is taken to have exercised her power to attach any incidental rights that would be required to give effect to the position of authority she has conveyed even if, in the real-world circumstances in which the grantor operated as owner, the grantor herself had had no need of that incidental right to take up and exercise the position (because she owned the adjacent land).[30] The simple presumption of *dat quod habet* is inadequate to the task of conveying full authority to the grantee where the grantee requires more than what the grantor herself had prior to subdivision. Prior to the subdivision, there were no separate lots, such that one could be understood to require such a benefit from the other: there was just undifferentiated authority to set the agenda for the whole of Blackacre.

The same principle of non-derogation, leading to the implication of incidental rights and privileges, is replicated in the context of grants of subordinate rights. Once a grant of something less than full ownership has been made, for example a lease or a profit, that grant is aligned as closely as possible to the ideal of a grant. The grantor is presumed to have conveyed the fullest authority consistent with that limited position. In the context of a lease for instance, it has been said: "where there is a demise of premises with which certain rights have been usually enjoyed it must be taken that the lessor has granted those rights." Thus, we imply what easements are reasonably required to put the lessee fully into that more limited position that the grantor intended to convey.[31]

Taken together, these presumptions—presumption of *dat quod habet* and the presumed grant of any additional rights reasonably necessary for purposes for which the authority is granted—align actual grants with the ideal of a grant of full authority. Both concern not the actual intentions of the grantor but what the grantor must be taken to have done for it to make sense as a grant.

B. Non-Derogation and Subordinate Rights

The presumption of *dat quod habet* is a rebuttable presumption: it yields where the grantor clearly holds back some of the authority she had to give, conveying only

[30] Sir William Blackstone, *Commentaries on the Laws of England* vol. 1, book 2: Of the Rights of Things (George Sharswood (ed.), J.B. Lipincott Company 1893) 36: "For when the law doth give any thing to one, it giveth impliedly whatsoever is necessary for enjoying the same. By the law of the twelve tables at Rome, where a man had the right of way over another's land, and the road was out of repair, he who had the right of way might go over any part of the land he pleased . . .".

[31] *Wong v. Beaumont Property Trust Ltd.* [1964] 2 All ER 119.

partial authority to the grantee. Property law allows a grant of partial authority but regulates the form it can take so that full agenda-setting authority with respect to a thing is wholly accounted for. One of the most important concerns in the law of property is the avoidance of a vacuum in authority with respect to things.[32] Through limiting the form and nature of subordinate rights that a grantor can create when they convey less than full authority, property law avoids a partial vacuum in which there are some aspects of a thing that no one is in charge of. This concern is reflected in the way property law conceives of subordinate rights in terms of complementary pairs: a lease is accompanied always by a reversion, a life estate by a remainder, the burden of an easement on a servient tenement by a benefit of an easement in the dominant tenement, a defeasible fee by a right of entry. Taken together, these complementary rights account for the full authority with respect to a thing even if, taken alone, each separate right-holder has only partial authority.

The ideal of a grant as a conveyance of full authority is in view in the limited ways available to owners to convey partial authority. A grant of ownership followed by instructions on how the grantee ought to deal with the property on her death is not a valid grant of partial authority: it is understood as a grant of authority from which the grantor has attempted then to claw back some power to control the disposition of the property, in derogation from the grant. What is it then about a grant of land burdened by an easement that escapes this worry about derogation in its most extreme form, repugnancy? I will focus here on how subordinate rights like easements align with the ideal of a grant. In brief, a grant of Blackacre burdened by an easement (the servient tenement) for the benefit of Whiteacre (the dominant tenement) is still a grant in which all authority with respect to Blackacre is accounted for. I will then contrast ownership of land burdened by an easement with a defeasible interest in land. A grant of a defeasible fee is a grant of partial authority where the remaining authority is not yet vested in anyone. As we will see, the law's concern with limiting the time during which a defeasible fee is subject to forfeiture is a concern about a vacuum in authority that is not certain to be resolved within a short-enough time frame.

Easements permit the owner of land (the dominant tenement) to make some use of her neighbor's land for a purpose related to the "*normal* enjoyment of the dominant tenement."[33] For a right to be an easement, it must be "reasonably necessary" to accommodate the benefited land. It must, in other words, make up for something about the benefited land that impairs its owner's ability to use and

[32] This is expressed in the old maxim that the law abhors a vacuum. See Katz (n 14).
[33] *Re Ellenborough Park* [1955] All ER 667 (CA) (my emphasis).

enjoy it to the usual extent. [34] The essence of an easement—and indeed the subject-matter of the right—is thus the *enhancement* of the authority of the owner of the dominant tenement. That enhanced authority, beyond the usual boundaries of the dominant tenement, places a burden on the owner of the servient tenement, and means that she enjoys less than full authority: she must adjust the agenda she sets for the servient tenement to accommodate this extension of the dominant tenement's authority. And yet property law accepts easements and the reduction in the servient tenement's authority because, taken together with the extension of the dominant tenement's authority, there is no vacuum in authority. The dominant and servient tenement, taken together, hold all of the authority that is to be had with respect to the servient tenement. By requiring that an easement benefit a dominant tenement (and treating easements in gross—easements that benefit people not land—as invalid), property law aligns the grant of land subject to an easement as closely as possible with the ideal of full authority.

An easement, in that it burdens the servient tenement only to the extent that it benefits the dominant tenement, avoids the vacuum in authority that might be created in the context of a conveyance of partial authority tout court. That problem emerges in the context of defeasible fees and the contingent future interests that accompany them. The common law traditionally took a very dim view of the creation of defeasible fees—an estate upon a condition, giving rise to the grantor's right of entry (originally an unassignable chose in action[35]) on the breach of the condition. A right of entry, once triggered, made it as though the grant had never occurred. The common law's stance was that an "estate upon a condition cannot be created by deed except where the terms of the grant will admit of no other reasonable interpretation."[36] In keeping with the principle of non-derogation, the common law's presumption was that a condition concerned with the use of land was best understood as a *covenant* relating to use, rather than a condition upon which the grantee held her position and then stood to have it taken back by the grantor. As with other presumptions that follow a principle of non-derogation this one was treated as rebuttable: some conditions clearly were accompanied by a right of entry, triggering forfeiture in case of breach. The creation of such contingent future interests, however, still represented a particularly troubling form of deviation from the ideal of a grant as the conveyance of full authority:[37] where

[34] C. J. Gale and T. D. Whatley, *A Treatise on the Law of Easements* (S. Sweet1839) 2.

[35] Washburn (n 11) vol. 2 para. 954 at 14 et seq. "But of conditions in deed no one but he who creates the estate . . . can take advantage by entering and defeating the estate. It is a right which can not be aliened or assigned . . . ", at 16: " a stranger cannot take advantage of a condition . . . it is a mere chose in action."

[36] Ibid. para. 938 at 5.

[37] Indeed, in England it is no longer possible to create defeasible interests outside of a trust, see Law of Property Act 1925 (abolishing of all forms of property but the leasehold and fee simple).

a condition is attached to a grant of authority, the violation of which leads to its forfeiture, the owner is constrained to exercise her authority only for purposes prescribed by the condition *and the remaining authority is not vested in anyone else*.[38] This is not a situation that property law can tolerate indefinitely because it creates a vacuum in authority with respect to a thing. The law aligns a grant of a defeasible fee more closely with the ideal of a grant first by construing the conditions attached to it as to operate as narrowly as possible and by subjecting any contingent future interests created in these situations to the rule against perpetuities. The rule against perpetuities limits the time during which there is only partial authority with respect to a thing by invalidating any conditions that might be triggered outside that period.[39] In *Keppel v. Bailey*,[40] Lord Brougham described the fundamental difference between a grant of partial authority, where full authority is still accounted for through the creation of a complementary vested right, and a grant of partial authority, where the remaining authority is simply left hanging. What distinguished the easement or covenant from the perpetuity created by a condition attached to an interest is the absence in the latter case of anyone who has the authority equivalent to what is held back in a grant of partial authority. He wrote: "But if . . . the party covenantee has the entire power of dealing with his interest in the subject matter, it is an obvious mistake to treat this as an instance of a perpetuity . . . [T]hough one of the parties interested, the owner of the party subject to the covenant . . . , may be fast, the other is loose; and so quoad both taken together, that is quoad all interested, the property is free."[41]

C. Non-Derogation Beyond the Grant

So far, we have seen the principle of non-derogation work mainly through presumptions to align a grant with the ideal of a grant. It concerns, in the contexts discussed above, the proper formulation of the grant itself. A principle of non-derogation also arises in a third context, where a grantor exercises her own clearly retained rights, privileges, and powers in ways that disable the grantee or her successor from taking up the granted position to its fullest extent. Sometimes these

[38] Anne Warner Law Forest, *Anger & Honsberger Law of Real Property* (3rd ed., Carswell 2019), § 9:30.20 "the law's abhorrence of the abeyance of seisin".

[39] See in the context of grants in wills, e.g., *Phipps v. Ackers et al.* [1558–1774] All ER Rep 381; *Abrahams' Will Trusts, Re, Caplan v. Abrahams* [1967] 2 All ER 1175.

[40] [1834] EWHC Ch. J77.

[41] Ibid. para. 29.

retained rights are not even proprietary in nature and so could not have formed part of the subject-matter of a grant. As it was put in *Browne v. Flower*:

> The implications usually explained by the maxim that no one can derogate from his own grant do not stop short with easements. Under certain circumstances there will be implied on the part of the grantor obligations which restrict the user of the land retained by him further than can be explained by the implication of any easement known to the law.[42]

In this context, a principle of non-derogation does not operate just through presumptions relating to the content of the grant because it cannot; rather, it operates by regulating the relationship between the grantor and grantee (and their privies) *inter se*.[43] On the basis that it would otherwise be a derogation from the grant, a grantor may thus be required to adjust the way he exercises his own clearly retained rights to allow the grantee the full enjoyment of the position for the purpose for which that authority was conveyed. Thus, courts have sometimes held that a grantor must adjust his exercise of his own retained rights, privileges, and powers so as to better enable the grantee to use and enjoy what was conveyed.[44] In *Griffin v. Keane*,[45] the defendant grantor sold the plaintiff a house with a right of way over a private road on land retained by the defendant. In the deed, the defendant was relieved of liability for maintaining the road. The defendant, who cut timber on his own land, used the road before the sale and retained the right to continue to use the road himself for purposes related to his business. After the sale, the defendant's timber business increased significantly, and so did his use

[42] *Browne v. Flower* [1911] 1 Ch. 219.

[43] This is the aspect of the principle of non-derogation that most closely resembles the doctrine of implied terms in contract law. The interpersonal, bilateral relationship of grantor and grantee is the foundation of the obligation the grantor may come under to adjust her rights for the benefit of the grantee. I want to resist thinking about this just in terms of contract, if only because (1) while the obligation not to derogate in this way often starts out with an agreement to sell or transfer property rights (e.g., shares), the obligation retains its character as a principle of non-derogation concerned with property not contract: these cases involve an equitable interest in the subject-matter of the contract that is created ahead of the actual conveyance of property and that attracts a principle against derogation in a way that foreshadows the operation of that principle in relation to the legal property right; (2) there is a proprietary or *in rem* character to the grantor's obligations that can bind the grantor's successors, in a way that is not easy to fit within the logic of contract law and implied terms.

[44] *Texaco Antilles Ltd. v. Kernochan* [1973] 2 All ER 117, 126 (in obiter: a claim by a vendor to enforce a covenant in a common development scheme against a purchaser would be a derogation from the grant where the vendor previously had used the premises in violation of the covenant and sold to the purchaser for the purpose of continuing that use. This is so even if other owners in the development could enforce the covenant against the purchaser).

[45] *Griffin v. Keane* (1927) 61 ILTR 177.

of the road. By driving heavy carts and felling timber on the road, the defendant caused the road to be unusable. The court found the defendant liable for damages (notwithstanding the waiver of liability in the deed) because the defendant's "excessive user," which in effect sterilized the grant of the right of way, would derogate from the grant. Here the wrong of non-derogation would have been constituted not by the improper retention of rights and powers but the failure to exercise rights that the grantor retained—his own right to continue to use the road free from liability for repair—in a manner that left the grantee in a position to exercise the authority granted for the purposes for which it was conveyed.[46] A more extreme version of this principle is found in the few cases that consider it a derogation from the grant for the grantor to use his land in a way that undermines the value of what he granted.[47]

A canonical statement of this strand of non-derogation is by Wood V-C:

> If a landowner conveys one of two closes to another, he cannot *afterwards* do anything to derogate from his grant and if the conveyance is made for the express purpose of having a building erected upon the land so granted, a contract is implied on the part of the grantor to do nothing to prevent the land from being used for the purpose for which to the knowledge of the grantor the conveyance is made.[48]

[46] The courts resist implying positive covenants as such. See *Halsbury's Laws of England, Landlord and Tendant* vol. 62 (2016) para. 411 < https://www.lexisnexis.ca/en-ca/products/halsburys-laws-of-england.page> accessed January 28, 2020: "Neither the express covenant for quiet enjoyment nor the implied covenant against derogation from grant can impose on the landlord positive obligations to repair which he would not otherwise be obliged to perform." See also *Halsbury's Laws of England, Animals* vol. 2 (2017) para. 70 < https://www.lexisnexis.ca/en-ca/products/halsburys-laws-of-england.page> accessed January 28, 2020, on grant of shooting rights—the usual use and management of land is retained: "But any act done with the intention of injuring the rights granted or any user of the land which does not fall within the ordinary course of its management, or which works a substantial change in its character is, if it substantially injures the rights granted, a derogation from the grant and a breach of the usual covenant for quiet enjoyment."

[47] *Hefazi v. Stiglitz*, 862 A.2d 901 (DC 2004) (doctrine of implied grants of easements for light and air considered, although no easement found on the facts). A widely held view is that grantors cannot destroy but can interfere with the value of the grant in the exercise of their own rights.

[48] *North Eastern Rly. Co. v. Elliot* 1860, 1 John & H 145, 153 (my emphasis). This strand of non-derogation is a general principle in property law but it is found most commonly in the context of landlord–tenant law—where the purposes of the grant tend to be more clearly articulated. See *Halsbury's Laws of England, Landlord and Tenant* vol. 62 (2016) para. 414 < https://www.lexisnexis.ca/en-ca/products/halsburys-laws-of-england.page> accessed January 28, 2020: "In addition to any obligation to give quiet enjoyment, the landlord is under an obligation not to derogate from his grant; and this obligation is not excluded by an express covenant for quiet enjoyment. Thus, where a lease is made for a particular purpose, the landlord is under an obligation not to use adjoining land retained by him in such a way as to render the demised premises unfit or materially less fit for that purpose.")

(The same principle applies in grants of partial authority, for example leases, easements, where the grantor is constrained not to prevent the grantee's exercising her authority for the purpose for which it was conferred.)[49]

The grantor's obligations to adjust her rights to the interests of the grantee can be understood as just another way in which property law makes sense of and preserves the integrity of a grant in light of the ideal of a grant as the conveyance of full authority. It is thus more concerned with rationality than the actual intentions of the grantor. As Lord Denning put it:

> it is a general principle of law that if one man agrees to confer a particular benefit on another he must not do anything which substantially deprives the other of the enjoyment of that benefit because that would be to take away with one hand what is given with the other . . . Sometimes it is rested on an implied term in the contract. But this is not correct. It is a principle evolved by the law itself.[50]

Lord Denning was talking about the obligations of a grantor of a lease in relation to its power to consent to an enforcement order from the city council that would subvert the purpose of the grant. The original grantor, a Crown corporation, had granted a lease for ninety-nine years for purposes of either residential or professional offices. After the grant, because of changes in local planning law, the tenants (the original grantee's successors) were required to get permission from the local council to change the use from residential to professional offices. The grantee's successors converted the space without permission (but in keeping with the purposes of their lease). Because the land was Crown land, the council required the consent of the original grantor in order to serve an enforcement notice on the tenant. The alleged derogation of the grant consisted in the grantor's exercising its power to consent to the council's enforcement notice, the service of which required the tenant to remedy breach of planning law. The obligation imposed on the grantor not to derogate from its grant would have required the grantor to exercise independent powers it retained as a Crown corporation, and to cooperate with the local council so as to deliver to the grantee and its successors the means of enjoying the grant: the ability to use the land for the purposes for which the grant is made.

[49] See discussion of *Paragon Finance Plc v. City of London Real Property Co. Ltd.* [2002] EGLR 97 in Jonathan Gaunt, *Gale on Easements* (20th ed., (Sweet & Maxwell 2016) para. 13-23 (limiting only the landlord's ability to destroy what was granted but not restricting all interferences).

[50] *Molton Builders Ltd. v. City of Westminster London Borough Council* [1976] 1 EGLR 150, 152.

This strand of non-derogation can be accounted for in terms of the integrity of the grant as the shared foundation of rights and duties of the grantor and the grantee and their successors. A grant establishes the authority of the grantee and her successor vis-à-vis the world at large: it is the basis upon which they ground their claim to be the ones entitled to set the agenda for that object, regulating how others can relate to it. But a grant is also the shared foundation of the rights and duties *as between* the grantor and grantee: the grant determines how things stand between them with respect to that thing. This shared foundation is a close analogue to the privity forged through contract, where two people each ground their normative position vis-à-vis the other with respect to that matter in the same contract. Like all relationships of privity, this one is maintained by principles of honesty and even loyalty that persist for as long as they stand on that shared foundation of right. The privity between a grantor and grantee, like that between the state as warrantor and owner as warrantee, or that between a seller and buyer in a contractual relationship reflects a vision of a shared juridical foundation for that interaction or relationship. It is this foundation that is being chipped away at when one person acts to undermine that shared foundation. It is a special kind of disloyalty that arises in these contexts of privity. When it comes to public law, the state warrants an owner's authority and so is bound to remain true to its own warrant in its future dealings with that owner. It would be dishonest and disloyal to do otherwise. And in the context of contract law there is a similar basis for treating a party who seeks to exercise her rights and powers in such a way as to undermine the very contract to which she and the defendant stand. A person who eats the horse she has promised to sell to another does not violate an implied term not to eat the horse.[51] She has acted disloyally to the buyer who stands in a relation of privity to her: she has undermined the very basis upon which the contract might continue to stand as the foundation of rights and obligations for both. She has made a dishonest transaction of it.

III. Conclusion

My account of a principle of non-derogation reveals also how it relates to other currents in private law that seem to pull in a different direction. Once the threshold for recognizing a change in legal relations is met, by a clear exercise of a power to bring about that change, the law's concern is then to make sense

[51] Robert Stevens offered this example in conversation.

of the transaction. Voluntarist as to whether a legal power is exercised, the law's approach is rationalist as to the effects of its exercise, making sense of particular grants in terms of the ideal of a grant. This explains both why there is a strong presumption against change in our relations with others (and the demand for juridical reasons to explain any change) and at the same time, once rebutted, a presumption that the grant conveys what is reasonably necessary for it to operate as the appointment of another fully to *that* position of authority.

3

The Hegemony of the Reasonable Person in Anglo-American Tort Law

Kenneth W. Simons

I. Introduction: Negligence, Reasonableness and the Reasonable Person

It is common to divide Anglo-American tort doctrine into three broad categories: intentional torts, negligence, and strict liability. In the last century, negligence has been ascendant. More precisely, tort liability has increasingly required proof either of negligence or of an intentional tort, while strict liability, in the sense of liability without fault, persists only for a small number of circumscribed categories.[1]

The increasing importance of negligence liability has been accompanied by the progressive dilution or elimination of doctrines that restricted such liability, including the privity requirement, sovereign immunity, and more limited duties to licensees or trespassers who enter one's land (discussed below). At the same time, a number of negligence doctrines have extended liability. Recovery is increasingly allowed for negligent infliction of emotional harm unaccompanied by physical harm. "Enabling" torts have expanded, imposing liability on a wide range of actors, including therapists for not warning potential victims of their patients' criminal acts; landlords, businesses, and universities for not preventing criminal acts; businesses (and occasionally social hosts) who serve liquor to obviously intoxicated persons; and those who leave keys in the ignitions of cars that are then stolen.[2] "Reasonable foreseeability"

[1] This story oversimplifies, because strict product liability expanded in the middle of the twentieth century and because intentional torts and negligence doctrines contain what might be characterized as "strict liability" elements. Examples include the irrelevance of fault as to the ownership of property in trespass to land, and the objective criterion of fault in negligence, which ignores an actor's mental incapacities.

[2] Robert L. Rabin, "Enabling Torts" (1999) 49 DePaul LR 435.

Kenneth W. Simons, *The Hegemony of the Reasonable Person in Anglo-American Tort Law* In: *Oxford Studies in Private Law Theory: Volume 1*. Edited by: Paul B. Miller and John Oberdiek, Oxford University Press (2020). © The Several Contributors.
DOI: 10.1093/oso/9780198851356.003.0003

of the harm is a decisive factor in establishing liability in these enabling torts.[3] Moreover, although the advent of strict products liability for manufacturing defects was widely expected to augur a general expansion of strict liability, this did not occur, and negligence was remarkably resilient.[4]

As a purer, more unqualified form of negligence has thus emerged, it becomes all the more critical to understand the meaning and scope of a central feature of negligence doctrine: the reasonable person.

In American tort law, jury instructions in negligence cases are typically rather perfunctory, asking whether the defendant failed to act as a "reasonably prudent person" or "reasonably careful person" or "reasonable person" would have acted under the same circumstances. Some instructions also indicate that negligence is the lack of "ordinary care."[5]

The reasonable person test is, to some extent, an idealized standard. Customary or average behavior is not necessarily reasonable behavior, except in limited circumstances such as professional negligence. It is improper, for example, to instruct members of a jury in a negligence case that they should decide whether they would have acted as defendant or plaintiff acted if they had been in his or her shoes. A compelling example (with which I am intimately familiar, after residing most of my life in Boston) is the typical Boston driver, who accelerates through a yellow traffic light or a light that has just turned red, without regard to traffic conditions. On the other hand, the way in which most ordinary individuals act surely seems relevant to what reasonable care demands.

The extent to which the reasonable person test is idealized and departs from ordinary or normal behavior is an important issue in describing and defending that test, as we shall see. But an initial question is why, if one is employing an evaluative criterion for legal liability, it would ever make sense to frame that criterion in terms of a reasonable person. Why not employ an evaluative criterion that explicitly invokes the relevant normative principle? That criterion might be "act in a way that shows equal respect for the interests of others" (as a corrective justice or contractualist theorist might say[6]) or "take the optimal

[3] Similarly, proximate cause is increasingly understood as extending to all "reasonably foreseeable" harms, an approach that is usually more expansive than the traditional directness test of proximate cause.

[4] G. Edward White, *Tort Law in America: An Intellectual History* (Expanded edn, OUP 2003) ch. 8.

[5] Benjamin Zipursky, "Sleight of Hand" (2007) 48 Wm. & Mary LR 1999, 2013–17; Patrick J. Kelley and Laurel A. Wendt, "What Judges Tell Juries About Negligence: A Review of Pattern Jury Instructions" (2002) 77 Chi-Kent LR 587, 595–612.

[6] For a recent discussion of Kantian theories of tort law, see Alan D. Miller and Ronen Perry, "The Reasonable Person" (2012) 87 NYULR 323, 348–61. Contractualist accounts include John Oberdiek, *Imposing Risk: A Normative Framework* (OUP 2017); Gregory Keating, "A Social Contract Conception of the Tort Law of Accidents" in Gerald J. Postema (ed.), *Philosophy and the Law of Torts* (CUP 2001).

precaution in light of the expected costs and benefits of all alternatives" (as the economists would have it[7]). It is not obvious why the reasonable person would make an appearance.[8]

A first answer to this preliminary question is that a reasonable person test performs a number of functions.[9] By personifying fault, it makes the requisite analysis of fault more concrete and vivid, which is especially valuable when the jury is the trier of fact. Moreover, many negligence cases do not involve advertent fault: the actor often has not made a conscious choice between alternative possible precautions. Consider cases of deficient skill, such as a surgeon whose hand slips or a rider who loses control of her bicycle despite utmost attention to the risk, as well as cases of inadvertent negligence, such as an automobile driver who forgets to check his side mirror before changing lanes. In these cases, the reasonable person test is especially appealing, and indeed no sensible substitute comes readily to mind.[10]

Furthermore, a reasonable person test can readily permit a significant degree of individualization. If we wish to make allowance for the fact that the actor is a child, is suffering from a physical disability, or confronts emergency circumstances permitting very little time to assess the risks of different alternatives (or very little time to think at all before acting), we can qualify the reasonable person to accommodate those special facts—thus, the reasonable child, the reasonable blind person, the reasonable person facing an emergency. And we can qualify the test even further—thus, the reasonable child of the actor's age, maturity, intelligence, and experience.[11] It is unclear how individualization could be achieved without employing a reasonable person test.

At the same time, the reasonable person test, unless supplemented with additional criteria, is extraordinarily vague. This creates a serious risk of inconsistency: presented with identical facts, a different judge or jury could easily reach a different conclusion about whether the actor failed to satisfy the test.

[7] Richard A. Posner, *Economic Analysis of Law* (9th edn, Wolters Kluwer 2014) ss 6.1 and 6.2; Steven Shavell, *Foundations of Economic Analysis of Law* (HUP 2004) ch. 8.

[8] Indeed, advocates of economic explanations of tort law have some difficulty explaining the point and value of the reasonable person test.

[9] The following analysis is drawn from Kenneth W. Simons, "Dimensions of Negligence in Criminal and Tort Law" (2002) 3 Theo. Inq. L. 283.

[10] For further discussion of deficient skill and inadvertent negligence cases, see Zipursky (n 5) 19–20; Kenneth W. Simons, "The Hand Formula in the Draft Restatement Third of Torts: Encompassing Fairness as Well as Efficiency Values" (2001) 54 Vand. LR 901, 931–33. Zipursky helpfully distinguishes the "performance-negligence" issue that arises in these cases from "precaution-negligence."

[11] Am. L. Inst., *Restatement, Third, Torts: Liability for Physical and Emotional Harm* (Am. L. Inst. 2010) § 10. Similarly, a reasonable person test can more readily accommodate excuses (such as duress or provocation) as well as justifications. Simons (n 9) 314; John Gardner, *The Reasonable Person Standard, The International Encyclopedia of Ethics* (Hugh LaFolette ed., 2nd edn, forthcoming 2020); John Gardner, "The Many Faces of the Reasonable Person" (2015) 131 LQR 563.

And insofar as a legal definition of negligence is intended to guide behavior, or at least provide notice of what is permitted and prohibited, such vagueness is highly problematic.[12]

There is much more to ponder about the reasonable person test in tort law. For now, I put off further general analysis and focus instead on four doctrinal examples that illuminate a range of descriptive and normative difficulties that the test poses.

II. Four Doctrinal Examples

A. Duties toward Land Entrants: Problematic Oversimplification

Historically, Anglo-American law drew a clear distinction between the duties owed by landowners and land possessors toward three different categories of entrants onto the land—invitees, licensees, and trespassers. The highest duty was owed to invitees, a lesser duty to licensees, and the least to trespassers. (For example, the owner owes a duty to inspect for hidden defects for the benefit of invitees but not for the benefit of licensees or trespassers; and she owes a duty to alert invitees and licenses, but not trespassers, about known dangers.) With respect to invitees and licensees, distinct rules specified the scope of the duty and thus whether the defendant was negligent. With respect to trespassers, the duty analysis identified the limited circumstances in which the defendant was liable for negligence, and clarified that in most circumstances, negligence was insufficient for liability, and "wilful or wanton conduct" or some similarly aggravated form of fault was required.

However, by the middle of the twentieth century, many courts became dissatisfied with these traditional rules. In the United Kingdom and many American states, the distinction between invitees and licensees was abolished by statute or by judicial decision.[13] The California Supreme Court went even

[12] Kenneth Abraham, "The Trouble with Negligence" (2001) 54 Vand. LR 1187. See also James Henderson, "Expanding the Negligence Concept: Retreat from the Rule of Law" (1976) 51 Ind. LJ 467, noting concern that negligence standards are 'polycentric,' i.e., open-ended and dependent on a variety of incommensurable factors; George Fletcher, "The Right and the Reasonable" (1985) 98 Harv. L. Rev. 949, 962, stating 'The reasonable person enables us to blur the line between justification and excuse, between wrongfulness and blameworthiness, and thus renders impossible any ordering of the dimensions of liability.'

[13] Occupiers' Liability Act 1957 (OLA 1957), s. 2(2), establishing "a duty to take such care as in all the circumstances of the case is reasonable."

further in *Rowland v. Christian*,[14] purporting to abolish not only that distinction, but also the distinction between those categories and the category of trespasser. The *Rowland* decision is worth considering in more detail.

In *Rowland*, the court began with a statement of the general duty to use ordinary care to prevent harm to others and articulated a multifactor balancing test to decide when it is proper to depart from this general duty. The traditional classification had, according to the court, led to strained and artificial distinctions,[15] problematic "subtleties and confusion" and "complexity,"[16] and application of rules that was "difficult and often arbitrary."[17] The court noted that California courts had characterized the rules as "unrealistic, arbitrary, and inelastic," involving "exceedingly fine distinctions."[18]

In a rhetorically powerful passage, the court explained:

> A man's life or limb does not become less worthy of protection by the law nor a loss less worthy of compensation under the law because he has come upon the land of another without permission or with permission but without a business purpose. Reasonable people do not ordinarily vary their conduct depending upon such matters, and to focus upon the status of the injured party as a trespasser, licensee, or invitee in order to determine the question whether the landowner has a duty of care, is contrary to our modern social mores and humanitarian values.

Notice the court's invocation of "reasonable people" as an independent criterion for evaluating the landowner duty rules, as if it is perfectly obvious that the reasonable person test is the presumptively correct legal test to employ in tort law.

However, in the process of announcing a new unitary reasonable person test to replace the traditional three-fold classification, the court seemed to want to have it both ways, for the court paid lip service to the potential relevance of the entrant's status:

> The proper test to be applied to the liability of the possessor of land . . . is whether in the management of his property he has acted as a reasonable man in view of the probability of injury to others, and, although the plaintiff's

[14] 443 P 2d 561 (Cal. 1968).
[15] Ibid. 565.
[16] Ibid. 566.
[17] Ibid. 567.
[18] Ibid. 567.

> status as a trespasser, licensee, or invitee may in the light of the facts giving rise to such status have some bearing on the question of liability, the status is not determinative.[19]

This is a maddeningly obscure concession. How, exactly, is status still relevant? To assert that it "may . . . have some bearing" without being "determinative" offers very little guidance.[20]

To be sure, the judicial rejection (or downplaying) of the traditional distinctions between entrants has much to commend it, especially with respect to the distinction between invitees and licensees.[21] What is striking about *Rowland*, however, is the court's confidence that switching to a unitary reasonable person test will solve all the problems that the traditional classifications engendered. Is a simple reasonable person jury instruction really sufficient to capture the policies and principles underlying the traditional categories, including the fair expectations of the parties, the rights of property owners, and the fault or illegal conduct of the victim?[22]

The evolving law concerning liability to different categories of land entrants displays increasing sympathy for the plight of victims, rejection of rule-based criteria in favor of the simpler standard of reasonable care, and an untested faith that triers of fact can incorporate into their reasonable person analysis those factual and normative features of the traditional categorical rules that are relevant and justifiable under contemporary norms.

[19] Ibid. 567.

[20] According to Dan B. Dobbs, Paul T. Hayden, and Ellen M. Bublick, *The Law of Torts* (2nd edn, updated June 2016) s. 378:

> Courts sometimes say explicitly that the status of the visitor remains relevant on the issue of the foreseeability of the harm or the landowner's reasonable expectations. That is a shorthand expression; it is not the status itself that is relevant but some of the facts that establish status.

[21] The Restatement, Third, Torts, adopted by the American Law Institute in 2010, rejects the invitee/licensee distinction. *Restatement, Third, Torts: Liability for Physical and Emotional Harm* (n 11) §§ 49–54. So does the statutory law of the United Kingdom, OLA 1957 .

[22] Other courts did not share *Rowland*'s confidence: very few went as far as *Rowland* in eliminating *all* of the status categories, including even trespassers. And in California itself, controversial cases arose after *Rowland* that permitted trespassers to sue landowners, including a case in which a trespasser successfully sued a school district after he fell through a skylight while attempting to illegally remove floodlights from the roof of a school gymnasium. These cases prompted the legislature to respond by precluding lawsuits by criminal felons. Cal. Code § 847 (West).

B. Assumption of Risk: The Problematic Merger into Comparative Fault

Another illustration of the ascendance of the reasonable person is how American courts dramatically changed their treatment of the defense of assumption of risk in the middle of the twentieth century. This development, too, resulted in increased liability of potential defendants. However, the expansion of the reasonable person test into this domain has also been problematic.

The basic story is familiar, but its implications are less well understood. The traditional contributory negligence doctrine was all-or-nothing: if the victim was even slightly at fault, he recovered nothing, even if the injurer was highly negligent. Over time, by legislation or judicial decree, almost all American jurisdictions adopted comparative fault, permitting the trier of fact to allocate legal responsibility in proportion to each party's fault. This change greatly benefited victims, who at least had the hope of partial recovery even if they acted negligently.

The elimination of the harsh traditional contributory negligence doctrine left open the question of the continued vitality of other victim-focused doctrines, especially assumption of risk. Under the latter doctrine, courts precluded any recovery if the victim knowingly and voluntarily chose to confront the risk that the injurer negligently created. With the advent of comparative fault, however, most jurisdictions abolished assumption of risk as an independent and complete defense and "merged" it within comparative fault.[23] Under merger, if the plaintiff's voluntary and knowing choice to assume a risk was unreasonable, the plaintiff would have a chance to recover at least partial damages under comparative fault, while if her choice was reasonable, she would recover in full. Thus, the plaintiff often would be better off under merger than under the traditional assumption of risk rule. For example, if the plaintiff intervenes to assist a person being roughed up by unruly patrons in a bar and thereby incurs their wrath and suffers injury, traditional assumption of risk would bar recovery, but under the merger approach, the plaintiff would likely obtain full recovery.[24]

Meistrich v. Casino Arena Attractions is a leading case espousing the merger approach. As the court explained:

[23] Similarly, in English law, the advent of legislation requiring apportionment of fault between negligent defendants and negligent plaintiffs has resulted in a narrowing of the assumption of risk defense. James Goudkamp, "Defences to Negligence" in C. Sappideen and P. Vines (eds.), *Fleming's The Law of Torts* (10th edn, Thompson Reuters 2011) 335. In Australia, by contrast, all states have enacted legislation expanding the scope of assumption of risk: Ibid. 343.

[24] *Fagan v. Atnalta*, 376 SE 2d 204 (Ga. App. 1988), applying traditional assumption of risk principles to deny recovery on these facts.

> [A]ssumption of risk . . . [as a defense to negligence] is a mere phase of contributory negligence, the total issue being whether a reasonably prudent man in the exercise of due care (a) would have incurred the known risk and (b) if he would, whether such a person in the light of all of the circumstances including the appreciated risk would have conducted himself in the manner in which plaintiff acted.[25]

Remarkably, the opinion pays no heed to one of the principal rationales for the traditional assumption of risk doctrine—that it reflects the plaintiff's consent to the risk that the defendant negligently created.[26] Contrast this explanation from the Rhode Island Supreme Court, which has bucked the trend of merger and retained the independent defense:

> [C]ontributory negligence and assumption of the risk do not overlap; the key difference is . . . the exercise of one's free will in encountering the risk. Negligence analysis, couched in reasonable man hypotheses, has no place in the assumption of the risk framework. When one acts knowingly, it is immaterial whether he acts reasonably. The postulate . . . that assumption of the risk is merely a variant of contributory fault, is not, to our minds, persuasive.[27]

Advocates of merger do not explain why consent should be ignored in the context of negligently caused harm when consent is universally understood to be a vital defense to intentional torts, whether or not the plaintiff's decision to consent was reasonable.[28] If Harry Houdini dares someone to punch him in the stomach as hard as he likes, the doctrine of consent would preclude Houdini's recovery for the resulting injury, whether we deem his invitation to be reasonable or foolish. And if I ask you to speed when you drive me to the airport, and your resulting dangerous driving injures me, in some jurisdictions the doctrine of assumption of risk would preclude my recovery, again without regard to the reasonableness of my encouraging you to speed.

[25] *Meistrich v. Casino Arena Attractions, Inc.*, 155 A 2d 90, 95–96 (NJ 1959).

[26] Indeed, in one passage, the court curtly states: "[W]e place beyond present discussion the problem raised by an express contract not to sue for injury or loss . . . and also situations in which actual consent exists, as, for example, participation in a contact sport." Ibid. 93. Yet the latter no-recovery category, in which plaintiff consents to what would otherwise be an intentional tort, is justified by the same basic consensual rationale as assumption of risk, according to advocates of an independent assumption of risk defense.

[27] *Kennedy v. Providence Hockey Club, Inc*, 376 A 2d 329, 76–77 (RI 1977).

[28] For a fuller exploration of the similarities and differences between the two consent contexts, see Kenneth W. Simons, "Exploring the Relationship between Consent, Assumption of Risk, and Contributory Fault" in John Oberdiek (ed.), *Philosophical Foundations of the Law of Torts* (OUP 2014); Kenneth W. Simons, "Reflections on Assumption of Risk" (2002) 50 UCLA LR 481.

To be sure, recognizing an independent assumption of risk defense has its dangers, especially the risk that the scope of the defense as applied will greatly exceed its legitimate underlying rationale.[29] In my view, the defense should be retained but interpreted narrowly.[30] Thus, in the case where the plaintiff attempts to rescue someone from a beating and suffers injury, the defense should not apply and the plaintiff should obtain partial or full recovery under comparative fault; but in the case where the passenger encourages a driver to speed, the passenger should be denied recovery.

Although the prevalent American approach to assumption of risk after the advent of comparative fault is abolition and merger, this does not mean that all fact patterns that traditionally would be handled by the defense of assumption of risk now result in complete recovery (if the plaintiff acted reasonably) or potential partial recovery (if the plaintiff acted unreasonably). Assumption of risk lives on as a complete defense even in many "abolitionist" jurisdictions, but it survives in altered form, as "primary assumption of risk."[31]

Under primary assumption of risk, courts decide, as a matter of law, that a particular category of activity is not subject to liability, or is subject only to limited liability,[32] based in significant part on the fact that many or most participants in the activity consent to the relevant risks. Primary assumption of risk is a type of no-duty or limited-duty rule.

[29] Jurisdictions such as Rhode Island that retain the defense often struggle over the question of scope and resort to artificial criteria, such as demanding that the defendant surmount a surprisingly high threshold to establish that a plaintiff's choice was "voluntary." Compare *Kennedy* (n 27) with *Hennessey v. Pyne*, 694 A 2d 691 (RI 1977) (jury question whether plaintiff voluntarily assumed risk of being hit by golf ball).

[30] I believe that assumption of risk should be retained in only two situations—when the plaintiff actually preferred, ex ante, the risky alternative that the defendant negligently created to the less risky, non-negligent alternative that would have avoided the plaintiff's harm; and when the plaintiff insisted on a relationship with defendant. See Simons, 'Reflections on Assumption of Risk' (n 28).

[31] Similarly, English courts have recognized limited duty rules in the context of sporting injuries. As stated in *Blake v. Galloway* [2004] 1 WLR 2844, "a breach of the duty of care will only be established where there has been recklessness or a very high degree of carelessness." See S. Deakin, A. Johnston, and B Markesinis, *Markesinis and Deakin's Tort Law* (7th edn, OUP 2013) 768. See also James Goudkamp, *Tort Law Defences* (Hart Publishing 2013) 58 (noting that when courts deny recovery based on assumption of risk, although they refer to the doctrine as a defense, "they are frequently holding that there is no negligence on the part of the defendant.").

Canadian courts also recognize limited duty rules in sporting and recreational activities cases, while at the same time recognizing only a very narrow conception of assumption of risk, one that requires that the plaintiff agreed to accept both the physical and legal risks (i.e., impliedly agreeing to waive one's right to sue in tort). See G. H. L. Fridman, *The Law of Torts in Canada* (3rd edn, Thompson Reuters 2010) 447–54, 457–59; A. Linden and B. Feldthusen, *Canadian Tort Law* (8th edn, LexisNexis Canada 2006) 508–13.

[32] A common way of limiting liability is to preclude recovery for simple negligence and to require the plaintiff to prove reckless or wanton conduct or conduct intended to harm. See, e.g., *Knight v. Jewitt*, 834 P 2d 696, 711 (Cal. 1992).

It is striking that if a jurisdiction aggressively employs the "no duty" approach, the supposed death of assumption of risk is greatly exaggerated. If abolishing the defense of assumption of risk is accompanied by expanding the limited duty rule of primary assumption of risk, then many victims are no better off, and some may indeed be worse off, than if neither change had been made.[33]

An intriguing alternative approach to both primary and secondary assumption of risk has been endorsed by a few American jurisdictions: employ an extremely flexible conception of what constitutes negligence on the part of an injurer, one that takes into account the policies and principles that underlie these assumption of risk doctrines.[34] Thus, in *Pfenning v. Lineman*, the Indiana Supreme Court rejected a limited duty rule for sports participants, and instead purported to adopt a negligence test: "[I]n negligence claims against a participant in a sports activity, if the conduct of such participant is within the range of ordinary behavior of participants in the sport, the conduct is reasonable as a matter of law and does not constitute a breach of duty."[35] The court then applied the test to several claims, including a claim that a golfer failed to yell "fore" and thus failed to give a reasonable warning to the plaintiff when the golfer's drive hooked to the left. The court concluded that, even if the golfer did not yell "fore" loudly enough, and even if he did not warn at all (an omission that violates conventional golf etiquette), as a matter of law such an inadequate warning "is within the ordinary behavior of golfers." But this reasoning, it should be clear, employs a stipulative definition of reasonable care, no different in substance from other courts' more candid formulation that mere negligence (here, in failing to shout a warning) is insufficient for liability to other participants in a sporting activity.

[33] They may be worse off in two respects. First, the plaintiff has the burden of proving duty (which is negated by primary assumption of risk), while the defendant has the burden of proving the defense of secondary assumption of risk. Second, primary assumption of risk is a wholesale judgment that an activity is not subject to liability in light of the preferences of many or most participants (as well as other factors), while the defense of assumption of risk is a retail judgment requiring the defendant to prove, case by case, that the individual plaintiff subjectively was aware of, and voluntarily chose to encounter, the risk.

Under primary assumption of risk, for example, a first-time spectator to a baseball game who knows nothing about the risks of being hit by a foul ball or by a flung bat would be precluded from recovery. The more subjective defense of secondary assumption of risk would not have that preclusive effect. See Simons, 'Reflections on Assumption of Risk' (n 28).

[34] See, e.g., *American Powerlifting Ass'n v. Cotillo*, 934 A 2d 27 (Md. 2007) (spotters failed to catch the bar during powerlifting competition); *Allen v. Dover Co-Recreational Softball League*, 807 A 2d 1274 (NH 2002) (errant throw in recreational softball game); *Auckenthaler v. Grundmeyer*, 877 P 2d 1039 (Nev. 1994) (plaintiff injured while riding horse by another rider's horse); *Lestina v. West Bend Mutual Ins Co*, 501 NW 2d 28 (Wisc. 1993) (plaintiff injured by collision during recreational soccer match).

[35] *Pfenning v. Lineman*, 947 NE 2d 392, 404 (Ind. 2011).

This unusually flexible "negligence" approach creates a more fundamental problem: it conceals the significant weight accorded to the preferences and consent of participants in an activity as reasons for precluding liability. I believe it would be more honest to recognize that such consent is an independently weighty reason for denying tort liability. Consider another claim asserted by the plaintiff in *Pfenning*: she had never played golf before and did not know anything about its safety or etiquette rules; thus, she could not subjectively appreciate the risks she faced. The court responded that the operator of the golf course had an "objectively reasonable expectation . . . that persons present on its golf course would realize the risk of being struck by an errant golf ball and take appropriate precautions."[36] But the operator surely knew that not all persons on the course fully appreciated that risk. The operator's justification for not taking further precautions to protect unaware victims deserves more careful analysis than this. Perhaps it would be unrealistic or unduly burdensome to take extensive precautions against the harms of mishit golf balls, because most participants in the activity would prefer an affordable and bucolic experience. Towering brick walls separating fairways from each other would effectively reduce these risks, as would replacing current golf balls with plastic whiffle balls. But such precautions would undermine the value of the sport to participants. Golf is a good walk, whether or not Mark Twain is correct that it is a good walk spoiled.[37]

C. Plaintiff's Negligence: The Problematic Symmetry with Defendant's Negligence

A third legal context in which the reasonable person test is more problematic than first appears is its use to characterize the negligence of a tort victim.[38] The reflexive judicial approach, in all Anglo-American jurisdictions, is to apply a symmetrical standard of care for victims and injurers: just as injurers are liable for failure to use reasonable care to prevent harm to others, victims receive reduced compensation insofar as they failed to use reasonable care to prevent harm to themselves. The advent of comparative fault has made this

[36] Ibid. 406.

[37] Alas, it appears that Mark Twain is not the original source of the quote. See: <http://quoteinvestigator.com/2010/05/28/golf-good-walk>.

[38] Much of the discussion that follows is drawn from Kenneth W. Simons, "Victim Fault and Victim Strict Responsibility in Anglo-American Tort Law" (2016) 8 J. Tort L. 29. See also Robert Stevens, "Should Contributory Fault Be Analogue or Digital?" in Dyson, Goudkamp, and Wilmont-Smith, *Defences in Tort* (Hart Publishing 2015).

symmetrical approach seem inexorable and unremarkable. And the standard of the reasonable person may seem to support this approach, insofar as it suggests a requirement that the actor exercise moderation between excessive and deficient attention to risk (whether to others or to oneself).

Quite often, however, the legal system does not actually adopt a symmetrical attitude toward victim and injurer conduct. Courts depart from symmetry in a number of ways. Thus, courts recognize several categorical doctrines that permit *full* recovery without regard to the possible fault of the victim (e.g., when the defendant has a duty to protect the victim from his own vulnerability or incapacity, or when the defendant is engaged to provide medical care or other services to the victim necessitated by the victim's own prior fault). Courts also recognize categorical doctrines that automatically preclude *any* recovery despite the supposed presumptive status of comparative fault (e.g., the illegality doctrine, the mitigation of damages doctrine, and, as we have just seen, the defense of voluntary assumption of risk).

Even when courts do permit the comparison of victim conduct with injurer conduct, the way in which victim conduct is relevant to tort liability is frequently qualitatively different from the way in which injurer conduct is relevant. Often, when legal rules characterize a victim as being "at fault," this does not mean that the victim should have acted differently, but only that he should be strictly responsible for his choice or action (e.g., because he justifiably forfeited his right to full damages). Indeed, sometimes, a victim actually has a moral or legal right *not* to take a precaution, yet it is appropriate to deny him full damages for the harm that the precaution would have averted. An example: a victim's religious beliefs counsel against following a doctor's advice about how to recover from surgery, with the result that the victim's injuries are vastly increased.

Nevertheless, symmetry is sometimes appropriate, especially when the actor's unreasonable conduct creates substantial risks both to others and to himself (e.g., when the actor drives an automobile carelessly). But in many other cases, symmetry is much less defensible, at least if one endorses a largely nonconsequentialist rather than a purely utilitarian account of tort law. On certain utilitarian accounts, especially those that evaluate legal rules according to whether they maximize economic efficiency, the only question is whether an actor made the optimal choice among alternatives; it is irrelevant whether the actor is endangering only others, only himself, or some combination of the two. A nonconsequentialist account, by contrast, might decline to treat an actor as unreasonable in the same sense, or to the same degree, when he endangers only or mainly himself, as when he endangers others: such an account might recognize a more robust duty to avoid injuring others than to avoid injuring oneself.[39]

Granted, the vagueness of the reasonable person test makes it difficult to know whether a fact-finder applying the test is interpreting it in symmetrical fashion to the negligence of an injurer and of a victim. Perhaps the jury or judge will usually treat unreasonable risk to others as a qualitatively more serious type of fault than unreasonable risk to self. However, if one shares my belief that these are indeed qualitatively distinct phenomena that often should be treated asymmetrically, it might be sensible to so instruct the jury or to have the judge apply different standards. The larger lesson is that articulating negligence *simply* in terms of the reasonable person may, once again, flatten analysis and ignore prominent features of the legal topography.

D. Liability Only if Plaintiff Responded "Reasonably": A Problematic Limitation

A number of tort doctrines (apart from contributory and comparative fault) make liability depend on how a reasonable or average person in plaintiff's position would react to defendant's conduct.[40] Thus, the invasion of privacy torts consider whether an intrusion on seclusion or the publication of a private fact "would be highly offensive to a reasonable person."[41] Fraud requires reasonable or justifiable reliance by plaintiff.[42] Products liability law employs a "reasonable consumer expectation" test in two contexts—when determining liability

[39] Indeed, it is doubtful that a victim has an actual "duty" not to unreasonably injure himself. Kenneth W. Simons, "The Puzzling Doctrine of Contributory Negligence"(1995) 16 Cardozo L. Rev. 1693, 1795; Stevens (n 38) 254.

[40] Benjamin Zipursky uses the term 'secondary qualities' to describe legal properties that depend on how others respond, in thought or emotion, to the defendant's conduct:

> The idea is that just as colors are defined in reference to the perceptual responses of normal persons, so too are certain legal qualities defined in reference to the affective responses of normal persons. For these kinds of qualities, the word 'reasonable' is typically used in defining moments.

Benjamin C. Zipursky, "Reasonableness In and Out of Negligence Law" (2015) 163 U. Pa. LR 2131, 2144.

[41] Am. L. Inst., *Restatement, Second, Torts* (Am. L. Inst. 1997) § 652B (requiring, for the privacy tort of intrusion on seclusion, that "the intrusion would be highly offensive to a reasonable person"); ibid. § 652D (requiring, for the privacy tort of publicity to private life, that "the matter publicized is of a kind that . . . would be highly offensive to a reasonable person").

[42] Am. L. Inst., *Restatement, Third, Torts: Liability for Economic Harm* (Am. L. Inst. 2020) § 11, cmt d; Jason Solomon, "Judging Plaintiffs" (2007) 60 Vand. LR 1749, 1765–67.

for food impurities[43] and, in some jurisdictions, when determining whether a product has been defectively designed.[44] A doctor's duty to disclose the risks of a proposed treatment depends, in most American jurisdictions, on whether a "reasonable patient" would find the risk material to the decision whether to choose the treatment.[45] A recent United Kingdom Supreme Court decision adopts a similar test, but also seems to support liability when the doctor should know that a particular patient would find a risk material, even if a reasonable patient would not.[46] And Title VII sexual harassment law considers whether a reasonable plaintiff (or perhaps a reasonable woman) would find the co-employee's advances unwelcome.[47]

In all of these contexts, employing a "reasonable person" test cuts against, rather than in favor of, liability. More precisely, it is more difficult for a plaintiff to satisfy such a test than to satisfy a purely subjective test that considers only the effect of the defendant's conduct on the individual plaintiff. The more objective test might preclude liability even though this particular plaintiff was highly offended by the intrusion upon seclusion, or actually relied upon the defendant's fraud, or considered an undisclosed risk from medical treatment material.

Many of these examples involve intentional torts. Indeed, the inclusion of reasonableness requirements in intentional torts extends further. For example, apparent consent precludes liability in American law when the defendant

[43] Thus, the Restatement Third of Torts: Product Liability provides that "a harm-causing ingredient of the food product constitutes a defect if a reasonable consumer would not expect the food product to contain that ingredient." Am. L. Inst., *Restatement, Third, Torts: Product Liability* (Am. L. Inst. 1992) § 7.

[44] Ibid. § 2, cmts g, h. The "consumer expectation" test of design defect, which tends to impose liability more readily than the competing risk-utility test, sometimes refers to the "reasonable" consumer and sometimes to the "ordinary" consumer. See, e.g., Restatement Second (n 41) § 402A, cmt i (product must be "dangerous to an extent beyond that which would be contemplated by the ordinary consumer").

[45] See, e.g., *Canterbury v. Spence*, 464 F 2d 772 (DC Cir. 1972). See also Dobbs, Hayden, and Bublick (n 20) s. 309 (jurisdictions are split between those that require only those disclosures that medical custom indicates should be disclosed, and those that require disclosures of information that a reasonable patient would want to have). In *Bernard v. Char*, 903 P 2d 667, 675 (Haw. 1995), the court endorses an objective test of causation but permits a great deal of individualization: "[V]iewing the question from a core of reasonableness establishes an initially uniform standard . . . from which adjustments for idiosyncracies may be made. . . . [T[he analytical exercise is grounded in objective reasonableness, but the standard may still flexibly accommodate the individual characteristics of each patient."

[46] See *Montgomery v. Lanarkshire Health Board*, [2015] UKSC 11 [87]:

> The doctor is . . . under a duty to take reasonable care to ensure that the patient is aware of any material risks involved in any recommended treatment, and of any reasonable alternative or variant treatments. The test of materiality is whether, in the circumstances of the particular case, a reasonable person in the patient's position would be likely to attach significance to the risk, *or the doctor is or should reasonably be aware that the particular patient would be likely to attach significance to it.* (emphasis added)

[47] See *Schiavo v. Marina Dist. Development Co., LLC*, 123 A 2d 272, 284 (NJ Super. (2015); Elizabeth L. Shoenfelt, Allison E. Maue, and JoAnn Nelson, "Reasonable Person Versus Reasonable Woman: Does It Matter?" (2002) 10 Am. UJ Gender Soc. Pol'y & L. 633.

reasonably (though mistakenly) believes that the plaintiff consented.[48] And a reasonable (though mistaken) belief in the facts that would establish a privilege such as self-defense typically precludes liability, in both the United States and Commonwealth jurisdictions.[49] In these instances, as well, reasonableness limits liability, as compared to a rule providing that, as between an innocent victim and a reasonable but mistaken defendant who causes harm, tort law should favor the victim.

Why do courts employ a reasonable victim test when the defendant's liability depends on the victim's response? One possible explanation is that the victim is expected to conform to a standard of appropriate behavior; therefore, we entirely preclude her from recovering if she fails to respond "reasonably." But this explanation is often quite implausible, both descriptively and normatively. It amounts to blaming the victim for failing to react "reasonably" to the defendant's intentional wrongdoing, a remarkable and unjustified extension of principles of comparative fault.

The most plausible rationale for employing a reasonable victim test in this context is fairness to defendants. It is arguably unfair to require defendants to mold their behavior to accommodate a plaintiff who possesses nonstandard preferences or who reacts to a defendant's conduct in an unusual way, when defendants could not reasonably expect that their behavior would have a legally cognizable effect on such a plaintiff. Moreover, problems of fraud might arise if a plaintiff knew that he or she could obtain a tort recovery based only on a subjective reaction that would not be shared by other similarly situated victims. Employing a reasonable person test also obviates the need for the judge to specify the conditions that limit defendant's liability, when the judge has the sense that some such limitation must be imposed. And finally, the reasonable person test is quite familiar to judges. Thus, invoking it in the "reasonable victim" context is an understandable extension.

When the law employs a reasonable person test for judging the reactions of plaintiffs, does "reasonable person" have the same meaning as when that criterion defines the necessary qualities of a defendant? It probably does

[48] See *Restatement, Second, Torts* (n 41) ss 50 and 892(2). In English law, however, authority appears to be divided concerning whether a reasonable mistake about consent will result in liability. See Sappideen and Vines (n 23), citing two cases as giving a negative answer, *Re F* [1990] 2 AC 1 and *Chatterton v. Gerson* [1981] QB 432 and one case as giving an affirmative answer, *Ashley v. Chief Constable of Sussex Police* [2008] 1 AC 962; [2008] 1 AC 974 (Lord Scott). An affirmative answer is given in Sir Percy Henry Winfield and John Anthony Jolowicz, *Winfield & Jolowicz on Tort* (W. Edwin Peel and James Goudkamp eds., 19th edn, Sweet & Maxwell 2014), but a negative answer in ibid. s. 26-013 (stating that the defendant's mistake about consent, even if reasonable, is not a defense, citing *Chatterton* (above)).

[49] See *Restatement, Second, Torts* (n 41) § 63; Sappideen and Vines (n 23) 99; Winfield and Jolowicz (n 48) s. 26-031.

not: "reasonable" in this context usually seems to mean average or customary, though the case law is sparse. Moreover, it often makes sense to employ a specialized meaning here. If the main purpose of such a test is fairness and notice to potentially liable actors, then "reasonable plaintiff" should be defined differently—not as a criterion of ideal behavior, but as a description of normal or typical behavior.[50] For we are asking, not whether the plaintiff acted responsibly or reasonably, but only whether the defendant had fair notice of how the plaintiff would act.

In many cases in this category, the distinction between a "reasonable" person test and a "normal" or "ordinary" person test will not affect the legal outcome, but in some cases, it might. At the extremes, it will be obvious that neither a reasonable person nor an ordinary person would care whether the nurse or doctor disclosed a one in a million chance of a mild side-effect from surgery such as constipation; while both the reasonable and the ordinary person will want to be informed about a 10 percent chance that paralysis will result. Similarly, in the self-defense context, either test would permit defensive force by an actor who is responding to an obvious, serious threat of force when no alternative seems to exist. However, in closer cases, the distinction can make a difference. Suppose a small drunk person suddenly approaches the defendant, swears at him and threatens to shove him, and the defendant immediately pushes the drunk away. A jury instructed to apply the reasonable person test to the actor's belief that the victim was making a genuine threat of force is somewhat less likely to support the claim of self-defense than if it is asked to apply an ordinary or average person test.[51]

An alternative possible approach for this general category is a subjective test, considering how the actual plaintiff reacted to the defendant's conduct. Thus, informed consent doctrine could employ a subjective test, inquiring whether the particular plaintiff would have attached importance to a particular risk in deciding whether to proceed with medical treatment.[52] In principle, a subjective test is the better approach, because it is the patient's individual profile that

[50] Zipursky (n 40) 2144 (characterizing the reasonable person test in these contexts as identifying "normal" responses).

[51] Self-defense reasonableness criteria should, however, be applied realistically, in light of the actor's need to make a quick decision based on incomplete information. One response to this problem is to examine the surrounding circumstances to determine whether the defendant's beliefs about necessity and proportionality were reasonable. Another response is to question the cognitive focus of these reasonableness requirements. See Kenneth W. Simons, "Self-Defense: Reasonable Beliefs or Reasonable Self-Control?" (2008) 11 New Crim. LR 51 (endorsing a reasonable self-control test in lieu of a reasonable belief standard in some self-defense cases).

[52] Some American jurisdictions do employ a subjective test. See, e.g., *Scott v. Bradford*, 606 P 2d 554 (Okla. 1979).

is most crucial in determining what information would be helpful to a decision about treatment. To be sure, practical difficulties might arise in applying the subjective test. How is the doctor or nurse to know the subjective desires of the patient? On the other hand, medical personnel and patients often have conversations about the risks and benefits of alternative treatments, and sound medical care calls for doctors and nurses to undertake at least some minimal investigation of the lifestyle choices and other preferences of the patient in order to ensure that risk disclosure is as useful as possible. Moreover, a reasonable person test is not necessarily easier to apply in this context than a subjective test. Given the opacity and vagueness of the reasonable person test, noted above, it is not at all clear that that test will result in more reliable and consistent jury verdicts on similar facts than the subjective test.

The law of offensive battery is another important illustration of this category of cases. Most American jurisdictions permit battery liability, not only for nonconsensual intentional physical contacts that cause harm, but also for those that cause offense. But what counts as offensive? The conventional answer is: those contacts that are offensive to a *reasonable* sense of dignity.[53]

In most situations, this answer is sensible. Suppose a woman shakes a man's hand after being introduced at a party, unaware that the man has a religious or other personal objection to touching any person of the opposite sex other than a family member. It would be unfair to find the woman liable for offensive battery, since she reasonably believed that the other person consented and did not find the touching offensive. But suppose the plaintiff has made his objection clear to the defendant in advance. What legitimate right does the defendant have to ignore his unusual, subjective preference? Similarly, suppose a guest at a wedding, for religious reasons, requests that she be served a meal other than pork. The caterer agrees to do so but later decides it is too much bother. Suppose he lies to the guest and asserts that the food does not contain pork.[54] If the guest then unknowingly consumes the pork, should there not be liability, since the caterer knows of the guest's special sensitivity, even though consuming pork might not be offensive to a "reasonable" sense of dignity? A compelling argument exists that offensive battery liability should be imposed, not only when the contact offends a reasonable sense of dignity, but also when the defendant knows that the contact will be offensive to a particular plaintiff's sense of dignity, even if the plaintiff's sense of dignity is unusually

[53] See *Restatement, Second, Torts* (n 41) § 19.

[54] See Am. L. Inst., *Restatement, Third, Torts: Intentional Torts to Persons* (Tentative Draft 4, April 1, 2019) § 3(b), illustration 5.

sensitive or is simply different from whatever the factfinder would characterize as "reasonable."

The tort of battery protects the autonomy rights of individuals, permitting them to decide which intentional contacts to permit and on what terms. A defendant must obtain the plaintiff's consent to a physical contact, even if the defendant in good faith believes that the contact will be beneficial to the plaintiff. Moreover, the right to choose embraces, not just "reasonable" or "ordinary" choices, but also choices that reflect unconventional cultural values, religious beliefs, or subjective preferences. An adult Jehovah's Witness has the right to refuse a blood transfusion that would save her life. A patient is free to reject any form of medical treatment even if 99 percent of patients would consent to it. A person is free not to engage in any form of sexual conduct even if almost all other people in the relevant situation would consent to the conduct. (Suppose the plaintiff expresses a preference not to kiss or engage in any intimate behavior with another until they have decided to marry.) It is difficult to square the very widely accepted requirement of deference to highly unconventional beliefs about medical treatment and other physical contacts with a standard under which the plaintiff must show that the contact offended a "reasonable" sense of dignity.

The Restatement Third of Torts: Intentional Torts to Persons (for which the author is chief Reporter) addressed this issue in an earlier draft, as follows:

> Section 3. Battery: Definition of Offensive Contact
>
> A contact is offensive . . . if:
>
> (a) the contact offends a reasonable sense of personal dignity; or
> (b) the contact is highly offensive to the other's unusually sensitive sense of personal dignity, and the actor knows that the contact will be highly offensive to the other.[55]

Section 3(b) proved very controversial, however. Opponents were concerned that expanding liability to situations in which the defendant knows that the plaintiff is unusually sensitive would create significant problems—for example, in workplaces where employees must interact. For examples, some employees might insist on unjustifiable or unduly burdensome accommodation of their peculiar sensitivities and idiosyncrasies. There were also concerns

[55] Am. L. Inst., *Restatement, Third, Torts: Intentional Torts to Persons* (Tentative Draft 2, March 10, 2017) § 3(b).

that the culpable state of mind required by this standard—that the defendant must know that the contact will be highly offensive to the plaintiff-—would be too easy for the plaintiff to prove or would too readily be left for the jury to decide. These are legitimate concerns, and the Reporters offered some limiting language in response.[56] In the end, however, the members of the American Law Institute rejected the knowledge prong of section 3(b).

The current status of the debate in the Institute over the definition of offensive battery is as follows. A new draft has been approved that, in many cases, will reach the same result of recognizing liability that the knowledge prong would have reached, but the rationale for the result has subtly changed. Many who opposed the knowledge prong favored a flexible reasonable person test, under which such characteristics as the plaintiff's religious beliefs and sexual preferences would be considered part of the inquiry into whether the defendant's touching of the plaintiff offended a reasonable sense of dignity. The new draft adopts this flexible approach, thus permitting liability in cases such as the caterer who knowingly serves pork to a wedding guest despite the guest's religious objection or the person who has unusually modest preferences with respect to sexual conduct; in these cases, a factfinder could conclude that under these distinctive circumstances, the contact would offend a reasonable sense of dignity.[57]

This approach might be criticized. Recasting the question in this manner—asking whether a reasonable person *with the plaintiff's religious beliefs* or *with the plaintiff's unusual sensitivity* would be offended—arguably is not intellectually honest and deprives the reasonable person test of objectivity. Consider a more extreme case. Suppose the plaintiff has an intense, irrational fear of butterflies or of shaking hands with anyone. If the tort principle of respecting autonomous choice justifies permitting such a plaintiff to recover from a defendant who is fully aware of this unusual characteristic, it is arguably more honest to employ a doctrinal test that directly expresses that principle, a test providing that it is tortious to contact a person when the actor knows of the person's unusual, subjective sensitivity to offense. Instead of asking the awkward question whether a reasonable person who is terrified of butterflies

[56] The final paragraph of § 3 attempted to ameliorate these concerns:

> Liability under (b) shall not be imposed if the court determines that such liability would violate public policy or that requiring the actor to avoid the contact would be unduly burdensome.

Ibid.

[57] Subsection 3(b) also provides for a narrow extension of liability to cases in which the actor knowingly and purposely causes a highly offensive contact, even if the contact would not be considered offensive to a reasonable sense of dignity. Ibid.

would be highly upset if someone placed a butterfly on her body, the inquiry under the known extrasensitivity approach is more straightforward: Did the actor know that the plaintiff would be offended by the type of contact that the actor caused?

Nevertheless, the evolution of the Restatement Third of Torts' definition of offensiveness demonstrates that the gravitational pull of "reasonable person" criteria is very strong. I now turn to a discussion of two more fundamental questions: why these criteria are so attractive to courts and when the use of such criteria is most justifiable.

III. Analysis

A. Why Are Reasonable Person Criteria So Widely Employed?

Over the last century, courts have increasingly employed reasonable person criteria in some areas and have persisted in employing them in many others. This section offers some possible explanations. The analysis that follows discusses the use both of reasonableness criteria generally and of reasonable person criteria in particular.

Earlier analysis suggested some particular functions of the reasonable person test—to make vivid and concrete the task of the jury or trial judge in analyzing fault; to address negligence when it takes the form of deficient skill or inadvertence; and to permit any desired degree of individualization. Let us now take a broader view of how and why such tests are employed.

1. Negligence Liability Has Expanded

As noted above, many American courts have moved toward a general presumption that negligence is the appropriate standard of care, unless a particular intentional tort or strict liability category applies. This development often reflects a more pro-victim orientation than prior doctrine. But insofar as the presumption endorses a fault requirement in lieu of a potential strict liability rule, it represents a more conservative judicial attitude toward the appropriate scope of tort liability.

Moreover, as we have seen, reasonable person tests are also employed to expand the scope of intentional tort privileges and defenses: a reasonable belief that one is under attack or that another person actually consented to one's conduct is usually a complete defense, even if that belief is mistaken. So used, these tests *limit* liability, as compared to a test that denies exculpatory significance to defenses if the actor was mistaken about whether he was justified.[58]

2. Inclusiveness: Considering All Relevant Facts and Reasons

Another reason why reasonableness and reasonable person tests are attractive is because they appear to permit all relevant facts and normative reasons to be brought to bear on the legal issue at hand. Many jury instructions specifically state the test as what a reasonable person would do "under the circumstances" or "under the same or similar circumstances" or "under all the circumstances."[59]

This inclusiveness seems, at first glance, to be an advantage. How could one object to considering all of the circumstances? But inclusiveness is only an advantage if the criteria of relevance are clear. Giving weight to everything is a vacuous and useless criterion, indistinguishable from giving weight to nothing.[60] And the criterion of relevance here—what a reasonable person would do in light of these circumstances—is troublingly vague, as we have seen.

3. The Benefits of Employing a Standard Rather than a Rule

The increasing use of reasonableness criteria in tort reveals the attraction of a simple, general standard, as opposed to more detailed negligence rules or the particularized criteria of intentional torts. Sometimes flexible standards such as the reasonable person are better than bright-line rules, for familiar reasons. Reasonableness tests avoid the artificiality and inaptness of such rules in cases at the margins. For example, landowner duty rules for different categories of entrants became increasingly complex when courts understandably created exceptions and qualifications that seemed better suited to serve the underlying purposes of the rules and to avoid injustice. Similarly, traditional all-or-nothing contributory negligence rules developed exceptions (such as last clear chance), and then exceptions to those exceptions.

However, if the reasonableness criterion itself does not sufficiently further the relevant tort goal (such as deterrence) or is not constitutive of a relevant tort principle (such as fairness or equal concern), then a rule, or a different standard, might be preferable. This is especially likely to be true when

[58] In the past, some jurisdictions did preclude invocation of defenses if the defendant was mistaken, even reasonably mistaken, about the facts apparently supporting the defense.

[59] See Kelley and Wendt (n 5), Appendix.

[60] Judge Richard Posner raises a similar concern about multifactor tests in his recent book. Richard A. Posner, *Divergent Paths: The Academy and the Judiciary* (HUP 2016) 117 (decrying the "pretense of analytical rigor" when courts employ open-ended multifactor tests).

reasonableness is merely a proxy for such a goal or principle. (Consider factor 6, below.)

Is the use of a general reasonable person standard an inescapable necessity, in light of the particularity, variability, and contextual nature of situations requiring tort liability judgments? That is the lesson that many American courts derive from Justice Oliver Wendell Holmes' famous and ill-fated effort to replace the general negligence standard with a set of specific rules, such as the requirement that a driver about to cross a train track must stop, look, and, if necessary, leave his vehicle to make sure that it is safe to proceed.[61] But we should be careful not to draw the wrong lesson from Holmes' failed effort. In a few situations, such as a driver falling asleep at the wheel, courts do adopt the Holmesian approach, treating a specified type of conduct as negligence per se. More importantly, even when a detailed rule is not suitable, it is still an open question whether the very general "reasonable person under the circumstances" test provides sufficient guidance. An intermediate solution between that test and Holmes' approach is quite feasible and is frequently employed by courts: define the duty with greater specificity but well short of the specificity of a "stop, look, and listen" rule. Examples include the duty owed by professionals such as doctors and lawyers; by land occupiers to trespassers; or to co-participants in recreational and sporting activities.

4. Moderation

The quality of being a "reasonable" person, like the quality of "reasonable" care or of "reasonable" foresight,[62] suggests moderation—neither too high nor too low a standard. Just as a "reasonable" rate means a rate that is not excessive, reasonable care means neither an extraordinarily high nor a very low standard of care.[63]

[61] In *Baltimore & Ohio Railroad v. Goodman*, 275 US 66 (1927), the Court, per Justice Holmes, endorsed this bright-line rule; in *Pokora v. Wabash Railway*, 292 US 98, 105 (1934), the Court, per Justice Cardozo, rejected the rule, relying on "the need for caution in framing standards of behavior that amount to rules of law."

[62] "Reasonable foresight" (of the type of harm suffered by the plaintiff) is the test used by many courts to define proximate cause or scope of liability limitations. Courts appear to view this as an attractively moderate test, intermediate between (1) "defendant is a proximate cause only if he subjectively foresaw the risk" (which is too pro-defendant) and (2) "defendant is a proximate cause so long as the risk was not freakish or extraordinary" (which is too pro-plaintiff).

[63] See Zipursky (n 40) 2139:

> "Reasonable" is a very common and well-worn adjective for referring to a moderate, or buyer-favorable price, and "reasonable" is comfortably and commonly used as a qualifier of time vaguely connoting a kind of Goldilocks "just right" quality.

See also ibid. 2146, noting that reasonableness often operates to convert a rule into a standard, ensuring a moderate level of the quality in question. Zipursky goes on to endorse a "moderation-based account" of reasonableness in negligence law. Ibid. 2153.

The language of "ordinary" care, used in many jury instructions, also suggests moderation.[64]

Economic tests of negligence often are not moderate in this sense, because they require a relatively high standard of care.[65] Specifically, many modern economic theories of tort law endorse an optimizing theory of reasonable care, one that seeks the precise level of precaution that will minimize the sum of accident costs and the costs of preventing accidents. We might call this optimizing account idealization-on-steroids: it condemns not only insufficient precautions, but also excessive precautions. In either case, the precaution falls short of the optimal, ideal tradeoff between prevention costs and accident costs. Driving a car that creates excessive safety risks is inefficient, but so, on this account, is driving a car that incorporates excessive safety precautions. Moreover, failing to take an easy precaution would sometimes be negligent, on the economic account, even if the precaution has only trivial safety benefits. Consider Benjamin Zipursky's example of a person who owns an all-wheel drive SUV, parked in his garage, and a new sedan, parked on the street. On a rainy night, the driver chooses to drive the slightly less safe sedan out of convenience and because the sedan is more fun to drive. Zipursky points out that negligence law is not so demanding of us that we always must drive the safer car that we own, yet economic theory might suggest otherwise.[66] These intuitively doubtful but inexorable consequences of many economic theories are good reason to doubt the principles underlying the theories.

The Learned Hand test of negligence is closely associated with the economic analysis of negligence. But the test need not be given a specifically economic interpretation.[67] Thus, the Restatement Third of Torts endorses a catholic interpretation of the Learned Hand test:

[64] A recent article systematically analyzes reasonableness and reasonable person tests and concludes that, as understood by ordinary persons and as frequently applied by legal actors, these tests are a hybrid, intermediate between (and partly reflecting) reasonableness as a statistical average and reasonableness as a prescriptive ideal. In the author's view, "normality" best expresses this hybrid standard. Kevin Tobia, "How People Judge What Is Reasonable" (2018) 70 Ala. LR 293.

[65] See Richard Wright, "The Standards of Care in Negligence Law" in David G. Owen (ed.), *Philosophical Foundations of Tort Law* (OUP 1995) 249, 255–63.

[66] Zipursky (n 40) 2165.

[67] See Winfield and Jolowicz (n 48) ss 6-022, 6-027, stating that Commonwealth courts employ a negligence calculus similar to the Learned Hand test, but explaining:

> Commonwealth courts generally have not reduced the breach of duty element to an economic question. McHugh JA summed up the position in Commonwealth jurisdictions as follows: "Negligence is not an economic cost/benefit equation. Immeasurable 'soft' values such as community concepts of justice, health, life and freedom of conduct have to be taken into account. [Citing *Western Suburbs Hospital v. Currie* (1987) 9 NSWLR 511, 523.]"

See also Simons (n 10) 925–26 (arguing that the Learned Hand factors need not be understood in utilitarian terms, and that courts typically do, and should, recognize that only the *socially recognized* advantages and disadvantages of taking a precaution should be compared).

> Primary factors to consider in ascertaining whether [a] person's conduct lacks reasonable care are the foreseeable likelihood that the person's conduct will result in harm, the foreseeable severity of any harm that may ensue, and the burden of precautions to eliminate or reduce the risk of harm.[68]

Moreover, section 6 of the Restatement, comment d, sets forth a fairness or corrective justice rationale as well as an economic incentive rationale for imposing negligence liability.[69]

Is the Learned Hand test nevertheless overly demanding, even if it is applied flexibly and even if the factors are not understood in a narrowly economic way? The worry here is that any balancing test that employs marginal analysis will be too demanding, if it deems any conduct to be negligent whenever the marginal advantages (in the form of risk reduction) of taking a precaution barely outweigh the marginal disadvantages (however understood). This way of understanding negligence seems to put an actor at the mercy of a quantitative formula, under the threat of liability if he slightly miscalculates either the inputs or the final computation.

But the worry is overstated. The more qualitative analysis called for by a fairness approach resists translation into purely quantitative variables. Moreover, a flexible Learned Hand test should consider the epistemic difficulties that actors routinely face (a) in determining what risks of harm are likely to occur, and with what probability, and (b) in judging whether a precaution will reduce those risks, and to what extent. Reasonable, not perfect, foresight is all that is required. In the end, the Hand test is flexible enough to express either a very demanding, a moderately demanding, or even an undemanding standard of care.

5. Normative Modesty (or Normative Evasion)?

When the trier of fact is empowered to decide whether the injurer or victim complied with the standard of the reasonable person, the appellate court (or the trial judge delegating to the jury) plays a more modest role in defining the legal standard. This position of deference is appealing insofar as the deferring actor doubts that it is legitimate, or wise, for her to devise more precise legal criteria reflecting her own views of justice or policy or the views of a group of unelected judges.

[68] *Restatement Third, Torts: Liability for Physical and Emotional Harm* (n 11) § 3. Cmt c clarifies that these primary factors must be supplemented or supplanted in certain cases, including emergencies, actors who are children, disabled actors, and inadvertent or inattentive actors.

[69] Ibid. § 6, cmt d.

Moreover, delegating this decision to the jury or trier of fact in terms of what reasonableness requires or what "reasonable person" means has a rhetorical benefit: the inquiry seems at least partly factual, and not purely normative. "What would a reasonable person have done?" sounds considerably less normative than, "What should *this* defendant (or *this* plaintiff) have done?"[70]

But normative modesty is sometimes normative evasion. Sometime, the tort law standard can and should be articulated more clearly, in order to assure greater consistency across similar cases and to give fair notice to primary actors. And, perhaps more importantly, often it is both desirable and perfectly legitimate for common law judges to play a prominent role in defining these standards ex ante. After all, negligence doctrine already contains numerous distinct rule-like doctrines that are widely accepted, including the customary standard for professionals, the general absence of an affirmative duty to prevent harm to strangers, numerous categories of special relationships (such as contract, family status, or creation of a risk), and distinctive standards for children and the physically disabled.

6. A Proxy for Other Values or Concerns

Sometimes, the reasonable person test is merely a proxy for other legitimate concerns. As we have seen, when the defendant's liability depends in part on how potential victims will react to the defendant's conduct, courts often reflexively ask how a "reasonable" victim would react—for example, they consider whether a reasonable victim would be offended by the breach of privacy or by the nonconsensual touching. But this approach is not meant to describe an actual standard of behavior for such a victim. The point, rather, must be to protect defendants from liability when they could not expect the victim to have reacted as he did.

Nevertheless, the approach is problematic, for reasons we have explored. It should normally be sufficient to show either that the plaintiff's reaction was normal (but not necessarily "reasonable" in a more ideal sense), *or* that defendant knew (or perhaps should have known) that the plaintiff would suffer the legally relevant type of harm, such as an interference with privacy or an offensive physical touching.

[70] Put differently, the reasonable person test might express a hybrid notion that gives weight to both statistically average and ideal behavior. See Tobia (n 64). Tobia's general account is problematic, however, in endorsing the use of a relatively uniform reasonable person test across widely varying legal domains. Yet (as he concedes) tort law might have especially strong reason to employ a largely prescriptive account. Ibid. 310.

In short, when reasonableness criteria are merely a proxy, they should be viewed with much more skepticism, for it is then an open question whether different or supplemental criteria should be employed in order to better serve the relevant policies or principles.

7. Simplicity

A reasonable person criterion is often much simpler than a more detailed set of rules or criteria. Employing this criterion as the central requirement of tort negligence is about as simple as one can get with a fault criterion. Any other imaginable criterion will have additional or more specific requirements, which the law-creator must carefully construct and define. Moreover, simpler criteria often have a practical benefit: they are easier to explain to the trier of fact, and their application to a particular set of facts is often easier for the parties to prove. (Compare proving whether a reasonable person would have taken a precaution that defendant driver neglected to take with proving whether the defendant, given all of his individual physical and mental capacities, was capable of taking that precaution.) Thus, if everything else is equal, simplicity is surely one virtue of a legal rule or standard.

But simplicity often comes at a cost. Consider self-defense. A very simple legal test of self-defense would be as follows: "Use only such force as a reasonable person would use in response to the threat." That would hardly offer sufficient guidance to judges, juries, and primary actors. At the same time, it is difficult to specify all of the requisite self-defense criteria with detailed rules governing triggering conditions, proportionality, and necessity. In both criminal and tort law, jurisdictions typically specify some aspects of self-defense but address others by a simple "reasonable person" criterion. Thus, the legal criteria are commonly fairly specific about proportionality requirements (e.g., deadly force only in response to a deadly threat or a threat of rape or kidnapping), less specific about necessity requirements (e.g., requiring imminence or necessity, and perhaps articulating a duty to, or no duty to, retreat), and quite unspecific about belief requirements (requiring only that the actor's beliefs about the facts demonstrating proportionality and necessity be "reasonable").

The last point is noteworthy. It is extremely common for legal standards to treat epistemic requirements very simply, requiring only that the actor "knew or should have known" some fact relevant to the underlying norm (such as what harms the actor's conduct risked, whether the injured person consented, or whether the actor was justified in self-defense). The epistemic meaning of the reasonable person test is typically parasitic on another legal norm, and it is often a fairly uncontroversial question whether the actor "should have known" the relevant facts. Even here, however, complications can arise. How much inquiry the actor should have made is not a straightforward question, for example.

Finally, the very simplicity of a reasonable person criterion may invite overuse. Sometimes more specific criteria are both feasible and desirable, but a reasonable person test is employed out of mere habit or intellectual laziness.

8. Preferable to Alternative Legal Tests

Most of the other explanations just mentioned support this all-encompassing explanation: a reasonableness or reasonable person test is better than other types of legal rules that one might consider applying to the problem at hand. Or, to paraphrase Winston Churchill: sometimes, a reasonable person test is the worst test of legal liability, except all the others.

This is not the occasion to identify every species of legal rule or standard that is available to a legislator or judge in laying out the content of tort law. But it is worth noting briefly some major competitors to a reasonable person test. One might employ a multifactor balancing test, such as the Restatement Second of Torts' test of abnormally dangerous activities.[71] Such tests are often problematic, however, in creating a mere illusion of determinacy.[72] One might employ a rule with clear necessary and sufficient conditions.[73] But such rules are difficult to formulate and frequently create significant problems of overinclusiveness and underinclusiveness. Or one might employ a vague criterion other than reasonableness or the reasonable person, such as "unduly burdensome" or "liable if factor A substantially outweighs factor B." No test is a panacea.

[71] See *Restatement, Second, Torts* (n 41) § 520:

> In determining whether an activity is abnormally dangerous, the following factors are to be considered:
>
> (a) existence of a high degree of risk of some harm to the person, land or chattels of others;
> (b) likelihood that the harm that results from it will be great;
> (c) inability to eliminate the risk by the exercise of reasonable care;
> (d) extent to which the activity is not a matter of common usage;
> (e) inappropriateness of the activity to the place where it is carried on; and
> (f) extent to which its value to the community is outweighed by its dangerous attributes.

[72] See Posner (n 60).

[73] Compare the *Restatement, Third, Torts: Liability for Physical and Emotional Harm* (n 11) § 20(b), test for abnormally dangerous activities:

> An activity is abnormally dangerous if:
>
> (1) the activity creates a foreseeable and highly significant risk of physical harm even when reasonable care is exercised by all actors; and
> (2) the activity is not one of common usage.

9. Familiarity and Caution

Often—probably too often—courts gravitate toward a reasonable person test simply because the test is so widely used in tort law (and elsewhere in the law). The test seems to be a safe choice, one that is unlikely to cause trouble or surprise. Such factors as moderation, normative modesty, and simplicity further support this tendency.

Familiarity and caution are hardly sufficient reasons for using this test, however, especially in light of the demonstrable risk that the test will be used indiscriminately in a range of distinct contexts that deserve careful differentiation.

B. When Should Reasonable Person Criteria Be Employed?

Let us now turn to the prescriptive question: how should the reasonable person test be employed? Many aspects of this question have already been addressed, but a more general discussion should prove helpful.

1. Establish a Standard of Behavior for Injurers

Reasonable person criteria are frequently used to establish a standard of behavior for those who cause injury to others. At first blush, it would seem that the reasonable person should be understood in this context as an ideal, a paragon of virtue, a person who never errs.[74]

Supporting this interpretation is the apparent defect of the major competing interpretation—the average or ordinary or normal person test. This test is problematic in potentially valorizing behavior that is conventional yet insufficiently attentive to the interests of others. Moreover, Mayo Moran points out another significant problem with the "ordinary" or "normal" person interpretation: it may perpetuate discriminatory stereotypes about gender, race, religion, ethnicity, and mental and physical disability.[75] On the other hand, the

[74] Recall A. P. Herbert's famous parody:

> [The reasonable person] is one who invariably looks where he is going, and is careful to examine the immediate foreground before he executes a leap or a bound; . . . who believes no gossip, nor repeats it, without firm basis for believing it to be true; . . . who never from one year's end to another makes an excessive demand upon his wife, his neighbours, his servants, his ox, or his ass; . . . who uses nothing except in moderation, and even while he flogs his child is meditating only on the golden mean. Devoid, in short, of any human weakness, with not one single saving vice, sans prejudice, procrastination, ill-nature, avarice, and absence of mind, . . . this excellent but odious character stands like a monument in our Courts of Justice, vainly appealing to his fellow citizens to order their lives after his own example.

A. P. Herbert, *Uncommon Law* (Capuchin Classics 2011).

[75] Mayo Moran, *Rethinking the Reasonable Person: An Egalitarian Reconstruction of the Objective Standard* (OUP 2003) ch. 5.

"ordinary" person test seems more justifiable in some of its applications. Thus, the "reasonable child" standard of care, an especially important qualification of the objective reasonable person test, is often justified on the basis that the status of childhood is a "normal" human condition through which all adults pass.[76]

The objective features of reasonable person tests, especially the controversial but long-standing tort position that mental disabilities and incapacities should be ignored in judging whether such a person acted with reasonable care, demonstrate that the reasonable person can be a very high standard of behavior—indeed, in some cases, an impossible standard to satisfy.[77] This might nevertheless be a defensible position for tort law to take in many contexts. After all, tort law, unlike criminal law, need not require as a condition of liability that the actor deserves moral blame.

One obvious way to split the difference between understanding the reasonable person as a (sometimes unattainable) ideal and as an (insufficiently demanding) description of ordinary or normal conduct is to characterize the reasonable person as one who has normal *capacities* for exercising care.[78] Even if the average Boston driver runs yellow (or even red) lights, almost all Boston drivers have the capacity for greater prudence. Oliver Wendell Holmes famously asserted that "when men live in society, a certain average of conduct, a sacrifice of individual peculiarities going beyond a certain point, is necessary to the general welfare."[79] This passage is best understood as asserting, not that acting with an average or customary degree of care is, as a matter of law, not negligence, but only that people are usually entitled to expect that others have average or normal capacities for acting with proper care.

Nevertheless, focusing on average capacities rather than average conduct does not dissolve the tension between the ideal and the ordinary person conceptions. Ordinary people with average capacities are, by definition, capable of achieving a more ideal level of care than ordinary care. Should they not be considered negligent if they fall short of that ideal?[80]

[76] See ibid. ch. 4.

[77] See Goudkamp (n 31) s. 8.3, thoroughly and sharply critiquing tort law's refusal to make significant allowances for insanity.

[78] See H. L. A. Hart, *Punishment and Responsibility* (2nd edn, OUP 2008).

[79] Oliver Wendell Holmes, *The Common Law* (Macmillan & Co 1881) Lecture III.

[80] Also, recall Mark Grady's point that when people must take repeated nondurable precautions, such as constantly paying proper attention while driving, it may be virtually impossible to achieve perfect compliance. Mark F. Grady, "Why Are People Negligent? Technology, Nondurable Precautions, and the Medical Malpractice Explosion" (1998) 82 NWULR 293, 319–20. Indeed, attempting to achieve perfect compliance might actually be less safe than, say, resting one's eyes from time to time.

Another possible way to bridge the gap between the normal and ideal, the descriptive and the prescriptive, is to appeal to community norms and values.[81] A number of courts and commentators consider the jury the conscience of the community and thereby try to justify the jury's dual role in negligence cases: first, identifying a community standard of care; and second, applying that standard of care to the actor. Even when a judge rather than a jury is the trier of fact, he or she might be expected to be familiar with community values about how reasonable people should behave when their conduct might endanger others (or themselves).

But the appeal to community or customary values poses problems of its own. Which community is relevant, either geographically or temporally? Should one look to historical or traditional values, to values that have endured, or to contemporary values? Is an appeal to such values at bottom an effort to disguise an evaluative judgment as a factual one? Would it be more honest to discuss and defend the so-called "community values" openly?

Whatever the answer to these questions, we should be skeptical of approaches that insist on an extremely demanding standard of reasonable care across the board, as the earlier discussion of economic analysis of negligence suggests.

Should the law move in the opposite direction? Some would advocate a relatively low standard of care, and would frame the question, not as whether the actor complied with an idealized standard, but as whether the actor's behavior was acceptable or permissible. Permissible behavior includes behavior that is just barely above the line of impermissibility, and such behavior is well short of ideal.[82] Instead of "the reasonable person," we might speak of the "not unreasonable person." "Ordinary" prudence is closer to this conception than is "reasonable care."[83]

Characterizing reasonable care as merely permissible conduct ordinarily identifies too low a standard, I believe. As a descriptive matter, tort law largely rejects that characterization, because in most circumstances it rejects

[81] See Stephen G. Gilles, "On Determining Negligence: Hand Formula Balancing, the Reasonable Person Standard, and the Jury" (2001) 54 Vand. LR 813; Kelley and Wendt (n 5) 591–92; Patrick J. Kelley, "Who Decides? Community Safety Conventions at the Heart of Tort Liability" (1990) 38 Clev. St. LR 315; Catharine Wells, "Tort Law as Corrective Justice: A Pragmatic Justification for Jury Adjudication" (1990) 88 Mich. LR 2348, 2402–13; Tobia (n 64) 312–16.

[82] See Kent Greenawalt, "The Perplexing Borders of Justification and Excuse" (1984) 84 Colum. LR 1897, 1904. "Justifiable" conduct or risk-creation is another concept sometimes employed here. But justifiable conduct could mean either conduct that one has good, affirmative reason to perform, or conduct that is merely permissible or within one's rights. Thus, substitution of this term does not resolve the debate noted in the text.

[83] See Zipursky (n 40) 2156.

customary or average care as a sufficient standard of care. The reasonable person is not merely a person who acts permissibly, but one who acts prudently, carefully, and with due care for the interests of others. She is at least minimally virtuous. She does not merely avoid acting impermissibly toward others. Zipursky elucidates this idea by stating that the reasonable person is "not wholly insensitive to the demands of others," "not wholly selfish and inconsiderate," and "somewhat fair-minded."[84] I endorse a slightly more demanding standard, one that treats the reasonable person as more admirable than these insipid descriptions suggest. However, I quite agree that the reasonable person need not be a paragon of virtue; nor must she select the best of several reasonable options.

2. Establish a Standard of Behavior for Victims

As discussed earlier, a symmetrical standard of care for injurers and victims is sometimes appropriate, especially when the actor's unreasonable conduct creates substantial risks of harm both to others and to himself. But when a victim creates "unreasonable" risks only or almost entirely to himself, his fault (if this is fault at all) is arguably qualitatively different. We might wish to recognize this difference in applying comparative fault rules: the fault of an actor who endangers only himself could receive much less weight than the fault of actors who pose significant risks to others.

3. Impose Liability Only If Plaintiff Responded "Reasonably"?

Although courts frequently preclude liability when a victim responds in an "unreasonable" way to the injurer's conduct, they should be cautious about how and even whether they use reasonable person criteria here. First, the "ordinary" or "average" person is often a more apt criterion than the "reasonable" person in these cases. Second, it is often preferable to use a narrowly tailored subjective test (one that, for example, permits offensive battery liability when the defendant knows of the individual plaintiff's susceptibility to offense), either alone or in conjunction with an average person test. However, in certain contexts, including some privacy and products liability cases, a "reasonable victim" test might be preferable: such a test might identify situations in which the plaintiff is able, and properly expected, to take care to prevent harm to himself.

[84] Ibid. 2161.

4. Supplement the Reasonable Person Test

A partial solution to the vagueness problems with an unadorned reasonable person test is to supplement that test with other general criteria, such as "equal consideration of the interests of others," community values, or balancing the burden of precaution against the risks to be prevented by the precaution; with general character traits, such as prudence or considerateness:[85] or with more specific criteria, such as the actor's specialized duty as a parent, therapist, veterinarian, or doctor. Similarly, a jury instruction might clarify that creating risks only to oneself is a less serious form of fault than creating risks to others.

On the other hand, to the extent that courts wish to be agnostic about the underlying principles and justifications of tort doctrine, supplementing the reasonable person test with general criteria such as cost-benefit balancing or equal consideration of interests might be counterproductive insofar as it takes a stand on controversial questions about the moral and legal principles underlying tort doctrine.[86] Whether it is desirable for courts to be normatively modest and catholic, here or elsewhere, raises fundamental questions about the judicial role in common law cases. If one concludes that judicial modesty about underlying principles is an overriding value or is essential to the legitimacy of the common law, then the reasonable person test is an especially attractive legal criterion.[87]

5. Individualize the Reasonable Person Test?

The appropriate degree of individualization of the reasonable person test—for example, according to age, physical or mental capacities, gender, occupation, or role—will depend in significant part on how one answers the other

[85] See Gardner (n 11) 580–81; Zipursky (n 40) 2156.

[86] See Gardner (n 11) 567:

> The reasonable person does not embody, nor does he fail to accommodate, any particular account of which reasons there are, or of how and when they come to be defeated or undefeated by each other. He does not stand for one justificatory standard rather than another, or for one type of justificatory standard rather than another. He is neither value-pluralist nor value-monist, neither consequentialist nor nonconsequentialist, neither actualist nor probabilist, neither Kantian nor Benthamite. He does not stand for "public justification", "impartial justification", "reasonable justification", or indeed any other "distinctive conception of . . . justification". He stands only for justification *tout court*. (footnotes omitted)

[87] Gardner makes a similar point in an arresting way: he claims that the principal function of the reasonable person test in tort law (and in law generally) is to import an extra-legal norm into the law. "[The reasonable person] exists to allow the law to pass the buck, to help itself pro tempore to standards of justification that are not themselves set by the law, and which therefore are only as good as the standards of justification used by the person or people to whom the buck is passed." Gardner (n 11) 568–69. Gardner is right to emphasize that the law's reasonable person criteria often are a partial reflection of standards of ordinary behavior and common-sense morality. But I am less convinced that such nonlegal standards fully determine the content of these legal criteria. Further discussion of this question must await another occasion.

questions addressed above.[88] For reasons of space, I do not explore this important issue further here.

IV. Conclusion

In conclusion, three points. First, reconsider the earlier question why reasonable person criteria are needed at all. Why not simply instruct the trier of fact to directly apply the fairness or economic criteria that render an actor's conduct negligent? In reply, I have offered several arguments, including the assistance an anthropomorphic test affords the fact-finder in making its task more concrete, the value of the reasonable person test in cases of deficient skill and inadvertence, the possible desirability of common law courts employing a stance of normative modesty, and the test's capacity to achieve the desired degree of individualization.

Zipursky offers a very different reply. In his view, it is a fundamental mistake to conceive of negligence as a matter of an unjustifiably low level of precaution against risk. Rather, the reasonable person criterion is the primary criterion of negligent conduct, while the idea of a reasonable level of precaution is secondary.[89]

In some cases, Zipursky is correct. When the question is whether an actor is negligent for displaying deficient skill (e.g., in conducting surgery or in riding a bicycle), it is unhelpful to frame the negligence inquiry as depending upon the justifiability of a particular level of precaution, in light of the advantages and disadvantages of selecting that level of precaution. That framing is similarly unhelpful in many cases of inadvertent negligence.

But when the question is whether the actor is negligent for choosing to drive at a high rate of speed for a particular purpose, or for not adding a safety feature to a product, or for building a fence of a particular height around a baseball or cricket field, an inquiry into the choices available to the actor, including their

[88] On individualization, see Moran (n 75); Peter Westen, "Individualizing the Reasonable Person in Criminal Law" (2008) 2 Crim L. & Philos. 137; Gardner (n 11) 578–79; Omri Ben-Shahar and Ariel Porat, "Personalizing Negligence Law" (2016) 91 NYULR 627.

[89] See Zipursky (n 40) 2162–63:

> The Hand Formula view [which Zipursky rejects] does not even consider the question of what a reasonable person is, or why we would want to use the idea of a reasonable person in determining whether the defendant was negligent. It is only concerned with the right or appropriate level of risk. . . . Of course, the reasonable person does enter the story, but only in a way that is reverse-engineered. The reasonable person is one who would not take unreasonable risks, and unreasonable risks are given content independently.

advantages and disadvantages, is critical to determining whether the actor was negligent. Although Zipursky purports to reject this balancing approach, portions of his discussion seem to favor it.[90] In my view, no coherent conception of advertent negligence can ignore the question of the socially acceptable level of precaution.[91]

Second, any serious discussion of the best way to formulate reasonableness and reasonable person criteria would greatly benefit from empirical research—specifically, research investigating how survey subjects (and, by extrapolation, juries) apply different reasonable person instructions, and whether supplementary or different criteria would actually improve consistency of evaluation of fact patterns or would otherwise lead to improved outcomes.[92] (Research would also be useful in exploring judges' understandings of these criteria.) Kevin Tobia's recent work is instructive. In three surveys, he finds that ordinary people understand reasonableness as an intermediate concept, setting a higher standard than a judgment of the relevant average but a lower standard than a judgment of the relevant ideal.[93] These experiments addressed ordinary understanding of the concept of reasonableness, not of the reasonable person. It would be helpful if future research also addressed the latter criterion.

Third, a powerful feature of contemporary tort doctrine too often goes unnoticed: reasonableness criteria, and the reasonable person test in particular, exert a very strong gravitational pull. Courts and legislators should resist succumbing to this force and should give careful consideration to whether other legal tests better serve the policies or better express the principles underlying contemporary tort law. Sometimes, reasonableness is the wrong standard to

[90] Thus, Zipursky suggests that the reasonable person criterion expresses "the capacity to constrain one's behavior and choices in a manner that is not wholly insensitive to others' needs and wishes, but rather displays some sense of mutuality." Zipursky (n 40) 2161. Somewhat more concretely, he says that "being reasonable requires constraining one's conduct by reference to the perils one creates for others," and that "[a] person who is reasonable in the mutuality sense and acts reasonably will choose to constrain his or her behavior in some fashion so that it is less likely to injure others." Ibid. 2162. These are gestures in the direction of a test focusing on the acceptable level of risk. Their practical guidance seems minimal, however, and their content is rather obscure.

[91] For a Rawlsian account of negligence that focuses on the reasonable level of precaution, not on the reasonable person, see Gregory Keating, "Reasonableness and Rationality in Negligence Theory" (1996) 48 Stan. LR 311, 369; Gregory Keating, "Is Cost-Benefit Analysis the Only Game in Town?" (2018) 91 So. Cal. LR 195.

[92] Compare Shen et al., "Sorting Guilty Minds" (2011) 86 NYULR 1306; Ginther et al., "The Language of Mens Rea" (2014) 67 Vand. LR 1327 (2014); Ginther et al., "Decoding Guilty Minds: How Jurors Attribute Knowledge and Guilt" (2018) 71 Vand. LR 241. In these studies, two of which I joined as co-author, the *mens rea* categories of the Model Penal Code were subjected to rigorous empirical testing. The results were not pretty: subjects were unable to accurately classify different scenarios in which actors possessed the mental state of recklessness from those in which they possessed the mental state of knowledge.

[93] Tobia (n 64) 316–29.

apply. Other times, although in principle it is an apt standard, more rule-like criteria are feasible and preferable to a reasonable person criterion.

For example, we have seen that it is often unwise to employ a reasonable person test when referring to a victim's response to the actor's conduct. At the same time, when we are analyzing a defendant's negligence toward others, the reasonable person formulation is quite useful as the primary legal criterion in cases involving inadvertence or deficient skill, while in cases involving advertent risky conduct and choices between risky alternatives, that formulation might be more useful as a supplement to a balancing test (such as the Learned Hand test) that evaluates when risk-creation is justifiable.

It is easy to slide from the almost tautological truth that people should act reasonably, to the much more debatable point that reasonable person criteria should presumptively apply throughout tort law. The hegemony of tort law's reasonable person should often be resisted.

4

Property as Intangible Property

Katrina M. Wyman

I. Introduction

For over two decades, prominent Anglo-American property scholars have sought to bury the idea that property is an infinitely malleable bundle of rights and revive a more determinate understanding of property as a legal category that provides owners with a broad measure of authority over things.[1] Scholars such as Thomas Merrill, James Penner, and Henry Smith have resurrected this "thing-based" understanding of property largely with tangible property, especially property in land, in mind.[2] They are by no means unique in focusing on tangible things as the paradigmatic objects of property. Historically, property theory generally has tended to focus on real property as the premier example of property, reflecting the long-standing importance of land as a source of wealth and political power.[3]

[1] I discuss the work of these scholars in Katrina Wyman, "The New Essentialism in Property" (2017) 9 JLA 183. This restatement of the thing-based view of property draws on Thomas Merrill's assertion that "[b]roadly speaking, the property strategy is one of decentralized control over resources." Thomas Merrill, "The Property Strategy" (2012) 160 U. Pa. L. 2061, 2063.

[2] See, e.g., Henry E. Smith, "Intellectual Property as Property: Delineating Entitlements in Information" (2007) 116 Yale LJ 1742, 1799. See also Lee Anne Fennell, "Fee Simple Obsolete" (2016) 91 NYU L. Rev. 1457, 1495, 1495 fn 156.

Smith is likely the contemporary scholar most closely associated with the idea that property is "the law of things" and indeed, he uses the term "thing-based." Henry E. Smith, "Property as the Law of Things" (2012) 125 Harv. L. Rev. 1691, 1694. Although Smith has applied his understanding of property to intellectual property, these applications indirectly underscore the primacy of real property in Smith's thinking. See, e.g., Smith, "Intellectual Property as Property" (n 2) 1745 (arguing that property relies heavily on what Smith calls "the exclusion strategy" and that "[t]he prototypical example" of this strategy "is trespass to land"); Henry E. Smith, "Institutions and Indirectness in Intellectual Property" (2009) 157 U. Pa. L. Rev. 2083, 2087 (using the law of trespass to land to illustrate the benefits of the exclusion strategy in property); Henry E. Smith, "Semicommons in Fluid Resources" (2016) 20 Marq. Intell. Prop. L. Rev. 195, 212 (distinguishing "'regular'" property from "intellectual" and "entity" property); Henry E. Smith, "Governing Intellectual Property" in Ben Depoorter and Peter S. Menell (eds.), *Research Handbook on the Economics of Intellectual Property Law: Volume I: Theory* (Edward Elgar Publishing 2019) at 48 (distinguishing "regular property" and intellectual property).

[3] Christopher Essert, "Property in Licences and the Law of Things" (2014) 59 McGill LJ 559, 566; Julie E. Cohen, 'Property as Institutions for Resources: Lessons from and for IP' (2015) 94 Tex. L. Rev. 1, 1–2, 5–7; Thomas C. Grey, "The Disintegration of Property" (1980) 22 Nomos 69, 73. See also Jeremy Waldron, *The Right to Private Property* (Clarendon Press and Oxford University Press 1988) 31 (property is a "system of rules governing access to and control of material resources").

Katrina M. Wyman, *Property as Intangible Property* In: *Oxford Studies in Private Law Theory: Volume 1*. Edited by: Paul B. Miller and John Oberdiek, Oxford University Press (2020). © The Several Contributors. DOI: 10.1093/oso/9780198851356.003.0004

This essay argues that it is time for property theorists to think of intangible property as a paradigmatic form of property, and to move away from focusing on land and tangible personal property as their main core cases. It makes three main points. First, it emphasizes the contemporary economic importance of intangible property, as well as its increasing social importance in everyday life, especially in highly urbanized, developed countries. Second, it posits that the currently prevalent thing-based understanding of property is sufficiently capacious to embrace intangible property, and thus that there is no reason to marginalize intangible property. Third, it speculates about why Anglo-American property theory has remained largely focused on land and tangible personal property, notwithstanding the economic centrality of intangible property and the ability to subsume intangible property within contemporary understandings of property. It concludes by underscoring two potential benefits of property theory paying greater attention to intangible property: an expanded focus on intangible property might lead to greater recognition of the constrained character of property in the modern interdependent, urbanized world;[4] and greater acknowledgment of the potential for property—albeit likely in a constrained form—to play a role in addressing the consequences of modern technology.

A few words are in order about how this essay relates to the long-standing debate about whether intellectual property is property. This is a debate between skeptics of propertizing intellectual property, who resist the idea that intellectual property is so-called "regular property,"[5] and proponents of strong intellectual property rights, who insist on the contrary that intellectual property rights are—or should be treated like—regular property.[6] Both sides in this debate associate the term "property" with a near absolutist conception of property rights

[4] See also Peter S. Menell, "Intellectual Property and the Property Rights Movement" (2007) 30 Reg. 36, 41 (arguing that intellectual property has little to learn from real property, and that "[b]ringing intellectual property into the 'property tent' will call attention to the interdependency conception of resources."). "68% of the World Population Projected to Live in Urban Areas by 2050, Says UN" *United Nations* (May 16, 2018) <www.un.org/development/desa/en/news/population/2018-revision-of-world-urbanization-prospects.html>. Menell's observation has influenced my thinking in important ways.

[5] I borrow the phrase "regular property" from Henry Smith, who uses it to refer to real and tangible personal property, as contrasted with intellectual property. See, e.g., Smith, "Semicommons in Fluid Resources" (n 2); Smith, "Governing Intellectual Property" (n 2).

[6] Smith refers to "fans and skeptics of strong intellectual property rights." Smith, "Intellectual Property as Property" (n 2) 1749. For some framings of the debate, see Richard A. Epstein, "The Disintegration of Intellectual Property? A Classical Liberal Response to a Premature Obituary" (2010) 62 Stan. L. Rev. 455, 456; Mark A. Lemley, "Property, Intellectual Property and Free-Riding" (2005) 83 Tex. L. Rev. 1031, 1033–40; Menell (n 4); Richard A. Epstein, "A Response to Peter Menell: The Property Rights Movement and Intellectual Property" [2008] Reg. 58; Peter S. Menell, "A Reply to Richard Epstein: Intellectual Property and the Law of the Land" [2008] Reg. 64.

in tangible assets such as land, in which owners have robust rights to exclude, protected by injunctions ("property rules"), and owners are not burdened by government regulation.[7] This is certainly not an accurate characterization of property rights in land today in many places given the emergence of extensive land use regulation in the twentieth century, a reality bemoaned by some of the proponents of treating intellectual property rights like "regular property."[8] This essay urges property scholars to assume that intellectual property, and property in other intangibles, is "regular property." Thus, the essay's project is the opposite of that of the proponents of strong intellectual property rights who want to transform intellectual property into "regular property": it suggests that we should update our image of property to reflect the significance of intangible property. In addition to intellectual property rights, other forms of intangible property include shares of stock and debts, and possibly government issued licenses and permits.[9] In general, we might think of intangible property as "[p]roperty that lacks a physical existence."[10]

II. The Centrality of Intangible Property

Intangible property is nothing new and commentary about it goes back hundreds of years.[11] In his history of property in America, Stuart Banner argues that intangible property was the leading form of property as far back as the

[7] Cohen (n 3) 9–10.

[8] See, e.g., Epstein, 'The Disintegration of Intellectual Property? A Classical Liberal Response to a Premature Obituary' (n 6) 462–80, 485; see also ibid. 497. Epstein acknowledges that even historically, "the boundary conditions on land have never been treated as absolute and inviolate either," which is why I say that property is used in this debate to refer to a "near absolutist conception" of property rights. Ibid. 496. See also Hanoch Dagan, "Property and the Public Domain" (2006) 18 Yale J. L. & Human. 84 (arguing that supporters of a large public domain for intellectual goods are misguided in rejecting property, because property values and doctrines can be used to support limits on ownership).

[9] For definitions of intangible property, see, e.g., Aaron D. Simowitz, "Siting Intangibles" (2015) 48 NYU J. Int'l Law & Pol. 259, 259 (referring to intangible assets as "[d]ebts, shares of stock, intellectual property, wire transfers, LLC interests, and all other intangible assets [that] have no physical location"); William B. Stoebuck and Dale A. Whitman, *The Law of Property* (3rd edn, West Group 2000) 10–11 ("The list of intangible 'things' that may form the subject matter of 'personal property' is long, including claims represented by bank accounts, promissory notes, corporate and government bonds, shares of corporate stock, life insurance policies, and annuities, as well as patents, copyrights, trademarks, and even the 'goodwill' of business enterprises.").

[10] *Black's Law Dictionary* (7th edn, West Pub. Co. 1999) 1233 ("*intangible property*. Property that lacks a physical existence. Examples include bank accounts, stock options, and business goodwill. Cf. *tangible property*."); see also ibid. 1234 ("*tangible property*. Property that has physical form and characteristics. Cf. *intangible property*.").

[11] See, e.g., Kenneth J. Vandevelde, "The New Property of the Nineteenth Century: The Development of the Modern Concept of Property" (1980) 29 Buff. L. Rev. 325, 331–32 (discussing Blackstone's treatment of incorporeal things); Greg Alexander, *Commodity & Propriety* (University of Chicago Press 1997) 140 (analyzing Blackstone's discussion of property in public debt).

eighteenth century, as "[m]uch of eighteenth century property consisted of nonphysical assets like labor or offices."[12] There also were intangible property rights in land.[13] Banner's argument notwithstanding, scholars generally suggest that intangible property became the dominant form of property in the late nineteenth or early twentieth century, as land became a less important source of wealth.[14] Tom Grey famously argued in 1980 that the significance of intangibles meant that property was no longer an important legal category.[15] I suggest instead that the rise of intangibles necessitates increasing the importance of intangible property in thinking, not abandoning the category.

There are sound reasons for thinking about intangible property as a core case of property in the early twentieth-first century in highly developed, urbanized countries. Most corporate assets in the United States are intangibles.[16] Intellectual property accounts for "[an] estimated 80% of the value of U.S. corporations."[17] Little of the value of leading companies such as Google comes from "servers, land, buildings, furniture and the like."[18]

For individuals too, intangible assets—especially financial property—also have become increasingly important.[19] Although the home is still an important source of household wealth, many individuals also have bank accounts, and shares in mutual funds and companies, for example in the retirement accounts that have replaced many defined benefit pension plans in the United States.[20] Cultural materials like books, music, television shows, and movies also are increasingly distributed online rather than in physical form; many individuals

[12] Stuart Banner, *American Property: A History of How, Why, and What We Own* (Harvard University Press 2011) 13.

[13] Ibid. 13; Alexander (n 11) 69–70.

[14] See, e.g., Katharina Pistor, *The Code of Capital: How the Law Creates Wealth and Inequality* (Princeton University Press 2019) 5, 24, 78.

[15] Grey (n 3) 69, 70, 81–82.

[16] Simowitz (n 9) 260 (citing Carol Corrado, Charles Hulten, and Daniel Sichel, "Intangible Capital and Economic Growth", Finance and Economics Discussion Series, Division of Research & Statistics and Monetary Affairs, Federal Reserve Board (2006) <www.federalreserve.gov/pubs/FEDS/2006/200624/200624pap.pdf>); see also Mary Juetten, "Pay Attention to Innovation and Intangibles—They're More Than 80 Percent of Your Business Value" *Forbes* (October 2, 2014) <www.forbes.com/sites/maryjuetten/2014/10/02/pay-attention-to-innovation-and-intangibles-more-than-80-of-your-business-value/#53ff559b1a67> ("non-tangible assets are over 80% of the average business' value") (referring to work of Andrew Sherman).

[17] Dan Breznitz and Michael Murphee, "What the U.S. Should Be Doing to Protect Intellectual Property" *Harvard Bus. Review* (January 27, 2016) <https://hbr.org/2016/01/what-the-u-s-should-be-doing-to-protect-intellectual-property>. See also Pistor (n 14) 115–16 (In "*Capitalism Without Capital*, Haskel and Westlake argue that the market value of leading corporations today is not determined by the physical assets that they own and use to produce goods, but by intangibles: the patents, copyrights and trademarks they own, and the branding and business processes they have developed.").

[18] Juetten (n 16) (referring to Andrew Sherman's use of Google as an example).

[19] Daniel Markovits and Alan Schwartz, "Who Owns What? Re-thinking Remedies in Private Law" (draft 2019).

[20] Ibid.

prefer to stream movies and music and listen to books, rather than to own DVDs, CDs, records, and hard copies of books.[21] People are much less inclined to compile physical photo albums; instead, they keep their photos online, on the cloud.[22] It is becoming harder to sustain the Hegelian-inspired argument that people realize their personhood through physical things. Online presentation of images on Facebook and Instagram sometimes seems more central to personhood today than tangible objects, at least among digital natives.

The law tracks developments in the marketplace and the wider world. Courts routinely treat intangible property, including intellectual property rights, as property.[23] Attorneys at major corporate law firms now recognize the value of knowing something about intellectual property. When a group of Harvard Law professors surveyed "124 practicing attorneys at major law firms" in 2013 about what classes Harvard Law School students should take, intellectual property, patent and copyright were among those recommended.[24] A few property law professors have even started to change the standard property curriculum to reflect the heightened importance of intangible property, and the lesser economic significance of land and other natural resources.[25] Perhaps these professors sense that if property law is not updated, it risks becoming the General Motors of the law school curriculum: a legacy, unable to keep up with newer, nimbler technology oriented entrants.[26]

To be sure, the rise of intangibles does not mean that tangible property is unimportant; it means that it is less important than it was historically in post-industrial developed countries where much of the population now lives in

[21] Aaron Perzanowski and Jason Schultz, *The End of Ownership: Personal Property in the Digital Economy* (MIT Press 2016) 35.

[22] Meg Mason, "Why Looking Through Old Memories Will Never Be the Same Again" *News.Com.Au* (March 5, 2016) <www.news.com.au/lifestyle/sunday-style/why-looking-through-old-memories-will-never-be-the-same-again/news-story/841b42853ecb96511e773930370317ab>.

[23] See, e.g., *Ruckelshaus v. Monsanto Co* 104 S. Ct. 2862, 2873 (1984) (trade secrets); *Phillips v. Washington Legal Foundation* 524 US 156 (1998) (interest); *Horne v. Department of Agriculture* 135 S. Ct. 2419, 2427 (2015) (patent (citing *James v. Campbell* 104 US 356 (1882)); *Armstrong v. United States* 364 US 40 (1960) (materialman's lien); *Starr Intern. Co. v. United States* 106 Fed. Cl. 50, *71 (2012) (equity interest); vacated on other grounds, *Starr Int'l Co. v. United States*, 856 F 3d 953, 973 (Fed. Cir. 2017).

[24] John C Coates, Jesse M Fried, and Kathryn Spier, "What Courses Should Law Students Take? Harvard's Largest Employers Weigh In" (2014) Harvard Public Law Working Paper No. 14-20, 5–6 <https://dash.harvard.edu/bitstream/handle/1/12911341/What-courses-should-law-students-take-Harvard-largest-employers-weigh-in.pdf?sequence=1>.

[25] James Grimmelmann, "Raze and Rebuild the Property Course" *L. & Pol. Econ.* (November 2, 2018) <https://lpeblog.org/2018/11/02/raze-and-rebuild-the-property-course/>; see also James Grimmelmann, "Real + Imaginary = Complex: Toward a Better Property Course" (Summer 2017) 66 J. Leg. Ed. 930. Grimmelmann uses the term "intangible property" more narrowly than I do, as he posits that intellectual property is a separate category from intangible property, while I include intellectual property within intangible property. Grimmelmann, "Real + Imaginary = Complex" (n 25) 935 fn.27.

[26] Neal E. Boudette, "Cadillac's Last Stand? Storied Brand Aims (Again) For Revival" *NY Times* (August 27, 2019) <www.nytimes.com/2019/08/27/business/cadillac-brand.html>.

urban areas—and than one might surmise by looking to the stock examples in property theory scholarship. Since humans "are embodied beings," we all need a physical place to live, as Jeremy Waldron explains in his work on homelessness.[27] We might not need to own that physical structure outright, and it might not need to be the proverbial single-family home of the American dream, but some physical space, and hence tangible property, is still necessary.[28] Then there are the physical accoutrements of daily life, such as clothes and food, which it is hard to imagine becoming virtual.[29] Even the cultural products that are distributed digitally require physical devices to enjoy, such as Amazon's Echo or the iPhone, although the extent to which people own these products might be up for debate, since a lot of the use value of these products comes from the software embedded within them, which consumers may merely be licensing.[30]

III. Intangible Property is Property

As suggested in the introduction, from one perspective, it should not be difficult to adapt property theory to reflect the economic and cultural importance of intangible property. The revived thing-based understanding of property is sufficiently capacious to encompass intangible property. Indeed, the 2018 partial, preliminary draft of the American Law Institute's Fourth Restatement of Property, whose lead reporter is Henry Smith, proposes to include intangibles as suitable objects for property.[31] This echoes the embrace of intangible property as a form of property in the First Restatement from 1936.[32]

To elaborate on these points, it is useful to consider for a few moments how property might be defined if one were thinking solely of intangible property. Then we can see how an intangible-inspired definition of property can be

[27] Jeremy Waldron, "Homelessness and the Issue of Freedom" (1991) 39 UCLA L. Rev. 295, 296. See also Larissa Katz, 'Corporate Shares as Shares' in Ben McFarlane and Sinéad Agnew (eds), *Modern Studies in Property Law: Volume 10* (Hart Publishing, Bloomsbury Publishing 2019) 107, 109.

[28] Property rights in land are likely even more important in areas where agriculture is more economically significant, such as rural areas in developed countries, or less urbanized developing countries. But intangible property will likely become more important in more places as the world becomes even more urban and post-industrial.

[29] Notably, people can rent clothes using apps, and thereby avoid owning them. Jessica Testa and Jonah Engel Bromwich, "Real Men Don't Rent" *NY Times* (January 8, 2020), <https://www.nytimes.com/2020/01/08/style/men-rent-rental-clothing.html>.

[30] Perzanowski and Schultz (n 21) 61–62.

[31] Am. L. Inst., *Restatement of the Law Fourth Property* (Preliminary Draft No. 4, 2018) vol. 1, div. 1, § 2 cmt.d ("Intangible items, even under some circumstances rights themselves, can be things for purposes of property law.")

[32] Am. L. Inst., *Restatement of the Law of Property* (Am. L. Inst. 1936) vol. 1, div. 1, ch. 1, intro note.

understood as merely a gloss on the prevalent thing-based understanding of property, suggesting that intangible property can be readily assimilated into that understanding, and therefore into contemporary property theory, without much difficulty.

A. What Is Property if we Focus on Intangible Property?

Drawing on the terminology used in intellectual property scholarship, if one conceives of property with intangibles front and center, one might describe property as a mechanism that delegates decision-making authority to individuals over a specific subject matter. As with any delegation of authority, whether by statute to an administrative agency, by contract to a corporate officer, or to a friend to care for one's child, that delegation has a number of elements, in particular: *the scope of the authority conferred* (e.g., do the owner's rights include the right to x, y, and z, or merely a?), *the duration of the delegation* (perpetual, time-limited like patents and copyright, or contingent on satisfying certain conditions like prior appropriation water rights?), and a "*subject matter*" (the "thing" over which authority is being delegated might be an abstract thing such as a right to profit from an image that someone has created instead of a tangible thing such as land).[33] In suggesting that property is a delegation, I might be taken as saying something similar to Larissa Katz and others, who have characterized property (or ownership) as an office through which authority to manage things is decentralized within society.[34] I see it as a grant of authority over a specific object.

The idea that property delegates authority over subjects to individuals ("owners") is evident in cases in which courts are determining as a matter of first instance whether someone has a property right in an intangible. In these cases, the courts are defining property with intangibles in mind, as they are trying to decide whether an intangible is the object of property. These decisions focus on whether the owner has sufficient authority over some subject matter that the courts should protect the owner, by requiring someone who is

[33] See Pascale Chapdelaine, "The Property Attributes of Copyright" (2014) 10 Buff. Intell. Prop. LJ 34, 34 (using the terms "duration, scope and subject matter" in referring to copyright); Lemley (n 6) 1066 (referring to the "scope, strength, and duration of intellectual property"); Cohen (n 3) 21-22, 36 (using the terms "subject matter" and "scope" similar to the above text).

[34] Larissa M. Katz, "Exclusion and Exclusivity in Property Law" (2008) 58 UTLJ 275, 306–08 ; Larissa M. Katz, "Governing Through Owners: How and Why Formal Property Rights Enhance State Power" (2012) 160 U. Pa. L. Rev. 2029, 2036–39; see also Christopher Essert, "The Office of Ownership" (2013) 63 UTLJ 418, 435–42 (referring to the work of Katz and Avihay Dorfman, "Private Ownership" (2010) 16 LEG 1).

interfering with that subject matter to compensate the putative owner, or cease the interference. In essence, the courts are seeking to determine whether there is someone with some degree of control, some sphere of authority, which the law should vindicate.

Consider two cases in which courts decide as a matter of first impression whether someone has a property right in an intangible. In the well-known case of *Kremen v. Cohen*, Kremen sued Network Solutions, which registers domain names, arguing that the company converted his sex.com domain name by transferring it to Cohen, a fraudster beyond the reach of the law.[35] To bring this conversion claim, Kremen initially needed to establish a property right in the domain name under the governing California law.[36] Writing for a panel of the Ninth Circuit, Judge Alex Kozinski used a combination of formalist and policy-based reasoning in determining that Kremen had a property right in his domain name. Judge Kozinski applied "a three-part test to determine whether a property right exists: 'First, there must be an interest capable of precise definition; second, it must be capable of exclusive possession or control; and third, the putative owner must have established a legitimate claim to exclusivity.' "[37] The court held that "a domain name is a well-defined interest"[38] because "[s]omeone who registers a domain name decides where on the Internet those who invoke that particular name . . . are sent."[39] It held that a domain name was "exclusive" because "the registrant alone [decides where a person goes on the internet when they enter a set of characters] . . . Moreover, like other forms of property, domain names are valued, bought and sold, often for millions of dollars."[40] Third, it held that "registrants have a legitimate claim to exclusivity. Registering a domain name is like staking a claim to a plot of land at the title office. It informs others that the domain name is the registrant's and no one else's."[41] The court further offered a policy justification for finding that the domain name registrant had an exclusive interest: "Many registrants . . . invest substantial time and money to develop and promote websites that depend on their domain names. Ensuring that they reap the benefits of their investments

[35] *Kremen v. Cohen* 337 F 3d 1024 (9th Cir. 2003).

[36] "To establish that tort, a plaintiff must show 'ownership or right to possession of property, wrongful disposition of the property right and damages.' " *Kremen* 337 F 3d at 1029 (quoting *GS Rasmussen & Associates v. Kalitta Flying Service Inc.* 958 F 2d 896, 906 (9th Cir. 1992)).

[37] *Kremen* 337 F 3d at 1030 (quoting *GS Rasmussen*, 958 F 2d at 903).

[38] Ibid.

[39] Ibid.

[40] Ibid.

[41] Ibid.

reduces uncertainty and thus encourages investment in the first place, promoting the growth of the Internet overall."[42]

To relate the Ninth Circuit's approach back to the definition of property I offered earlier, in investigating whether Kremen had a property interest in his domain name, the Ninth Circuit searched for, and found, a delegation of authority (the registrant makes a determination), over a subject matter (where someone entering a set of characters goes on the internet) that binds others (the domain name owner has an "exclusive interest"). Its policy reason for recognizing that Kremen had exclusive control—encouraging investment in websites—is a standard utilitarian justification for private property.

Kremen is a classic "private law" case involving the horizontal assertion of a property interest in an intangible in a case brought by one private actor against another. The courts also demonstrate intuitions about what intangible property is in vertical contexts, in which a private actor asserts a property interest against a government. In US jurisprudence, a prominent example is Takings cases, where plaintiffs assert that governments owe them compensation because the governments have taken their private property without paying the compensation mandated by federal and state constitutions when governments take private property.[43] Takings cases are a particularly interesting context to look for judicial intuitions about what counts as property because the courts have the last word in these cases, unlike in common law cases such as Kremen, and cases where parties seek to define "property" when the term is used in statute.[44] In the common law and statutory cases, the courts might be inclined to expansively interpret property because they know that they can be reversed by legislatures if they define property too broadly for the public to bear.[45] In addition, the courts might be more cautious in defining property in Takings cases

[42] Ibid. The court held that Kremen only needed to establish a property interest to sue for conversion, and did not need to establish that this interest had been merged into a document as the Restatement (Second) of Torts requires to sue for the conversion of intangibles. However, Judge Kozinski ruled in the alternative that if California law requires merger into a document, then Kremen had satisfied the merger requirement. 337 F 3d at 1033–36.

The November 2018 partial draft of the Property Restatement would allow suits to be brought for conversion of intangible property without requiring that the intangible be merged with a document, as the 1965 Second Restatement of Torts had required. Restatement (Second) of Torts § 242 (1965). Am. L. Inst., *Restatement of the Law Fourth Property* (Preliminary Draft No. 4, 2018) vol. 2, div. I, ch. 5 (Conversion: Prima Facie Case); ibid. § 1 (Conversion in General); ibid. cmt b; ibid § 2 (Elements of Conversion); ibid. cmt g (Intangibles).

[43] US Const. amend. V, cl. 4 ("nor shall private property be taken for public use, without just compensation").

[44] e.g., the term "property" is used in the federal Internal Revenue Code and there is consequently case law interpreting the meaning of "property" under the statute. Thank you to Professor Steve Johnson for this observation. See, e.g., *United States v. Craft* 535 US 274 (2002).

[45] The Takings cases also are unlike Due Process cases invoking constitutional protections against deprivations of property without due process. In these cases, the courts often are pursuing objectives other than protecting property per se, including a commitment to transparent governmental

because holding that an individual has a property interest helps to clear the way for an individual to obtain financial compensation from the government, provided the individual satisfies the other required elements for a successful Takings claim.[46] The likelihood that courts are more cautious in defining property in Takings cases means that they are cases where the courts may be most apt to restrict the property label to interests that they think fall most squarely within the bounds of property.

In the United States, the rise of Uber, itself a symbol of the increasing importance of intangible property, led to a series of Takings cases where the owners of once-valuable taxicab licenses sued city and state governments that allowed Uber to operate for compensation for the decline in the value of their taxicab licenses. The licenses became less valuable with the arrival of Uber because cities and states allowed Uber-dispatched vehicles to pick up passengers for hire in competition with taxis without purchasing one of the limited number of taxicab licenses that taxis have to hold. As passengers migrated to Uber, taxicab drivers also shifted to driving for Uber, meaning there also was less demand from drivers to lease the licenses from owners, in addition to reduced demand from passengers for the incumbent taxis. The taxicab license owners' suits were a new chapter in an old story: the development of a new form of transportation economically harms an incumbent transportation provider that thought it had a monopoly franchise, and the incumbent then sues the government in vain for the harm to its business.[47]

The taxicab license owners claimed that in allowing Uber to operate, governments had taken their property, and therefore that the license owners were entitled to compensation for the loss in value of their property under the Takings Clause. In bringing their claims, taxicab license owners needed to assert a private property interest, to satisfy the predicate for invoking the Takings

decision-making. The remedy available to a successful plaintiff is an injunction, not a payment of compensation by the government. One consequence is that it is easier to establish a property interest for Due Process than Takings protection. Thomas W. Merrill, "The Landscape of Constitutional Property" (2000) 86 Va. L. Rev. 885.

[46] The Federal Circuit explicitly refers to the chilling effect on government action of finding a regulatory taking in *Maritrans Inc. v. US* 342 F 3d 1344, 1357–58 (Fed. Cir. 2003).

[47] See, e.g., *Charles River Bridge v. Warren Bridge* 36 US 420 (1837) (upholding the dismissal of a claim by the owners of the Charles River Bridge, which charged tolls, that their contract rights were violated when Massachusetts subsequently chartered the Warren Bridge, which siphoned away much of the business of the Charles Bridge because passage was free on the Warren Bridge). Dissenting, Justice Story held that suits brought by incumbent ferries for grants to new ferries provided precedents for the suit by the Charles River Bridge. Thanks to Henry Smith for suggesting I look at *Charles River Bridge*, and to John Greil for conversations about the historical precedents to the Takings litigation prompted by the emergence of Uber; see also John Greil, "The Unfranchised Competitor Doctrine" (draft).

Clause. They could not simply assert that their licenses had been taken, because the licenses (which themselves are a form of intangible property) had not literally been taken by the government; their value had merely been diminished by the competition from Uber drivers. None of the license owners' Takings claims prevailed,[48] but some of the decisions dismissing the claims demonstrate judicial intuitions about property in intangibles.

Consider the Seventh Circuit decision, authored by Judge Richard Posner, upholding the dismissal of the Takings claim of Chicago taxicab license owners.[49] Judge Posner characterized the property right that the license owners were claiming as "a right to be free from competition."[50] He held that no such right inhered in the taxicab licenses as a matter of positive law; these merely authorized the license owners to "own and operate taxis," not to restrict the number of taxis (the City "reserved the right . . . to issue additional" licenses) or to restrict competition from other types of transportation providers.[51] Moreover, Judge Posner emphasized that there was no policy reason for recognizing the taxicab license owners as having a right to exclude new competitors; the court might have read in such a right by holding that in licensing the operation of taxis, the government was implicitly precluded from authorizing the licensing of competitors to the taxis, without compensating the original license owners.[52] In Judge Posner's view, welfare would be promoted by denying the taxicab license owners a right to block new competitors. Sounding like Chief Justice Taney in 1837 when he rejected the claims of the owners of the Charles River Bridge who had lost much of their business to the new Warren Bridge, Judge Posner explained, "Were the old deemed to have a constitutional right to preclude the entry of the new into the markets of the old, economic progress might grind to a halt."[53]

Reading between the lines of Judge Posner's opinion, we see the same intuition about what counts as an intangible property right as in Kremen. Judge Posner, like Judge Kozinski, identifies property with a delegation of authority over a subject matter; thus Judge Posner finds that the license owners lack a property right because they did not have the authority to block the entry of

[48] Katrina M. Wyman, "Taxi Regulation in the Age of Uber" (2017) 20 NYU J. Legis.& Pub. Pol. 1, 6 fn. 9

[49] *Illinois Transportation Trade Ass'n v. City of Chicago* 839 F 3d 594 (7th Cir. 2016).

[50] Ibid. 596.

[51] Ibid. 597.

[52] This is a variation of the argument that Justice Story developed in dissent on behalf of the Charles River Bridge in *Charles River Bridge v. Warren Bridge*. Writing for the majority, Chief Justice Taney rejected the argument.

[53] *Illinois Transportation Trade Ass'n* 839 F 3d at 597; see also *Charles River Bridge v. Warren Bridge* (1837) 36 US 420, 552–53.

new competitors under the terms of their licenses. The absence of this right to exclude means that the license owners lack the binding authority that they assert against the world. The City of Chicago retains the authority to determine the number of taxis, and whether Uber and Lyft will be able to dispatch cars that compete with the incumbents; the taxicab license owners have not been delegated this function.[54]

B. The Delegation and Thing-based Definitions of Property

I hope that I have convinced you that if you think of intangibles as the motivating example, (1) property can be understood as a delegation of authority over a subject matter, and (2) courts are searching for such a delegation when they are deciding whether someone has a property right in an intangible in a novel case such as Kremen or Illinois Transportation.

As I mentioned before, I think that this definition of property is essentially a gloss on the thing-based understanding of property that scholars have revived in the past few decades.[55] Recall that the thing-based understanding of property characterizes it as providing owners with a broad measure of authority over things by according owners a right to exclude others from the things, subject to some limitations. There is little difference in practice in saying that property delegates authority, and saying that it provides owners with a broad measure of authority. "Things" might simply be understood as the "subject matter" of property, especially when one remembers that contemporary scholars generally have a broad understanding of the things that can be the object of property, and include intangibles as well as land and

[54] Many Takings cases adopt a much more formalist approach to determining whether a plaintiff has the necessary predicate of a private property right to seek just compensation than Judge Posner in *Illinois Transportation*. For example, in *Phillips v. Washington Legal Found.*, the Supreme Court held that the owner of principal in a bank account also owns the interest generated from the deposit of their funds, based on a common law rule that "interest follows principal." *Phillips v. Washington Legal Foundation* 524 US 156, 165 (1998). The Court did not meaningfully inquire into whether the interest satisfied certain proxies for property (as the Ninth Circuit did in *Kremen*). Nor did it inquire (as the Seventh Circuit did in *Illinois Transportation*) whether there was a policy justification for holding that the owner of the principal also had private property in the interest even though the small amounts of principal involved likely would not have accrued "net interest" without being commingled with other funds. The Federal Circuit also uses a formalist test for determining whether a plaintiff has a private property right in an intangible, such as fishing permit, to ground a Takings claim. *Members of Peanut Quota Holders Ass'n v. United States* 421 F 3d 1323, 1331 (Fed. Cir. 2005). This test uses three proxies to, in my view, identify if there is a delegation of authority over a subject matter that binds others.

[55] For more on the thing-based definition of property, see Wyman (n 1), which refers to this definition as the new essentialist definition of property.

other physical things.[56] Perhaps it is not surprising that the understanding of property evident in court decisions determining whether someone has a property right in an intangible focuses fundamentally on the same attributes as the revived thing-based definition; the courts, like the thing-based scholars, are likely thinking of property in land or other tangible resources even in defining property in intangibles.[57]

Assuming that property seems to amount to roughly the same thing regardless of whether one uses the thing-based definition of property, or a definition developed to deal with intangible property claims, why might property scholarship still think predominantly about land and other tangible property? And why might this focus on tangible objects matter? I turn next to my hypotheses for why land, cars, and other physical things remain the standard frame of reference in contemporary property theory. In the conclusion, I address why it matters that property theorists continue to focus on tangible property, by identifying some of the potential benefits of paying more attention to intangibles.

IV. Why Property Theory Is Still Focused on Tangibles

There are likely pragmatic reasons why property theory remains focused on land and other tangible resources. For one, many property scholars were educated before intellectual property, one of the most familiar forms of intangible property, became the fashionable subject that it is in law schools today and thus as students they did not learn much about it. Other forms of intangible property, such as financial assets including shares and debt, may not be have been presented in their legal education as forms of property.[58] A second reason is that prominent intellectual property scholars reject the idea that intellectual property has much to learn from "regular" property and are uninterested in engaging in the field.[59] The disinterest in regular property may be related to the emergence of intellectual property as a scholarly discipline in the shadow of legal realism, which mocked the idea that "property" has any

[56] Wyman (n 1) (citing sources). Some recent scholarship argues that only tangible things can be objects of property but this is definitely a minority view. Simon Douglas and Ben McFarlane, "Defining Property Rights" in *Philosophical Foundations of Property Law* (Oxford University Press 2014).

[57] e.g., Judge Kozinski expressly analogized to real property in holding that Kremen had a property right in the domain name. *Kremen* 337 F 3d at 1030.

[58] On the coding of capital, see Pistor (n 14) 47–107. For arguments that shares are not property, see Arianna Pretto-Sakmann, *Boundaries of Personal Property* (Hart Publishing 2005); Katz (n 27).

[59] See, e.g., Menell (n 4); Menell (n 6).

particular meaning.[60] Whatever the explanations of the siloing of property and intellectual property, the consequence is that there is generally little cross-pollination between traditional and intellectual property scholarship. Only a few scholars, such Shyam Balganesh and Henry Smith, research and write in both areas.[61] The American Law Institute today has separate restatement projects for "Property" and "Copyright," although there are some individuals who are involved with both projects.[62]

Digging deeper, I suspect that there are some conceptual hurdles that have delayed the pace at which property theory is re-orienting itself to acknowledge the centrality of intangible property. Even Henry Smith, who knows much more about intellectual property than many "regular property" scholars, seems ambivalent about the extent to which intellectual property is property, although, as already mentioned, the Smith-led fourth restatement of property project seems likely to recommend that intangibles are a proper object of property. On the one hand, Smith has applied his understanding of property to intellectual property, most notably in a lengthy 2007 article.[63] Yet even this article does not portray intellectual property as exactly the same as regular property.[64] In subsequent work emphasizing the preeminence of the "thing" to property, Smith argues that "property and ownership lie along a spectrum,"[65] and that "as we get away from tangible things, we get further from property and into adjacent areas—contract, tort, unjust enrichment—not that that's a bad thing."[66] In still more recent work, Smith describes information as a "fluid resource" that, like water, is hard to bound, and contrasts intellectual property with "regular

[60] See, e.g., Felix Cohen, "Transcendental Nonsense and the Functional Approach" (1935) 6 Colum. L. Rev. 809. Thanks to Shyam Balganesh for the hypothesis about the impact of legal realism.

[61] On specialization within intellectual property, see Shyamkrishna Balganesh, "Copyright as Legal Process: The Transformation of American Copyright Law" (forthcoming 2020) 168 U. Pa. L. Rev. (manuscript at 19).

[62] 'Current Projects' *American Law Institute* <https://www.ali.org/projects/ >.

[63] Smith, "Intellectual Property as Property" (n 2). Smith argues in this article that intellectual property, like other forms of property, embodies a combination of the right to exclude and governance (Smith's term for limitations on owner authority), with the mixture between exclusion and limitations on it varying depending on the type of intellectual property. Patent law, Smith maintains, relies more on the exclusion strategy than copyright because of information costs. Ibid. 1817–19; Smith, "Institutions and Indirectness in Intellectual Property" (n 2) 2088, 2087–88, 2090, 2120.

[64] Smith, "Intellectual Property as Property" (n 2) 1745 (referring to "intellectual property's close relationship to property"); ibid. 1749 (referring to "copyright's more regulatory and less property-like character as compared to patent law").

[65] Henry E. Smith, "The Thing About Exclusion" (2014) 3 Brigham-Kanner Prop. Rts. Conf. J. 95, 107.

[66] Ibid. 123. He refers to "choses in action and equitable rights" as "borderline cases . . . because they deal with legal objects that are thing-like but less thing-like—less separable and depersonalized—than legal things that correspond more straightforwardly to tangible objects." Ibid. 121. For a succinct discussion of the property status of choses in action, which argues that they are *in personam*, see Kelvin F. K. Low and Jolene Lin, "Carbon Credits as EU Like It: Property, Immunity, TragiCO_2medy?" (2015) 27 JEL 377, 387–88.

property."[67] Merrill, Smith's frequent coauthor, has expressed doubts about the potential for there to be property in intellectual goods distributed digitally, while recognizing intellectual property as property in other contexts.[68]

If not for the pragmatic reasons identified earlier, why might property theorists such as Smith and Merrill be reluctant to recognize intangible property (or some forms of it) as regular property, and bring intangible property more comfortably into the property fold? I offer three more fundamental hypotheses for why property theory remains focused on property in tangibles such as land and other physical things.

A. Tangible Property and Owner Sovereignty[69]

The first hypothesis is normative. As mentioned above, the thing-based understanding of property asserts that property provides owners with a broad sphere of authority over their things. To be sure, the thing-based understanding recognizes that there are limits on the owner's sphere of authority—for example, to address the negative externalities that one landowner's decision to build a smokestack may impose on other landowners and non-owners.[70] Nonetheless, the proponents of the thing-based understanding tend to downplay the breadth of the limits on owner authority allowed under their understanding of property.[71] Indeed, some, although by no means all, of those who have revived a thing-based understanding of property appear to have been partly motivated by a sense that such an understanding will better protect private property against government regulation than the bundle of rights picture of property associated with legal realism.[72]

[67] Smith, "Semicommons in Fluid Resources" (n 2) 212 (distinguishing "'regular'" property from "intellectual" and "entity" property); Smith, "Governing Intellectual Property" (n 2) 48 (distinguishing "regular property" and intellectual property).

[68] Thomas W. Merrill, "Possession as a Natural Right" (2015) 9 NYU J. L. & Liberty 345, 365–67; Thomas W. Merrill, "Property and the Right to Exclude" (1998) 77 Neb. L. Rev. 730, 749 (appearing to endorse the idea that "copyrights, patents, trademarks and trade secrets" are property).

For a defense of treating "material resources" as the starting point for theorizing about property, see Waldron (n 3) 33–37. For a defense of treating land as the paradigmatic case for property theory, see Katz (n 27) 109–11.

[69] The heading is a reference to Morris Cohen's well-known article "Property and Sovereignty" (1927) 13 Cornell L. Rev. 8.

[70] Wyman (n 1) 201–02.

[71] Ibid. 212.

[72] Ibid. 189–90. Ironically, in the nineteenth century, before the bundle picture was associated with legal realism, it provided the intellectual apparatus for robust protection for private property; more recently, Richard Epstein also has used to the bundle picture to protect private property. Ibid.; Banner (n 12) 45, 71–72.

Using real property as the core case of property may help to make the case that property provides a broad measure of control over things. There is a longstanding perception, certainly in the United States, that landownership is a source of freedom and independence. The Jeffersonian idea that widespread fee simple landownership would provide a sound foundation for a republic rests on the idea that such landowners are independent of the influence of others; it is that independence that will enable them to freely participate in politics.[73] Given the cultural understanding of landownership as a source of autonomy, it would seem to make sense to use land as the core case of property to advance the idea that property conveys robust, and largely, untrammeled authority.

Of course, the reality of contemporary landownership is more complicated than the mythical, cultural ideal on which thing-based scholarship about property seems to implicitly trade.[74] The residents of urban areas, where most American now live, often have constrained property rights in land.[75] Many city dwellers are tenants in multi-family buildings and are constrained by lease provisions to protect other tenants from fumes, noise, or other disturbances; their landlords also likely are regulated by governments to protect the safety and quality of life of building inhabitants, and in some places to keep rents affordable.[76] Public land use regulation, such as zoning, and privately agreed covenants, also constrain landowners in urban and suburban areas to address the impacts of property uses on others and to realize community preferences.[77] These and other components of property rights in land, which developed over the nineteenth and twentieth centuries in reaction to industrialization, urbanization, and suburbanization, mean that real property rights in urban areas provide something much less than a robust right to exclude or set the agenda for land. Notably, urbanites may also have constrained rights in some forms of tangible personal property due to modern communications technology. Such technology makes it possible for people living in dense cities to rent items such as cars and power tools for short periods of time through internet-based services such as Zipcar and Uber, and to therefore avoid buying these items outright.[78] Thus, property theory arguably conveys an inaccurate, and

[73] Alexander (n 11) 34; Lance Banning, *The Jeffersonian Persuasion: Evolution of a Party Ideology* (Cornell University Press 1978) 51; Drew R. McCoy, *The Elusive Republic: Political Economy in Jeffersonian America* (University of North Carolina Press 1980) 68, 126–28.

[74] Cars are another form of tangible property that are associated with freedom in American culture but whose use is heavily regulated. Sarah A. Seo, *Policing the Open Road: How Cars Transformed American Freedom* (Harvard University Press 2019) 10-12.

[75] Merrill recognizes the constrained character of urban property rights. Merrill (n 1) 2069.

[76] Banner (n 12) 107, 165–67, 197–201.

[77] Ibid. 182–97.

[78] To be sure, this "slicing and dicing" does not eliminate ownership. Someone or some company still owns the cars and tools (or rooms and apartments) that are being rented out for short periods

exaggerated, notion of owners' rights by focusing on real property and other forms of tangible property to the extent that these forms of property have historically been associated with freedom and autonomy.

B. The Reification of Physical Objects

The second hypothesis for the predominant focus on tangible property is the central role that some prominent contemporary proponents of the thing-based understanding assign to physical objects in maintaining a property system. Smith portrays the thing—the object of property—as a visual cue that triggers the non-owner's duty to stay off. The thing acts as a red flag, telling non-owners that there is a boundary that they must not cross or they will be liable for trespass.[79] Smith does not explicitly limit the things that can be propertized to physical things, but since only tangible things can play the role that he attributes to things, he implicitly conceives of property in physicalist terms.[80] As Smith recognizes, the "thing" in intellectual property is an abstraction, created by law.[81] In some cases, the intangible "thing" is embodied in a physical thing, as with patented inventions manifested in an iPhone, or a copyrighted story on the printed page. The physical product may help to provide notice of the patented invention or copyrighted creation, but not in every case and even then, the physical thing is merely one representation of the abstract, intellectual thing and a poor signal of its boundaries.[82] Not surprisingly, the stock example that

of time, and technology companies own the algorithms that are the basis of the platforms. Lee Anne Fennell, "Slicing Spontaneity" (2015) 100 Iowa L. Rev. 2365. See also Shelly Kreiczer-Levy, *Destabilized Property: Property Law in the Sharing Economy* (Cambridge University Press 2019) 5, 80. Thanks to Matt Harding for suggesting I consider how individuals now interact differently with tangible property.

[79] Smith (n 65) 119; Henry E. Smith, "The Elements of Possession" in Yun-chien Chang (ed.), *The Law and Economics of Possession* (Cambridge University Press 2015) 82, 85.

[80] Essert also argues that Smith can be interpreted as suggesting that things must be physical things because it is easier for people to recognize that they must abstain from interfering with something that is physically instantiated. Essert (n 3). However, Essert denies that it will be easier to avoid interfering with physical things, such as land, than a non-physical thing, such as a license. Ibid. 582–83.

Newman defines things more broadly to cover intangibles as well as tangibles. Christopher M. Newman, "Using Things, Defining Property" in James Penner and Michael Otsuka (eds.), *Property Theory: Legal and Political Perspectives* (Cambridge University Press 2018).

I borrow the term "physicalist" from Vandevelde, who uses it in describing Blackstone's conception of property (n 11) 325.

[81] Smith, "Intellectual Property as Property" (n 2) 1755, 1795; Smith, "Institutions and Indirectness in Intellectual Property" (n 2) 2094.

[82] See Smith, "Institutions and Indirectness in Intellectual Property" (n 2) 2123; Cohen (n 3) 23; Grimmelmann, "Real + Imaginary = Complex" (n 25) 941, 947; Jeanne Fromer, "Claiming Intellectual Property" (2009) 76 U. Chi. L. Rev. 719, 725–26. Smith refers to the greater difficulty of "keeping off" intangibles than tangibles. Smith, "Intellectual Property as Property" (n 2) 1782.

Smith in solo and coauthored work with Merrill uses to illustrate the mediating function of things involves physical objects, cars in the parking lot:[83]

> If I am walking through a parking lot, I know not to drive off with others' cars, and I do not need to know who the owners are, how virtuous (or not) they are, or whether they are actual people or corporations. Likewise, the owners of the autos need not know much about me or the vast crowd of duty-holders—the "rest of the world" against whom in rem rights avail. Our interactions can be relatively anonymous precisely because they are mediated by a thing—in this instance, the cars.[84]

In solo-authored work, Merrill is more explicit in suggesting that property can exist only in physical objects because only they can actually be possessed.[85] He suggests that intellectual property rights may not be enforceable in digitally distributed goods, such as online music or movies, because they are incapable of being physically possessed. According to Merrill, otherwise law-abiding young people "who would not think of stealing a book from a bookstore or a videotape from a video store apparently think there is nothing wrong with downloading pirated movies and TV shows from the internet" partly because "digital downloads are completely severed from any perception that one is interfering with possession established by another."[86] Merrill's comments reflect his broader view that property is rooted in possession, and that possession is hard-wired into human nature; he maintains that "there is a strong [biological] predisposition toward recognizing and respecting possession"[87] and that

[83] Smith argues that the thing mediates between owners and non-owners. Smith (n 65) 107, 113, 119; Smith, "Institutions and Indirectness in Intellectual Property" (n 2) 2100.

[84] Smith, "Intellectual Property as Property" (n 2) 1746–47. See also Smith, "Institutions and Indirectness in Intellectual Property" (n 2) 2093 (citing James Penner, *The Idea of Property in Law* (Clarendon Press 2000) 75–76); Thomas W. Merrill and Henry E. Smith, "The Morality of Property" (2007) 48 Wm. & Mary L. Rev. 1849, 1853–54; Smith (n 65) 97; Am. L. Inst., *Restatement of the Law Fourth Property* (Preliminary Draft No. 4, 2018) vol. 1, div. 1; ibid. § 1 (Property); ibid. cmt c ("In and through a thing").

Smith acknowledges in later work that it is easier to define the boundaries of tangible personal property—such as cars—than land. Smith, "Semicommons in Fluid Resources" (n 2).

[85] Merrill, "Possession as a Natural Right" (n 68) 363–65.

[86] Ibid. 366. See also Grimmelmann, "Real + Imaginary = Complex" (n 25) 941, 947. Notably, there are historical precedents for the increase in online music piracy that followed the technological innovation of disseminating music through the internet. The development of "long-playing records in 1948" led to more bootlegging of records; "record piracy" further increased in the 1960s when the spread of cassette tapes facilitated copying records by eliminating the need to have record pressing equipment. Banner (n 12) 127–28. The increases in music piracy that followed prior technological innovations in the physical objects for disseminating music reinforce the idea (suggested later in the text) that piracy is driven substantially by changes in the costs and benefits of illegally obtaining music, not the ability to physically possess the music per se.

[87] Merrill, "Possession as a Natural Right" (n 68) 363.

it may not be possible to have property in digitally distributed goods because people cannot tangibly possess them.

There are several problems with the just described reifications of physical objects in property theory. The argument that physical objects such as cars play a mediating function ignores the likelihood that it is not the "car" that is telling people to leave it alone, but rather property law, or social norms that are consistent with that law. Under this understanding, human decisions to avoid touching the cars in the parking lot flow from legal rules or social norms against touching objects that belong to others, and theorists are making a category mistake in attributing significance to the physical objects.[88] Thus, online piracy might not be an insoluble problem, but rather an issue that can be dealt with through the development of new norms that reinforce the legal protections that copyright owners enjoy. If one accepts the theory that norms sometimes evolve in response to changes in costs and benefits, new norms of online law-abidingness might emerge over time as the cost of legally accessing music online continues to decline and technological advances increase the probability of being caught for illegal downloading.[89]

Smith and Merrill's argument might be reframed as a suggestion that physical objects such as cars and fences trigger a keep-off response in humans, rather than as a statement that such objects actually play a mediating role. However, even this more plausible interpretation of the significance that they attribute to physical objects is problematic in light of technological advances that have reduced the need for physical objects to trigger the keep-off response. In the twenty-first century, boundaries can be virtually signaled, without a physical fence. Since the latter part of the last century, companies have used digital rights management (DRM) technology to establish virtual fences that stop consumers from doing things with products that they have purchased, such as reading an ebook bought from Amazon on a different company's device; DRM's usefulness to companies seeking to protect their copyrights was strengthened by 1998 Congressional legislation prohibiting consumers from

[88] Thanks to participants at an NYU workshop for observing that individual behavior in parking lots is constructed.

[89] See, e.g., Robert C. Ellickson, "The Evolution of Social Norms: A Perspective from the Legal Academy" in Michael Hechter and Karl-Dieter Opp (eds.), *Social Norms* (Russell Sage Foundation 2001) 35–75. Somewhat consistent with this hypothesis, a 2019 article suggested that piracy had largely disappeared because it "became easier" to stream movies, television shows, and music due to technological advancements but warned that piracy might increase again because the ongoing proliferation of streaming options increased the difficulty and cost for consumers of legally accessing online content. Brian Feldman, 'Piracy is Back' *New York Magazine* (June 26, 2019) <https://nymag.com/intelligencer/2019/06/piracy-is-back.html>.

tinkering with it.[90] In the future, technology-based "content filters" may significantly reduce illegal sharing of copyrighted music and movies through sites such as YouTube without a license from the copyright holder.[91] Going forward, new technology may render obsolete the idea that a physical "linchpin" is necessary for property[92] because virtual fencing, backed by law, may gradually replace physical fences in shielding owner authority.[93]

C. The Artificiality of Intangible Property

The third hurdle that I think has made it harder for property theory to embrace intangible property cannot be overcome through technology. I suspect that lurking behind the reluctance to embrace intangible property is a vague sense that intangible property is artificial, perhaps because, as in the case of intellectual property, it is often legally constructed pursuant to legislation, not solely created from the bottom up, Lockean-style, by an individual physically seizing something in the wild, such as a fox, in an act that is then ratified by the courts in a private law suit between two individuals like *Pierson v. Post*.[94]

There are several reasons why intangible property might be perceived as artificial, although none is convincing. One concerns the nature of information, the object of the leading category of intellectual property rights. As the opponents of robust intellectual property rights emphasize, these rights are created by law to promote certain activities, such as creation or invention, not to manage natural scarcity. Unlike the tangible objects to which property attaches, information is naturally non-rivalrous.[95] My neighbor knowing my chocolate chip cookie recipe does not keep me from baking the recipe; on the

[90] "DRM" *EFF* <www.eff.org/issues/drm> accessed 5 September 2019. The example comes from the Electronic Frontier Foundation's website. See also Chapdelaine (n 33).

[91] Gus Rossi, "The Copyright Directive Is SOPA Part 2, and It's Coming For Your Internet" *Public Knowledge* (April 8, 2019) <www.publicknowledge.org/news-blog/blogs/the-copyright-directive-is-sopa-part-2-and-its-coming-for-your-internet>; Andy Malt, "EU Council Gives European Copyright Directive the Final Nod" *CMU* (April 15, 2019) <https://completemusicupdate.com/article/eu-council-gives-european-copyright-directive-the-final-nod/>.

[92] Smith (n 65) 96 (arguing that the thing is the "linchpin" of property, although not limiting things to physical things).

[93] On the relationship between property and enforcement technology, see generally Henry Hansmann and Reinier Kraakman, "Property, Contract, and Verification: The Numerus Clausus Problem and the Divisibility of Rights" (2002) 31 JLS S373, S403 (arguing that "the structure" of property rights is "influenced by the limits on feasible verification rules"); Chapdelaine (n 33) 58 ("Expansionist views of the scope of copyright are increasingly made possible through new technological means of control.")

[94] The Ninth Circuit may have readily accepted that domain names are properly partly because it could characterize Kremen as having staked a claim, similar to Pierson. *Kremen* 337 F 3d at 1030.

[95] Lemley (n 6) 1050–51.

other hand, the chocolate chips are congestible—if my neighbor takes mine, there will be none for me to enjoy. Intellectual property makes the information that is propertized rivalrous, by giving its owners time-limited monopolies to induce people to create new information or disseminate it.[96] If I patent an invention before you, then you cannot access it without first getting my consent, for which I might demand a fee that you cannot afford; much like the chocolate chips, the first to get the invention gets to control it, at least for the period that the patent lasts, and that is likely to trigger a race for the patent.

However, the fact that information is naturally non-rivalrous does not mean that the property that is created in it is more artificial than the property in naturally rivalrous things such as land, foxes, or fishes of which there is a limited supply and one person's use diminishes the amount available for others. Property itself is artificial, in the sense of being human-made, regardless of whether the object to which it attaches is rivalrous. Property only exists when there is a state willing and able to back up people's entitlements[97]—and a state is a collection of people governed by human-made rules. Moreover, property is always established to advance human purposes—whether it is promoting creativity and inventions, or internalizing externalities, promoting human flourishing and autonomy, or some other goal.

A second reason why intangible property might be (inaccurately) seen as artificial in contradiction to property in land and other physical objects concerns the source of the law. The law governing intangible property, especially intellectual property, is often made or influenced by legislatures and administrative agencies, and so is not purely common law, developed by courts adjudicating cases between private parties using judge-made rules.[98] In the United States, Congress passed the first Copyright and Patent Acts in 1790, one year after the adoption of the federal constitution, and these statutes have been amended since in ways that have strengthened their regulatory dimensions.[99] Some intellectual property scholars embrace the "regulatory" or "public law" aspects of the field; others seek to keep these aspects at bay and to reaffirm the similarities

[96] Ibid. See also ibid. 1057.

All property rights, even rights in land, are grants of a monopoly. Eric A. Posner and E. Glen Weyl, *Radical Markets* (Princeton University Press 2018). The fee simple, the paradigmatic form of private property in land, grants owners a perpetual right to decide how to use a particular parcel of land (subject to government and other forms of regulation). Whether the monopoly of the fee simple owner is harmful depends on whether there are adequate substitutes for that land; the social costs of intellectual property rights also depend on the extent to which there are substitutes for the propertized information.

[97] Felix S. Cohen, "Dialogue on Private Property" (1954–55) 9 Rutgers L. Rev. 357, 374.

[98] See, e.g., Balganesh (n 61) (manuscript at 14–15).

[99] Ibid. (manuscript at 23).

between intellectual property and conventional private, property law.[100] The latter skepticism of the public law dimensions of intellectual property is consonant with the long-standing tradition in some quarters of thinking of the common law as purer, superior, or more efficient than laws made by legislatures and agencies because judges are supposedly less susceptible to interest group pressures than legislatures and agencies.[101] Justice Scalia's decision in *Lucas v. South Carolina Coastal Council*[102] embodies this reverence for the common law in holding that government restrictions on land use are most secure against regulatory takings claims when the restrictions are grounded in historically common law doctrines such as nuisance law.

It has always struck me as odd to think of the common law as purer or less susceptible to interest group pressures in the American context, given that the common law is elaborated in a good number of US states by elected state court judges who need campaign contributions and votes.[103] But assuming for the moment that the common law is for some reason purer than public law, it is erroneous to think of land law as purely common law in the United States in the early twentieth-first century. While property theory often seeks to elaborate the field through common law property (and tort) law doctrines such as trespass and nuisance, landowner rights are regulated by zoning in all large American cities except for Houston; even Houston has other forms of land use regulation, such as subdivision control.[104] On a day-to-day basis, "public" land use regulation, usually established at the local level by agencies, such as city planning departments, and elected city councils, is probably more important in the urban areas where most people live in determining landowner rights than trespass and nuisance. For example, in New York City, construction typically requires a government building permit;[105] the owner of a historically

[100] *Compare* Mark A. Lemley, "Taking the Regulatory Nature of IP Seriously" (2014) 92 Tex. L. Rev. 107, 107 ("Modern IP is certainly more like regulation that it is like property, at least as people traditionally think of property") *with* Statement of Professor Adam Mossoff on *Oil States v. Greene's Energy, Center for the Protection of Intellectual Property*, Antonin Scalia Law School (April 24, 2018) <https://cpip.gmu.edu/2018/04/24/statement-of-professor-adam-mossoff-on-oil-states-v-greenes-energy/> (criticizing the Supreme Court for holding that patents are "regulatory grants similar to monopoly grants for bridges or toll roads").

[101] In the American context, this association of the common law with purity and legislation with corruption goes back at least to the latter nineteenth century to the era of "Legal Formalism" and "Classical Legal Thought." Balganesh (n 61) (manuscript at 22–25). For sources discussing the public choice dynamic in intellectual property, focusing on copyright, see, e.g., Lemley (n 6) 1046, 1046 fn. 68, 1062–63, 1062 fn. 130.

[102] 505 US 1003 (1992).

[103] "Partisan Election of Judges" (*BallotPedia*) <https://ballotpedia.org/Partisan_election_of_judges> accessed September 5, 2019.

[104] "Development Regulations" (*City of Houston Plan. & Dev.*) <www.houstontx.gov/planning/DevelopRegs/> accessed September 5, 2019.

[105] "Building Construction or Alteration Permit" (*NYC*) <https://portal.311.nyc.gov/article/?kanumber=KA-02104> accessed September 5, 2019.

landmarked building cannot even change the windows without the approval of a special government agency.[106] Such regulation can be analogized to the public law governing intellectual property, with the main difference being that "public" intellectual property is often federal law while "public" land law is often local law, in some jurisdictions subject to state oversight. In both contexts there are statutes (Copyright and Patent Acts, zoning resolutions), passed by legislatures (Congress, city councils), administered by expert agencies (Copyright Office,[107] Patent and Trademark Office, planning departments or commissions), which provide a backdrop for extensive litigation in the courts.

Even the original acquisition of property in land bears a public law imprint, not entirely dissimilar to the initial acquisition of important forms of intellectual property.[108] Much land in the United States came to be privately owned through the grant of federal patents.[109] Today, patents for inventions are granted by the federal Patent and Trademark Office.[110] Copyright is acquired by "in an original work of authorship once it is fixed in a tangible medium," and does not require registration or approval from the federal Copyright Office to obtain, but "registration (or refusal) is necessary to enforce the exclusive rights of copyright through litigation."[111] Thus there is no basis for seeing intellectual property, at least, as more artificial than real property law even if a public role in making the law is considered a marker of artificiality. The role of public law in creating and enforcing real as well as intellectual property suggests that intangible property merits the same academic respect as more traditional forms of tangible property.

V. Conclusion

By way of conclusion, I want to address what might be gained by thinking of intangibles as a core case of property, in addition to land and other tangible

[106] "Performing Work on a Landmarked Property" (*NYC Business*) <www1.nyc.gov/nycbusiness/description/performing-work-on-a-landmarked-property> accessed September 5, 2019.

[107] Unlike the Patent Office, the Copyright Office is a branch of Congress. Balganesh (n 61) (manuscript at 65, 72).

[108] Banner (n 12) 221.

[109] Ibid.; see also *Summa Corp. v. California ex rel. State Lands Com'n*, 466 US 198, 202–04 (1984) (describing issuance of federal patent affirming boundaries after California became part of the United States).

[110] "General Information Concerning Patents" USPTO <www.uspto.gov/patents-getting-started/general-information-concerning-patents#heading-2> accessed October 2015.

[111] USPO, "Copyright Basics" (2017) 4 <www.copyright.gov/circs/circ01.pdf>. But see Balganesh (n 61) (manuscript at 73 fn. 425) (The "courts undertake the first real scrutiny of the existence and scope of [copyright] protection" because registration is not required "for protection").

personal property. If the revived thing-based understanding of property covers intangibles and tangibles, as suggested above, why bother increasing the profile of intangible examples in property thinking, other than to make it seem more *au courant*?

For one, a greater focus on intangible property likely would lead property theory to more accurately convey the kinds of property rights that individuals enjoy today, especially in urban, post-industrial societies. With intangible property as a motivating example, the limits on owner authority might be more salient because many intangible rights, such as copyrights and patents, often lack permanence or broad exclusivity. To be sure, it is not necessary to focus on intangible property to see that modern property often does not provide an unlimited realm of authority. As already mentioned, the residents of cities frequently have constrained property rights in land. Nevertheless, greater focus on intangible property would further underscore that limited property rights are more the norm than the exception, contrary to the thrust of prominent thing-based accounts of property.

In 2007, in rejecting the idea of treating intellectual property and real property as a unitary whole, intellectual property Professor Peter Menell warned that doing so "will call attention to the interdependency conception of resources."[112] I favor more focus on intangible property rights precisely because their lack of absoluteness is likely more representative of the state of contemporary property rights. The qualified character of intangible property rights also may be an apt model for the future of property rights in land and other tangible resources as well. Real property likely will need to become even less absolute as urbanization spreads and people come to live more interdependently in denser areas just as the earth's physical land mass is changing due to the warming of the climate.[113]

Second, incorporating intangible property more fully into property theory also may benefit thinking about intangible property, not merely tangible property. Consistent with the utilitarian purposes for which patents and copyrights are authorized in the US constitution, American intellectual property scholarship tends to be consequentialist.[114] Treating intellectual property as a species of property may lead to more and deeper discussion of the non-consequentialist attributes of intellectual property, which are increasingly important in the digital age when people define themselves partly online.

[112] Menell (n 4) 41.

[113] See, e.g., Fennell (n 2).

[114] Menell (n 4) 38 ("patents and copyrights emerged largely through legislative enactments pursuant to a specific utilitarian directive: 'to promote the Progress in Science and the useful Arts' ").

Amid public concern that corporations such as Facebook and Google are assembling vast troves of individual data and threatening personal privacy, there are proposals to give individuals some form of "property rights" in their "data," such as the information that individuals actively generate when they enter health data into an app or shop online, and passively create by moving around with cell phones.[115] Indeed, dissenting in *Carpenter v. US*, US Supreme Court Justice Neil Gorsuch suggested in 2018 that individuals already may have property vis-à-vis the government in the location data generated by their cell phones that requires governments to obtain a warrant under the Fourth Amendment prior to acquiring that data.[116] From a utilitarian perspective, it may be difficult to justify recognizing individual property rights in data that could be asserted against private companies because individuals already are compensated to some degree for giving up their data through the search, communication, and other services that they receive from companies such as Google and Facebook.[117] Also, creating individual data rights could significantly reduce collective welfare by empowering individuals to hold up societally beneficial projects such as medical research.[118] Arguably, however, the proposals to provide individuals with property rights in data exercisable against private actors make more sense from the perspective of increasing autonomy, protecting personhood, and promoting distributive justice, which are traditional concerns of non-economically oriented property scholarship.[119] If regular property theorists were to embrace intangible property as a core concern, they would be well positioned to assert these values in debates about propertizing online data often dominated by utilitarian thinking. The theoretical apparatus built up around real and other forms of tangible property

[115] Sarah Jeong, "Selling your Private Information is a Terrible Idea" *NY Times* (July 5, 2019) <www.nytimes.com/2019/07/05/opinion/health-data-property-privacy.html>; Steve Lohr, "Calls Mount to Ease Big Tech's Grip on Your Data" *NY Times* (July 25, 2019) <www.nytimes.com/2019/07/25/business/calls-mount-to-ease-big-techs-grip-on-your-data.html>.

[116] *Carpenter v. US*, 138 S. Ct. 2206, 2272 (2018) (Gorsuch, J. (dissenting)). On private sector use of "cell-site location information," see Stuart A. Thompson and Charlie Warzel, "Twelve Million Phones, One Dataset, Zero Privacy" *NY Times* (December 19, 2019) <https://www.nytimes.com/interactive/2019/12/19/opinion/location-tracking-cell-phone.html>.

[117] Lohr (n 115).

[118] See, e.g., Jorge L. Contreras, "Genetic Property" (2016) 105 Georgetown LJ 1, 7–10 (discussing genetic data).

[119] Dagan (n 8). *Compare* Jorge L. Contreras, "The False Promise of Health Data Ownership" (2019) 94 NYU L. Rev. 624, 626 ("some health law scholars have raised concerns regarding individual autonomy, privacy, and distributive justice in arguing for the propertization of genetic and other health information") *and* Christopher Odinet, "Data and the Social Obligation Norm of Property" (2020) Cornell J. L. & Pub. Pol'y <https://papers.ssrn.com/sol3/papers.cfm?abstract_id=3492648> (human flourishing theory implies that individuals and corporations should share control of individual data generated through platforms) *with* Jeong (n 115) (arguing that individual data ownership would undermine autonomy, privacy, and distributive justice).

emphasizes that utilitarianism is not the only frame for considering novel issues such as individual property rights in data.

It made sense for property theory to focus almost exclusively on topics related to land and other tangible objects in the late nineteenth and early twentieth centuries when vast industries were created based on land and extracting resources from it. To take an example, it was logical to focus on the meaning of possession in that era, as possession was the main way that the common law historically allocated property rights in new and unowned resources in the tangible objects which were important sources of wealth.[120] Today, however, topics such as the meaning of possession have a slightly musty feel to them, notwithstanding their innate intellectual interest. It is time for property scholarship to focus greater attention on the intangibles at the heart of the digital age.

[120] See Am. L. Inst., *Restatement of the Law Fourth Property* (Preliminary Draft No. 4, 2018) div. III; ibid. introductory note, 63, § 7 (Possession); ibid. cmt i (Physical Things); ibid. 69, 83.

5

Third Party Effects in Private Law

Form and Function

Ben McFarlane and Andreas Televantos

I. Introduction

A core task of private law is to determine the degree to which the terms of a transaction between A and B, whereby a right arises in favor of B, can affect strangers to that transaction. Private law rules therefore govern what we will term the "third party effect" of the A–B transaction. There are a number of different aspects to the broad issue of third party effect. It includes, for example, the question of when a stranger can take the benefit of the right acquired by B, perhaps as a result of an assignment by B. This chapter examines a particular aspect of third party effect: the circumstances in which the A–B transaction may affect C, who has no pre-existing right, but who rather enters into a subsequent transaction with A, or otherwise interferes with the right claimed by B.[1]

Our goal is to show the range of means by which private law controls and determines this aspect of third party effect. We make three key points. First, such effects are controlled not only by rules relating to legal property rights and equitable interests, as is often supposed, but also by parts of the law of agency, partnership, and tort, for example. This means that insights into the operation of legal property rights and equitable interests may also be relevant when considering these other areas. Secondly, whilst a range of doctrines share this *function* of controlling third party effects, it is important to distinguish between the precise legal *form* used by each doctrine. We argue, for example, that the form of a legal property right differs in significant ways from that of an equitable interest and that these differences are not mere technicalities, or jurisdictional hangovers, but are rather based on the different nature of each type of right, and that those differences in turn reflect different ways in which A and B might

[1] Our focus here is on the initial question of when C will owe a duty to B, or come under a liability to B, rather than on the posterior question of the remedies available to B against C.

Ben McFarlane and Andreas Televantos, *Third Party Effects in Private Law* In: *Oxford Studies in Private Law Theory: Volume 1*. Edited by: Paul B. Miller and John Oberdiek, Oxford University Press (2020). © The Several Contributors.
DOI: 10.1093/oso/9780198851356.003.0005

choose to transact. As will be seen in section III, attention must also be paid to the interaction between the different forms used to govern third party effect, as there are many relationships in which more than one such form may be relevant. Thirdly, even when considering one particular form, such as that of a legal property right, third party effect is determined by the interaction of different types of rules, with the practical operation of one type of rule modified by the application of a different type. So the third party effect of rules as to B's acquisition of a legal property right from A, for example, are modified by rules which instead determine when C might have a defense to B's right.

On our approach then, doctrines which are seen as closely related, because they perform the same broad function, may also need to be carefully distinguished, as each has a distinct form. We argue that an appreciation of the law's pluralistic approach to third party effect is crucial to maintain coherence in the law. We also identify two key tensions in this area: first, private law offers A and B a number of distinct ways to structure their relations, and thus significantly promotes the parties' autonomy;[2] yet, as shown by the rules governing the effect of such relations on third parties, the autonomy of C must also be considered. Secondly, there is a higher order tension between maintaining the different concepts and devices which allow for such diversity in the parties' legal relations and, at the same time, ensuring that the rules of private law are simple and clear enough to be used by parties in their planning and to be applied consistently by the courts. We argue that the law is justified in recognizing a range of forms of third party effect where the distinctions between such forms track distinctions between the different transactions entered into in practice and are thus capable of being comprehended by the parties themselves.[3]

Private law, and in particular the law of contract and property, can play an important role in enhancing parties' autonomy, by conferring powers to enter into diverse forms of legal relations with others. To allow parties to exercise such autonomy, however, the law should provide "stable secure frameworks for one's life and actions" and should itself be "a stable and safe basis for individual planning."[4] The potential tension between these aims is evident when considering third party effect. Imagine A owns an art gallery, and sells a particular painting to B. It is agreed that B will become owner of the painting

[2] See, e.g., H Dagan and M Heller, *The Choice Theory of Contracts Pt I* (CUP 2017) esp ch. 1; H Dagan, "Autonomy and Pluralism in Private Law" in A Gold et al. (eds.) *Oxford Handbook of the New Private Law* (OUP 2020).

[3] This argument is relevant, e.g., when considering the requirement that, if C is to be bound by B's pre-existing equitable interest in relation to a right acquired by C from A, C must have some knowledge of A and B's relationship: see section II.B.

[4] J. Raz, *The Authority of Law* (2nd ed., OUP 2002) 220.

immediately, but A will keep possession of it until B makes appropriate storage arrangements. The general rules as to sales allow A and B to structure their legal relations in that way: in such a transaction, where the relevant property is adequately identified, the intent of A and B governs when property passes,[5] without any requirement that B must take possession, and without the need to satisfy any formal requirements. Later, C sees the same painting in the gallery and, knowing nothing of the earlier A–B transaction, pays A the price, and takes it away. B argues that she has a better right to the painting than C, who should be left to a claim against A; C responds that he has a better right, and it is B who should be left to a claim against A. Whatever solution the law reaches in such a case, the ability of either B or C to plan his or her actions rationally must be impaired. In the context of competing claims to title to property, it has been said that security is an "elusive ideal,"[6] and a distinction has been made between the goals of "static security" (which would favor B) and of "dynamic security" (which would favor C).[7]

In English law, the solution to our example is provided by the "seller in possession" rule: a common law rule given statutory effect and now set out in the Factors Act 1889, s. 8 and the Sale of Goods Act 1979, s. 24. Provided that C dealt with A, and acquired possession of the goods, in good faith and without notice of the earlier sale to B, C is protected from B's pre-existing but hidden title to the painting.[8] It is important to see the interaction of different parts of the law: whilst the *acquisition* rules allow B to acquire A's legal ownership of the painting without taking possession, further rules, such as the seller in possession provision, can provide C with a defence to B's right and thus regulate the *enforceability* of B's right. The third party effect of the A–B transaction is a product of the interaction of those different types of rule, and the rules can only be evaluated together: thus the power of a sale in allowing a legal property right to be transferred without any formality, registration, or transfer of possession, whilst commercially very useful to A and B, would be hard to justify if there were no provisions for protecting a third party, such as C, from the effects of such a sale. The "seller in possession" rule depends in essence on a simple distinction, comprehensible to the parties, between a sale where the vendor keeps possession and one where the vendor does not. B's willingness to allow A to

[5] See, e.g., Sale of Goods Act 1979, s. 17; Uniform Commercial Code (UCC), § 2-401(1).

[6] T.W. Mapp, *Torrens' Elusive Title: Basic Principles of an Efficient Torrens System* (University of Alberta Faculty of Law 1978) 63.

[7] R. Demogue, "Security" in A. Fouillée et al. (eds.), *Modern French Legal Philosophy* (1916), discussed by P. O'Connor, "Registration of Title in England and Australia" in E. Cooke (ed.), *Modern Studies in Property Law: Volume 2* (Hart Publishing 2003).

[8] C would also be protected under Uniform Commercial Code § 2-403.

retain possession, whilst it does not prevent B's acquiring title (and so being protected if, for example, A goes into insolvency), creates an evident risk for C which is then dealt with in a tailored fashion: not by denying B title at all, but rather by providing C with a defense against the assertion of B's title.

We will consider here further examples of how different private law rules interact to perform the vital role of controlling the third party effect of an A–B transaction. First, in section II, we will examine some core conceptual building blocks, before considering in section III examples of how those doctrines combine to regulate third party effects in the case of agency, trusts, and partnership.

II. Building Blocks: Types of Rights

A. Legal Property Rights

Perhaps the most dramatic form of third party effect occurs where the A–B transaction confers on B a legal property right, such as ownership of goods, or a freehold of land. Such rights have the striking effect of imposing immediate, strict duties on the rest of the world, with the consequence that "persons deal with the property in chattels or exercise acts of ownership over them at their peril."[9] B's legal property right can be seen as depersonalized; not only because it is only contingently held by B, but also because it can be enforced against potentially anyone.[10] The duty thus imposed on a third party is not based on any specific relationship between the claimant and defendant, and exists without any triggering event or specific conduct by the defendant;[11] it arises immediately on B's acquisition of the legal property right.[12] It is also clear that the duty owed by C is a primary one, as it does not depend on the breach by A of any duty to B. Indeed, a legal property right can be acquired in some cases by B's unilateral action[13] and so need not be the product of an A–B transaction. B's

[9] Cleasby J. in *Fowler v. Hollins* (1872) LR 7 QB 616, 639, cited with approval by Lord Hoffmann in *OBG v. Allan* [2008] 1 AC 1, [9].

[10] See, e.g., J. Penner, *The Idea of Property in Law* (OUP 2000) ch. 5 and H.E. Smith, "Emergent Property" in J. Penner and H.E. Smith (eds.) *Philosophical Foundations of Property Law* (OUP 2013) 320, 338, referring to such "two-way depersonalization."

[11] This feature of standard property rights is emphasized by S. Balganesh, "Quasi-Property: Like, But Not Quite Property" (2012) 160 U. Penn. L. Rev. 1889, 1892, where it is contrasted with the more limited third party effect of "quasi-property" rights (such as the right in hot news recognized by Justice Pitney in *INS v. AP* (1918) 248 US 215, 236): see further text at n 42 below.

[12] Of course, particular conduct of C is required in order for C to breach that duty, but the duty exists prior to any specific conduct of C.

[13] As is the case, e.g., where B takes possession of an object and thereby acquires a title to it: see, e.g., R. Epstein, "Possession as the Root of Title" (1979) 13 Georgia L. Rev. 1221.

legal property right will also have an important effect on creditors of A: even if A has possession or control of the property, its value will not generally[14] be available to A's creditors.[15]

The dramatic impact of a legal property right on C is mitigated in four ways. First, the binding effect of such a right is not absolute: B's legal property right is prima facie binding on C, and so it may be possible for C to establish a defense to it. The absence of a general bona fide purchase for value defense is significant,[16] but, as our art gallery example shows, there are circumstances where a good faith acquisition for value of rights in a resource may play a role in allowing C to avoid liability to B. It is notable that where such defenses apply, they generally[17] identify particular situations where the law protects C's reliance on a reasonable belief for which B, through B's voluntary action, is at least partly responsible.[18] Second, even where no such defense is available to C, the third party effect of a legal property right is limited by the nature of the duty imposed on C. Whilst that duty is strict, it is simply a duty not to interfere with the particular resource in which B has a legal property right: if C merely interferes with B's use of the resource, without interfering with the resource itself, C is not, without more, liable to B.[19] Third, formality and other rules regulating the circumstances in which B may acquire a legal property right can also provide some protection to C, [20] although the power of a sale in allowing A to transfer a legal property right in goods to B without any formality remains a striking

[14] There are of course "claw-back" and preference provisions allowing for the setting aside of an A–B transaction in particular circumstances (see, e.g., Insolvency Act 1986, ss, 127, 238, 239; US Bankruptcy Code 11 USC §§ 547–551), and registration requirements which may mean registration is necessary if B's non-possessory legal property right is to be enforced in A's insolvency (see, e.g., Companies Act 2006, s. 859A).

[15] Note this was not always the case. For over 350 years property in a bankrupt's possession or control with the consent of its owner would vest in the bankrupt's estate under the doctrine of reputed ownership, 21 Jac. I c. 19 s. 10 (1623), which was abolished by amendments in the Insolvency Act 1985, consolidated in the Insolvency Act 1986. See G. Moss, "Should the British Eagle be Extinct?" (2011) 24 Insolvency Intelligence 49.

[16] See, e.g., *Farquarhson Bros. v. King* [1902] AC 325; D. Baird and T. Jackson, "Information, Uncertainty, and the Transfer of Property" (1984) 13 J. Legal Stud. 299, 302, noting the starting position that: "Anglo-American law assumes for the most part that an individual's interest in enjoying property that is acquired, in good faith, from someone else who appears to be the owner is not as important as recognizing the rights of the person who first owned it or who last owned it by wholly consensual transfers."

[17] Defenses may be based on other, more general concerns, such as those behind limitation statutes, or they may be specific to ownership of a specific type of property (as is the case in relation to currency: see, e.g., *Miller v. Race* (1758) 1 Burr 452).

[18] In our art gallery example, B allowed A to retain possession of the painting (in the terms of Uniform Commercial Code § 2-403(2) and (3), B thus "entrusted" possession of the painting to A). See too Factors Act 1889, ss. 2–4 and 8–9; Sale of Goods Act 1979, ss. 21, 24 and 25.

[19] See, e.g., *Spartan Steel & Alloys Ltd. V. Martin & Co. Ltd.* [1973] 1 QB 27; *Byrd v. English* 43 SE 419 (Ga. 1903); S. Douglas and B. McFarlane, "Defining Property Rights" in Penner and Smith (n 10).

[20] Such rules are of course prominent in relation to land: see, e.g., Law of Property Act 1925, s. 52; Land Registration Act 2002, ss. 4 and 27.

example of the law's commitment to facilitating parties' informal dealings with almost all forms of goods.

As well as regulating the enforcement and acquisition of legal property rights, the law also controls the content of legal property rights. Indeed, some of the most significant academic work on third party effect relates to the operation of the *numerus clausus* principle, which limits the content of legal property rights.[21] In so doing, the principle limits the range of duties A and B can impose on third parties through agreements in respect of property and thus reduces the risk of C incurring liability to additional parties, and hence for additional losses, when interfering with a resource.[22] It should be noted that, as seen in our art gallery example, that aim of shielding a third party from the effects of difficult to discover A–B transactions can also be furthered by providing C, in particular circumstances, with a defense to B's recognized proprietary right. The diversity in the means by which the law may deal with the question of third party effect thus plays a role in promoting the autonomy of A and B: in the absence of controls on the enforcement and acquisition of legal property rights, controls on the content of such rights would necessarily be tighter.

B. Equitable Interests

Private law's nuanced approach to third party effect, we contend, requires a distinction to be carefully drawn between legal property rights on the one hand and, on the other, equitable interests, such as the rights of a beneficiary of a trust, or the holder of an equitable charge. This important point is often overlooked, for example in discussions of the *numerus clausus* principle;[23] the term "equitable property right" may suggest an unwarranted assimilation of the two types of right and it is for that reason that we instead refer here to equitable interests.

Where an A–B transaction gives B an equitable interest,[24] rather than a legal property right, the most obvious change in third party effect is provided by the

[21] See, e.g., B. Rudden, "Economic Theory v Property Law: The *Numerus Clausus* Problem" in J. Eekelaar and J. Bell (eds.), *Oxford Essays in Jurisprudence, 3rd series* (Clarendon Press 1987); T.W. Merrill and H.E. Smith, "Optimal Standardization in the Law of Property: The *Numerus Clausus* Principle" (2000–2001) 110 Yale LJ 3; B. Edgeworth, "The *Numerus Clausus* Principle in Contemporary Australian Property Law" (2006) 32 Monash U. L. Rev. 387.

[22] See, e.g., *Hill v. Tupper* (1863) 2 H & C 121, 159 ER 51. See too B. McFarlane, "The *Numerus Clausus* Principle and Covenants Relating to Land" in S. Bright (ed.), *Modern Studies in Property Law: Volume 6* (Hart Publishing,2011) 311.

[23] See n 46 below.

[24] Note the analysis here applies, *mutatis mutandis*, where: (i) B's equitable interest arises by operation of law, without A having exercised a power to give B that right (as may occur, e.g., where A, a trustee,

availability to C of a general defense of bona fide purchase of a legal property right for value without notice of the limit on A's ability to deal with the property (referred to here as the "general bona fide purchase defense"). If, for example, A, rather than selling a painting to B, declares that he holds that painting on trust for B, then a later sale of the painting by A to C, even if not authorized under the terms of the trust, will give C a defense against B's assertion of that equitable interest if C acquired A's title to the painting in good faith and without notice of A's lack of authority.[25] Our point, however, is that an equitable interest is *not* equivalent to a legal property right subject to the general bona fide purchase defense: there are significant further differences in enforceability between legal property rights and equitable interests.[26] Most importantly, whilst a legal property right imposes an immediate prima facie duty on the rest of the world not to interfere with a particular resource, an equitable interest does not.[27] In considering the third party effect of an interest under a trust, for example, Lord Sumption recently stated that the beneficiary's interest is:[28]

> good against third parties into whose hands the property or its traceable proceeds may have come, subject to the rules of equity for the protection of bona fide purchasers for value without notice . . .

It is notable that Lord Sumption there identified a *particular* class of third parties subject to the beneficiary's interest: the right does not immediately bind the whole world, but rather may affect those who later acquire the trust property or its traceable proceeds. This limit is clear in some cases: if the A–B transaction arises where A, the vendor, is under a duty to transfer her estate in land to B, for example, then it is possible that not only A but also C (a party later acquiring A's estate) will come under that duty to B;[29] but of course X, a trespasser, could not

holds on trust for B assets acquired in breach of trust); and (ii) B's equitable interest arises as a result of a transaction between S and A (as may occur, e.g., where S, a settlor of a trust, transfers a right to A to hold on trust for B). In each case, a relevant "transaction" gives rise to rights and duties as between A and B, even if A and B are not the sole authors of that transaction, and C remains a stranger to that transaction.

[25] See, e.g., *Pilcher v. Rawlins* (1872) 7 Ch. App. 259.

[26] See too F. Maitland, "Trust and Corporation": see D. Runciman and M. Ryan (eds.), *Maitland: State, Trust and Corporation* (CUP 2003) 75, 94. The essay was first published in German: Maitland, "Trust and Corporation" (1905) *Grunhut's Zeitschrift fur das Privat- and Offentliche Recht* 1. Maitland there exposes the problems with the "ordinary thought of Englishmen [that] 'equitable ownership' is just ownership pure and simple, though it is subject to a peculiar, technical and not very intelligible rule in favour of bona fide purchasers."

[27] See, e.g., *The Lord Compton's Case* (1587) 3 Leo 197; *The Aliakmon* [1986] AC 785 (HL); *Restatement (Third) of Trusts* (2003) §§ 107–108.

[28] *Akers v. Samba* [2017] AC 424 (SC), [82].

[29] B acquires an equitable interest under a distinct form of vendor–purchaser constructive trust: see, e.g., *Lysaght v. Edwards* (1876) 2 Ch. D. 499; *Jerome v. Kelly* [2004] 1 WLR 1409 (PC), [28]–[32].

come under such a duty to B.[30] Even in the case where A holds on trust for B, where B might be thought of as the "equitable owner" of the property, B has no direct claim against X if X simply damages the trust property: the claim against X, if available, belongs to A, even if B can force A to make it.[31]

Further, in the *Akers* case, Lord Sumption stated that when an asset subject to an equitable interest is transferred to C, "the question becomes whether the conscience of the transferee is affected."[32] The position is clearly different where C receives an asset in which B has a legal property right: C can then be liable to B even if C deals with that asset innocently, in the reasonable belief that there are no competing claims to it, and even if C retains no property representing that original asset.[33] In contrast, if C is the innocent donee of property transferred by A in breach of trust, and C disposes of that property and its traceable proceeds before gaining any knowledge of A's lack of authority, B has no claim against C.[34] Indeed, even if we consider the "equitable proprietary claim" that B can make where C, an initially innocent donee, still holds the trust property or its traceable proceeds, C's duty to B can be seen as arising not at the time of the innocent receipt of the property, but only at the later point when C acquires sufficient knowledge of B's equitable interest.[35] On this view, references to conscience when considering the impact of an equitable interest on a third party are not an unfortunate historical hangover, but rather signify that C's duty arises only if B can show that the A–B relationship that gives rise initially to B's equitable interest is in some way replicated as between B and C, as C now holds a specific right and, because of her own conduct, is under a duty to B in relation to that right.

Further, the general bona fide purchase defense, when applied to equitable interests, does not have the same form as seemingly similar defenses, also based on a good faith acquisition of rights, available against legal property rights.[36]

[30] See W. Swadling, "Property" in A. Burrows (ed.), *English Private Law* (3rd ed., OUP 2013) 4.23.

[31] See the authorities in n 27 above. The Court of Appeal's decision in *Shell UK Ltd. v. Total UK Ltd.* [2011] QB 86 may cast some doubt on this point, but note that there the effect of B's equitable interest on a third party interfering with property was distinguished from the effect of a legal property right, as the loss suffered by B was characterized as purely economic loss: ibid. [132]–[136]. See too n 120 below.

[32] [2017] AC 424 at [89]. See too Lord Browne-Wilkinson in *Westdeutsche Landesbank Girozentrale v. Islington LBC* [1996] AC 669, 705.

[33] As made clear by, e.g., Lord Nicholls in *Kuwait Airways Corp. v. Iraqi Airways Co. (Nos. 4 and 5)* [2002] 2 AC 883, [79].

[34] *ITS Ltd. v. GP Noble Trustees Ltd.* [2013] Ch 91 (CA), [76] (Lloyd LJ): "to the extent that, before she had notice of the claim to the funds, she had disposed of any of the money without receiving traceable proceeds, she would not be liable [to B]." See too *Agip (Africa) Ltd. v. Jackson* [1990] Ch 265, 290–91 (Millett J.).

[35] See S. Agnew and B. McFarlane, "The Nature of the Equitable Proprietary Claim" in B. McFarlane and S. Agnew (eds.), *Modern Studies in Property Law: vol. X* (Hart 2019).

[36] See I. Samet and A. Nair, "What Can 'Equity's Darling' Tell Us About Equity?" in D. Klimchuk et al. (eds.), *Philosophical Foundations of the Law of Equity* (OUP 2020).

For example, the "seller in possession" rule, as applied in our art gallery example, may be seen as concerned with the question of title: it provides in effect that A has the power to pass B's good title to the painting to C, and thus prevents B from invoking against C the logic of *nemo dat*.[37] It is often assumed that the general bona fide purchase defense, when applied against B's equitable interest, operates in the same way.[38] The error of that view was recently exposed by the UK Supreme Court in *Akers v. Samba*. It was confirmed there that, if A holds property on trust for B, and then transfers that right to C, who, as a bona fide purchaser for value without notice takes free from B's interest, there is in fact no disposition from A to C of B's equitable interest. C is protected from any claim of B, and C is thus free to use the property for C's own benefit, but this is because of the inherently limited third party effect of B's equitable interest,[39] and not because of any transfer of B's equitable interest to C.[40]

The legacy of the jurisdictional divide between common law and equity is that the modern law has an additional means of determining the question of third party effect and that A and B thus have a further option as to the legal relations they may create. Even if an A–B transaction does not give B a right that imposes an immediate prima facie duty on all third parties, it may still give B an equitable interest, and thus have significant third party effect. Indeed, in re lation to some third parties, such as creditors of A, the effect of B's equitable interest will be no different from the effect of a legal property right.[41] Yet, as shown by our discussion of enforceability against third parties other than A's creditors, it is clear that the third party effect of an equitable interest is more limited than that of a legal property right. It is limited to a particular group of third parties (those who acquire from A the right to which B's equitable interest relates) and its effect is not automatic (B must show that C's conscience has been affected). In those ways, an equitable interest, even the supposed "equitable ownership"

[37] In the Sale of Goods Act 1979, ss. 21–26 are gathered together under the heading "transfer of title": s. 24, which applies in our example, operates to give the sale from A to C "the same effect as if [A] were expressly authorised by [B] to make the same"; UCC § 2-403(2) states that the effect in our example of B's entrusting of possession to A is that A has "power to transfer all rights of the entruster [B] to a buyer in ordinary course of business [C]." The model in each case, then, is of A having the power to transfer B's rights in the goods to C.

[38] See, e.g., P. Birks, "Notice and Onus in *O'Brien*" (1998) 12 TLI 2, 5.

[39] [2017] AC 424 (SC) at [51] (Lord Mance) and [89] (Lord Sumption).

[40] See too *Vandervell v. IRC* [1967] 2 AC 291 (HL): a transfer of the trust property by A to C, carried out with B's permission, is not a "disposition" of B's beneficial interest and so is not caught by the writing requirement laid down in the Law of Property Act 1925, s. 53(1)(c).

[41] See further text at n 76 below. It is therefore clear that the third party effects of a trust differ from those that can be achieved through purely contractual arrangements between A and B: see, e.g., H. Hansmann and U. Mattei, "The Functions of Trust Law: A Comparative Legal and Economic Analysis" (1998) 73 NYU L. Rev. 434, 466, 469–71 and R. Sitkoff, "Trust Law as Fiduciary Governance Plus Asset Partitioning" in L. Smith (ed.), *The Worlds of the Trust* (CUP 2013).

of a trust beneficiary, meets Balganesh's criteria for "quasi-property": it operates "against a *specified class of actors*, and only ever upon the occurrence of a *specific triggering event*"[42] and thus lacks the *erga omnes* exclusionary force of a legal property right. Milsom stated that: "equity has proved that from the materials of obligation you can counterfeit the phenomena of property."[43] Yet, like all counterfeits, the match is not perfect.

In our discussion of legal property rights, we noted that the question of enforceability is intrinsically linked to those of acquisition and content. The same is true in relation to equitable interests, and this has important consequences for the internal coherence of private law. In short, the differences between the rules as to the acquisition and content of equitable interests and their common law counterparts need not be seen as a mere accident of history, nor as a result of a different attitude to the enforcement of moral values, but can instead be explained as depending on the different third party effects of equitable interests on the one hand and legal property rights on the other. For example, as to acquisition, it is striking that A, the holder of a right, has the power to give B an equitable interest simply by orally and gratuitously expressing an intention that A now holds that right for B's benefit: as Hackney memorably puts it "No other device in the legal system approaches the massive power of these spoken words in Equity: 'I declare myself trustee of this for you.'"[44] The lack of formal or other requirements limiting A's power can only be understood once the limits on the enforceability of B's equitable interest are appreciated.

In our view, it is the role played by C's knowledge, rather than the availability or otherwise of the general bona fide purchaser defense, which is the key difference between a legal property right and an equitable interest. The role can be explained by the specific form of an equitable interest: it does not consist of a right correlating a duty of others not to interfere with a specific resource, but is rather focused on a specific right held by A. The distinction, we would argue, is not a mere technicality or a source of undue complexity. Rather, it tracks the difference between A transferring a right to B, and A instead keeping that right and coming under a duty to B in relation to the right. There is thus a difference in principle between the creation of a legal property right and of an equitable interest which is sufficiently comprehensible to parties such as A, B, and C. It would be odd for parties to expect that, if A owns property and simply comes

[42] Balganesh (n 11) 1892 (emphasis in original); see too B. McFarlane and S. Douglas, "Property, Analogy, and Variety" (2020) OJLS forthcoming.

[43] S.F. Milsom, *Historical Foundations of the Common Law* (2nd ed., Butterworths 1961) 6.

[44] J. Hackney, *Understanding Equity and Trusts* (Fontana 1987) 109. Indeed, A can exercise that power to create a trust without using the term "trust": see, e.g., *Paul v. Constance* [1977] 1 WLR 527 (CA).

under a duty to B in relation to it, B would acquire the same rights against third parties as in a case where A instead transfers A's ownership to B. As an equitable interest is based on A's being under a particular type of duty to B, there is no obvious reason why the existence of A's duty to B should immediately affect C who, after all, continues to owe duties to A in relation to the property. Certainly, the circumstances in which A can come under a duty to B are far more varied than those in which A can transfer a right to B, and are thus often more difficult for C to discover. If, however, C *knows* of the duty A owes to B, and thus of the limits, as against B, of A's powers to deal with the property, then the picture changes in a significant way.

The distinctive third party effect of equitable interests is also crucial when considering the content of such rights, and this has important consequences for our understanding of the *numerus clausus* principle. On the one hand, it might seem that the principle is undermined by equity's greater willingness to recognize B's right as "proprietary": A cannot give B a legal property right with the content that B has exclusive use of A's watch on a Monday;[45] but A *can* set up a trust, of which B is one of the beneficiaries, and under the terms of which the trustee must allow B to have exclusive use of the trust property (the watch) on a Monday.[46] B's right will then be proprietary in the sense that it will be protected from creditors of the trustee; but its effect on a party acquiring title to the watch from the trustee, or on a party interfering with the watch, will be limited and quite different from that of a legal property right. It would, we contend, be an error to think that the *numerus clausus* principle is not a feature of those legal systems (such as English law and those based on it) which allow A and B the flexibility to create equitable interests whilst imposing very few controls on the content of such interests.[47] The point is that, in such systems, the need to limit the third party effect of an A–B transaction (the key concern of the *numerus clausus*) is chiefly achieved by controlling the enforceability, rather than the content,[48] of equitable interests.

[45] An example given by Merrill and Smith (n 21) 27.

[46] It is notable that many discussions of the *numerus clausus* principle, such as that of Merrill and Smith (n 21), or of H. Hansmann and R. Kraakman, "Property, Contract, and Verification: The *Numerus Clausus* Problem and the Divisibility of Rights" (2002) 31 J. Legal Stud. S373, devote no or relatively little attention to the diversity permitted in the content of equitable interests under trusts.

[47] For possible skepticism as to whether common law systems such as English law feature a *numerus clausus* principle, see, e.g., the contrast drawn between such systems and civil law systems in P. Matthews, "The Compatibility of the Trust with the Civil Law Notion of Property" in L. Smith (ed.), *The Worlds of the Trust* (CUP 2013) 313, 320.

[48] This is not to say there are *no* restrictions on the content of an equitable interest: see, e.g., B. McFarlane and R. Stevens, "The Nature of Equitable Property" (2010) J. Eq. 1, 10–15.

C. Personal Rights

It is universally acknowledged that if an A–B transaction gives B only a personal right against A, rather than an equitable interest or a legal property right, then the third party effect of B's right is limited. This is emphasized by the fact that an unsecured personal right of B will not reduce the overall assets available to A's creditors.[49] The difference is also apparent in relation to non-creditor third parties; but some care must be taken.

First, it would be a mistake to say that B's personal right against A can have *no* effect on third parties. For example, if that right arises in a contract, then the tort of procuring a breach of contract gives it a form of weak third party effect.[50] As the tort recognizes a form of accessory liability,[51] it requires an initial breach by A, and so cannot assist B in a case where the A–B transaction gives B no right at all against A. The tort therefore depends on the existence of the A–B right: if B instead suffers some economic loss from C's conduct, but that loss does not involve any breach by A of a contractual duty to B, the tort does not apply and B's protection is correspondingly limited.[52] Equally, the third party effect recognized by the tort is different from that arising where the A–B transaction instead gives B a legal property right (as C cannot be strictly liable for interfering with B's purely contractual right)[53] or an equitable interest (as C cannot be liable simply because of acquiring property from A with knowledge that A had entered into a contract with B to allow B to use that property).[54] Private law can thus recognize some limited third party effect of B's personal right, without undermining the distinction between such rights and equitable interests or legal property rights. The same tension between promoting the

[49] It is of course possible however for certain unsecured personal rights to be given priority in A's insolvency and thus to limit indirectly the assets available to meet A's other debts: see, e.g., the categories of preferential creditors in the Insolvency Act 1986, s. 386 and Sch. 6 (including, e.g., employees of A). This point is of practical importance, as shown by the UK government's recent proposal to re-introduce priority for debts owed by an insolvent party to the tax authorities: see "Protecting Your Taxes in Insolvency" HMRC Consultation Document, February 26, 2019.

[50] See, e.g., *Lumley v. Gye* (1853) 2 El & Bl 216. Indeed, that effect has even been said to depend on treating contractual rights "as a species of property which deserve special protection": see *OBG v. Allan* [2008] 1 AC 1, [32] (Lord Hoffmann). Note too that, where A is under a fiduciary duty to B, C may be liable for dishonestly assisting A to breach that duty: see, e.g., *Royal Brunei Airlines v. Tan* [1995] 2 AC 378.

[51] See *OBG v. Allan* (ibid.) [8] (Lord Hoffmann).

[52] B may have a claim in such a case if, e.g., C has used independently unlawful means with the intention of causing loss to B. Such protection for B is extremely limited: see, e.g., *OBG v. Allan* (ibid.) [45]–[64].

[53] See, e.g., *OBG v. Allan* (ibid.), where the majority rejected the contention that the strict liability tort of conversion can apply where C deals with a purely contractual right of B.

[54] See, e.g., *Keppell v. Bailey* (1834) 2 My & K 517, 547, 39 ER 1042, 1053; *Port Line Ltd. v. Ben Line Steamers Ltd.* [1958] QB 146; Z. Chaffee, "Equitable Servitudes on Chattels" (1928) 41 Harv. L. Rev. 945.

autonomy of A and B on the one hand, and of C on the other, must inform the nature of the protection given to a personal right of B, and we can again see the interaction between rules of enforceability, acquisition, and content. The very limited nature of the third party effect of a personal right of B is part of an overall private law strategy which places relatively few limits on the acquisition and content of such rights, and therefore the risk of incoherence arises if courts are tempted to extend the enforceability of such rights without also modifying rules as to their acquisition and content.[55]

III. Forms of Relationships: Three Examples

The law regulates third party effect not only through the rules governing different types of rights, but also by imposing particular rights and duties on parties who enter into particular sorts of relationships. Here we will consider three examples, and look at how the types of right examined in section II interact in the context of these relationships.

A. Agency

Where B authorizes A to enter into contracts on her behalf, to dispose of B's property, or both, then in law B is said to engage A as her agent.[56] Whereas a trustee exercises powers over trust assets derived from her own (usually legal) title to those assets, it is distinct from agency: an agent exercises her principal's powers to contract or dispose of property, and not her own powers to do so.[57] This explains why, unlike a trustee, an agent who exercises her principal's powers usually[58] "drops out" of the transaction and incurs no liabilities toward third parties.

[55] An example of such incoherence is provided by the view of the minority in *OBG v. Allan* (n 50): Lord Nicholls, having emphasized the requirements of intention that must be met before C can be liable for procuring a breach of contract (at [191]–[193]), undermined that very control on third party effect by finding (at [233]) that C could instead be strictly liable in the tort of conversion for dealings with B's contractual right.

[56] P. Watts (ed.), *Bowstead & Reynolds on Agency* (21st ed., Sweet & Maxwell 2017) 1-001.

[57] R. Leow, "Understanding Agency: A Proxy Power Definition" (2019) 78 CLJ 99.

[58] There is an exception where C enters into a contract with A, unaware that A is acting as an agent for B. In such a case C has a power to impose contractual duties on A or B, see Watts (n 56) Art. 82. Similarly, where an B enters into a contract with C on behalf of A, and guarantees C's performance to A, B will have exercised her own powers in giving the guarantee and so would not "drop out," see R. Chorley, "Del Credere" (1929) 45 LQR 221.

Agency raises an important issue of third party effect. The A–B transaction giving rise to the principal–agent relationship will contain agreed limits on A's powers, and there is a question as to the effect those limits should have on C, a party who later deals with A. The answer is provided by the doctrine of ostensible or apparent authority.[59] This provides that where B holds out A as having authority to bind her, and C deals with A in reliance on this representation, then A is treated as having authority to bind B regardless of the terms of her actual authority.[60] For example, where B has legal title to goods, and holds out A as having authority to dispose of them, any disposition A makes of those goods within the terms of her ostensible authority will bind B automatically. This remains true even where B has instructed A not to dispose of the property, provided C has no notice of the limitation. In such cases, the more extensive protection C receives under the ostensible authority rules effectively supersedes the rules which automatically govern both legal property rights and equitable interests.

The doctrine thus governs the extent to which the internal aspect of an agency relationship—the actual terms of A's authority—will bind third parties. It is an important means of promoting security for C, and can limit the effect on particular third parties of an initial legal property right or equitable interest of B. As a result, private law also makes use of the doctrine even in cases where there is no genuine agency relationship between A and B. For example, when considering in section II.A our art gallery hypothetical, we saw that ostensible authority reasoning is employed to justify protecting C when C acquires title from a "seller in possession," even though B did not give A any actual authority to deal with B's title to the property. The doctrine thus applies whenever B can be said to have held out A as having authority to bind B, even if there is no real agency relationship. Its justification is conventionally said to lie in the logic of estoppel by representation: it protects C where C has relied on B's representation as to A's powers. In a true estoppel by representation, however, there is no loss of B's right, much less a transfer of a right from B to C; B retains the right but is simply prevented from asserting it. In contrast, ostensible authority, as seen in our art gallery example, can operate to "transfer a real title" from B to C.[61] Further, in many of the cases the traditional elements of estoppel are

[59] Distinctions are sometimes drawn between "ostensible authority," "ostensible ownership," and "usual" or "inherent" authority, although judges and commentators do not all use the terms in the same way, or indeed as discrete categories. For an overview of the different uses of the terms see Watts (n 56) 3-004–3-005, 8-126–8-128.

[60] Watts (n 56) Arts. 76, 83, 84. For the relationship with actual authority see, ibid. 3-004.

[61] See, e.g., UCC § 2-403(2) which operates to give A, in our example, the "power to transfer all rights of the entruster [B] to a buyer in ordinary course of business [C]." As noted by Devlin J. in *Eastern Distributors Ltd. v. Goldring* [1957] 2 QB 600, 609–10: "ostensible authority to sell is an exception to the

present in only a weakened form; conversely some, but not all, of the statutory codifications of the doctrine appear to introduce a further requirement that C is protected only where A was acting in the ordinary course of A's business when dealing with C.[62]

The estoppel rationalization of ostensible authority thus remains open to debate,[63] and we contend that the doctrine can best be understood instead in terms of the tension between the autonomy of A and B on the one hand, and C on the other, present in any case concerning the third party effect of an A–B transaction. First, B has chosen to enter into a particular form of transaction with A (either a genuine agency relationship, or, in our art gallery example, a purchase of goods not involving an immediate transfer of possession) and thus to take the benefits of such a transaction. By permitting such A–B relationships, private law increases the range of options open to A and B, and indeed to C;[64] but it also creates the risk that C will be misled as to the extent of A's powers. It may therefore make sense that, in some cases at least, B should bear the loss caused by this risk's materializing. Secondly, by providing that C's expectations will be honored, the rules increase the confidence with which third parties may deal with agents; this in turn benefits those who, like B, choose to act through agents and is of particular use to corporations, which can act only through agents. Further, shifting loss onto principals in such cases encourages careful selection of agents, theoretically reducing the number of cases in which C is misled. In the art gallery example, the same reasoning does not apply, as B has not chosen to act through an agent, but B does benefit from the power to acquire title through a sale and, as discussed in section II.A above, a limit of the enforceability of title thus acquired may be necessary to justify that acquisition rule.

At one level, it might seem that the doctrine of ostensible authority has much in common with the general bona fide purchase defense available against an equitable interest: in each case, C's protection depends on a lack of awareness of a limit, arising from an A–B transaction, on A's powers. There are certainly

maxim *nemo dat quod non habet*; and it is plain from the wording that if the owner of the goods is precluded from denying authority, the buyer will in fact acquire a better title than the seller . . . We doubt whether this principle . . . ought really to be regarded as part of the law of estoppel . . . the effect of its application is to transfer a real title and not merely a metaphorical title by estoppel."

[62] Watts (n 56) 8-024, 8-028, 8-127, 8-130; for the "ordinary courses of business" requirement (which does not apply to the provisions of English law governing our art gallery example) see, e.g., UCC § 2-403(2); Factors Act 1889, s. 2.

[63] For an overview see Watts (n 56) 8-028.

[64] As, e.g., it can be convenient not only for B to be able to sell goods to C using A as an agent, but also for C to buy goods from B by dealing with A as B's agent.

some similarities in relation to the role in such cases of C's knowledge:[65] this is consistent with our thesis as, where there is a concern as to C's ability to plan being limited by particular A–B dealings, then C's knowledge of such dealings makes a clear normative difference. Nonetheless, ostensible authority rules must be carefully distinguished from the limits on the enforceability of equitable interests. First, the agency rules operate to allow B to exercise a power of A, such as a power to transfer property, whereas, as discussed in section II.B above, a transfer by A, a trustee, to a bona fide purchaser for value without notice does not pass B's equitable interest to C: C acquires rights from A, not B, and is protected by B's inability to make a claim against C. Second, C is better protected when she purchases from an agent than from a trustee, as C then need only show that she relied on a holding out by B that A had authority to bind B: there is no need for C to have acquired the property for value, or to have acquired legal title to the property.

The differences in the rules governing purchases from agents and from trustees depend on two points. First, the existence of a trust does not mean that there is an agency relationship between A and B: put simply, the trust depends on A's being under duties to B in respect of particular rights, rather than on B's having given A any powers to affect B's legal relations.[66] Again, we would see this not as an arbitrary distinction, but rather as reflecting a comprehensible difference between two quite different types of A–B transaction. Actions by a trustee, even if not authorized by the trust, may have the *effect* of causing loss to a beneficiary, just as actions of an agent, even if not within the scope of the agent's actual authority, may have the effect of causing loss to the principal; the legal form of each relationship, however, is different. Second, and in contrast to the case where B buys goods from A but allows A to retain possession of those goods, the courts have not chosen to extend the logic of ostensible authority to the trust. Beneficiaries have instead been seen as the passive recipients of the fruits of assets managed by the trustees, without a "duty of watching" over those trustees.[67] The decision to allow trustees to manage the assets, and the

[65] e.g., just as the courts have been careful to limit the circumstances in which a commercial party may be found to have had notice of B's equitable interest, so have they been reluctant to find such notice where C attempts to invoke ostensible authority: see, e.g., *Quinn v. CC Automotive Group Ltd. (t/a Carcraft)* [2010] EWCA Civ. 1412, [23] and [27] (Gross LJ), adopting the approach of Lord Neuberger in *Thanakharn Kasikorn Thai Chamchat v. Akai Holdings Ltd.* [2011] 1 HKLC 357, [52]. The doctrines appear to be very similar if not identical, though the matter has not been fully settled.

[66] Of course a trustee can *also* be an agent of the beneficiary, but a trustee will not be treated as an agent simply by virtue of being a trustee: *Rimmer v. Webster* [1902] 2 Ch. 163; *Burgis v. Constantine* [1908] 2 KB 484 (CA).

[67] *Shropshire Union Railways and Canal Co. v. R* (1875) LR 7 HL 496, 507–08; *Smith v. Anderson* (1880) 15 Ch. D. 247.

selection of the trustees, is traditionally made by the settlors of trusts, not by the beneficiaries, and so the beneficiaries have not been seen as holding out trustees as having authority to bind them.

As a result, it is only in limited circumstances that beneficiaries can incur liability through the trustees' actions.[68] Again, the lesson is that, whatever the functional similarities between doctrines such as ostensible authority and the general bona fide purchase defense, we need to distinguish carefully between different A–B transactions and the different effects they may have on third parties. In particular, courts can fall into error if they treat a trust relationship per se as giving a trustee ostensible authority to bind the beneficiaries.[69] Conversely, if a trustee appoints an agent, even in breach of trust, courts must avoid the mistake[70] of thinking that the agent has no actual or ostensible authority validly to exercise the trustee's powers.[71]

B. Trusts

In section II.B above, we considered the particular means by which an equitable interest, such as that of a beneficiary of a trust, can have third party effect on C, a party to whom the trustee, A, transfers the trust property.[72] It is also important to consider the position where A, acting in discharge of A's functions as trustee, incurs a debt to C: for example, if A holds land on trust for B and contracts with C for necessary repairs to a roof of a house on that land.[73] As noted in section III.A, the fact that A is a trustee for B does not by itself mean that A is also B's agent and so, even when acting with authority under the terms of the trust, A has no power to bind B to the contract with C. Instead, the standard

[68] For when the beneficiary becomes liable to indemnify the trustee in respect of debts (in the absence of an agency relationship), see text at n 78 below.

[69] This error seems to be present in the reasoning in *Wishart v. Credit and Mercantile Plc* [2015] EWCA Civ. 655: see A. Televantos, "Trusteeship, Ostensible Authority, and Land Registration" (2016) Conv. 181.

[70] That mistake is present in *Niak v. Macdonald* [2001] 3 NZLR 334, [18]–[21]; *Ponniah v. Palmer* [2012] NZCA 490, [28]; *Finnigan v. Butcher (No. 2)* [2012] NZHC 2463, [42]–[43]: see P. Watts, "Some Aspects of the Intersection of the Law of Agency with the Law of Trusts" in P. Davies and J. Penner (eds.), *Equity, Trusts and Commerce* (Hart 2017) 29, 34–44.

[71] It is important to distinguish between the question of whether the agent can exercise the trustee's powers, and whether the agent can exercise the beneficiary's powers.

[72] Note that a standard trust involves a combination of different types of right: as well as an equitable interest, B will have distinct personal rights against A (such as, e.g., a duty to invest the trust property) which will not directly bind C, even if C acquires the trust property with knowledge of the trust: see R. Nolan, "Equitable Property" (2006) 122 LQR 232. If C however dishonestly assists A to breach one of those personal rights, C may be liable to B for dishonestly assisting a breach of fiduciary duty: see n 50 above.

[73] This example is used by L. Smith, "Trusts and Patrimony" (2008) Revue Générale de Droit 379, [9].

position[74] is that A is personally liable to C, and C has no direct claim on the trust assets in the event of A's default.[75] This is the case even if C knows that A is contracting as a trustee, and the rule flows from the fact that C is treated as a creditor of A, and, as noted in section II.B, A's creditors cannot claim the trust assets. The historical rationale is the simple one that, just as A is, in equity, barred from making free use of the trust assets, so are A's creditors.[76] A's custodial duty[77] to B not to dispose of assets without authority under the terms of the trust is seen as part of B's equitable interest (rather than as a distinct purely personal duty owed by A to B) and is thus enforced in A's insolvency. Again, the distinction between trusts and agency is crucial: in contracting with C, A is not acting as B's agent and thus does not give C a direct claim against B, or to the trust assets.

This is not, however, the end of the story, as there are again further nuances in private law's handling of this aspect of the third party effect of a trust. If, as in the roof repair example, the debt is incurred consistently with the terms of the trust, A will acquire a right of indemnity against B in respect of the debt, secured by a lien over the trust property.[78] In the event of A's insolvency, C can then be subrogated to that lien, and take the benefit of A's indemnity and lien in priority to A's general creditors.[79] C's access to the trust property is, however, indirect, and so vulnerable to any limits on A's indemnity and lien.[80] This means that if A (deliberately or mistakenly) exceeded his authority under the terms of the trust in contracting the debt, A will typically[81] acquire no right of indemnity or lien, and C will have no way of levying judgment against the trust assets. This is of particular concern to C where A is a poorly capitalized corporate sole trustee of a trading trust.[82] Likewise, if A has committed an unrelated breach of trust, then A's liability to B will be set off against any indemnity A has, and this may

[74] This has been modified by statute in some jurisdictions, e.g., in relation to statutory business trusts. See text at nn 89–92 below.

[75] See, e.g., Smith (n 73) [13]; *Investec Trust v. Glenalla Properties Ltd.* [2018] UKPC 7, [59].

[76] *Carter Holt Harvey Woodproducts Australia Pty Ltd. v. The Commonwealth of Australia and Ors* [2019] HCA 20, at [27]. Also see A. Televantos, *Capitalism Before Corporations: The Morality of Business Associations and the Roots of Commercial Equity and Law* (OUP 2020, forthcoming) chs. II and VI.

[77] C. Mitchell, "Stewardship of Property and Liability to Account" (2014) 78 Conv. 215.

[78] Note that, where B is a sole, *sui juris* beneficiary, the indemnity is a personal right against B and its value is not limited to the value of the trust assets: see *Hardoon v. Belilios* [1901] AC 118, 124 per Lord Lindley. See also L. Tucker et al., *Lewin on Trusts* (20th ed., Sweet & Maxwell 2020), paras. 27-059–27-060.

[79] Presumably the creditor could also be subrogated to a personal claim against the beneficiary.

[80] See, e.g., Lord Hodge's analysis of English law on this point in *Investec* (n 75) at [59].

[81] For the view that the creditors' right of subrogation may not be limited to particular kinds of liability as regards which a trustee is entitled to indemnity see Tucker et al. (n 78) para. 19-052.

[82] See NZ Law Commission, *Some Problems in the Law of Trusts* (2002) NZLR 79, at [27]–[29]; H. Tjio, "Lending to a Trust" (2005) 19 Trust Law International 75.

again prevent C from claiming the trust assets.[83] As Lionel Smith has noted, the traditional position, preserved in English law, is that there is no distinct trust patrimony, and so trust liabilities are not matched to and enforced against trust assets.[84] As far as C is concerned, the identification of trust assets is relevant only in two senses: first, even if the debt owed by A was incurred with authority under the trust, the trust assets are not available to meet A's debts; second, A's assets may include a right to indemnity from B, secured over the trust assets, and, if the debt owed by A was incurred with authority under the trust, C can have access to the trust assets by means of subrogation to that lien.

The point for present purposes is the nuanced way in which private law again handles the question of third party effect. The key asset-partitioning feature of the trust, the insulation of the trust assets from claims by A's creditors, is achieved without needing to vest legal title to those assets in a party with a legal personality distinct from A. Parties can thus enjoy the benefits of asset partitioning informally—in that trusts can be created without the registration or regulatory requirements which apply to corporations. As Maitland noted,[85] and as continues to be the case, parties often prefer to manage their arrangements through informal structures.[86] Private law thus increases the autonomy of A and B by allowing them greater freedom to determine the internal aspects of their relationship, to avoid potentially unsuitable default or mandatory rules applying to formal structures,[87] and to avoid corporate regulation and entity-level taxation.[88]

These nuances, and that distinct function of trusts law, are lost when a trust is treated as an entity separate from the legal personality of the trustee. For this reason, as Lionel Smith has argued, so-called statutory business trusts in the United States are not "trusts" in any orthodox sense.[89] The Delaware Statutory Trust, which formed the model for statutory trusts in other states, provides that neither trustees nor beneficiaries are to be personally liable for debts contracted by the trust; that the trust creditors instead have direct claims against the trust

[83] See, e.g., *re Johnson* (1880) 15 Ch. D. 548. Also see *Investec* (n 75) at [223].
[84] n 73 above.
[85] In "Trust and Corporation" (n 26) 75. See too Hansmann and Mattei (n 41) 472–73.
[86] Examples given by Maitland (ibid.) of unincorporated bodies include Lincoln's Inn and the Jockey Club. Similarly, today parties may prefer a trust or a partnership to incorporation.
[87] One example occurs where a charity is established as a company. The presumption then is that a donation to the charity is simply owned outright by the company, whereas if a gift is made to trustees of an unincorporated association the presumption is that the gift is held on trust for the charitable purpose. A difficulty can then arise if the charitable company is dissolved: its assets can be applied cy-près only if a general charitable intention can be found; if the gift was intended specifically for that company, it will fail and instead be held on resulting trust for the donor: see *re Finger's Will Trusts* [1972] Ch. 286.
[88] See, e.g., L. Ribstein, "Why Corporations?" (2004) 1 Berkeley Bus. LJ 183.
[89] L. Smith, "Mistaking the Trust" (2010) 40 HKLJ 787.

assets; and that the trust can sue and be sued.[90] Such "trusts" are simply a type of corporation, and Hansmann, Kraakman, and Squire argue they should be seen as such because of their asset-partitioning effects.[91]

We do not take a position here on whether statutory business trusts are to be welcomed; our point is rather that whilst it may often be a convenient shorthand to talk of an orthodox trust as though it were a distinct entity, that does not reflect the historical basis of the trust and also misrepresents its third party effect.[92] The point is far from academic, as of course the question of how best to characterize particular legal relationships continues to be important in the conflict of laws. In *Investec Trust (Guernsey) v. Glenalla Properties Ltd.*, for example, the issue of whether a Jersey trust was to be understood as an entity for the purpose of selecting a choice of law rule split the Judicial Board of the Privy Council, hearing appeals from the Court of Appeal of Guernsey.[93] A trustee of a Jersey trust contracted a debt and wished to rely on a provision of the Jersey Trust Law, which limits the assets to which a creditor may have access when enforcing a contractual claim against a trustee. The provision states that the creditor's claim "shall be against the trustee as trustee and shall extend only to the trust property" if the debt is incurred on behalf of the trust, and with authority under the trust's terms, as long as the creditor was aware that the trustee was acting as such when incurring the debt.[94] The initial question for the Privy Council was to decide, as a matter of the private international law of Guernsey,[95] which law governed the question of which assets were available to meet the debt. That in turn depended on how to characterize the issue. One argument was that the issue was one of the discharge of the debt, and so should be governed by the law of the contract between trustee and creditor which, it was agreed, was not Jersey law. As part of his rejection of that argument, Lord

[90] Delaware Code, Title 12, ss. 3803 (liability of beneficial owners and trustees); ss. 3804 (trust's capacity to sue and be sued). For discussion of the rise of such entities see R. Sitkoff, "The American Statutory Business Trust: A Research Agenda" in H. Tjio (ed.), *The Regulation of Wealth Management* (National University of Singapore 2008) 17.

[91] H. Hansmann, R. Kraakman, and R. Squire, "The New Business Entities in Evolutionary Perspective" (2007) 8 European Business Organization L. Rev. 59.

[92] We would therefore object to the grouping by Hansmann and Kraakman (n 46) S376 of the traditional trust with corporations and partnerships as cases in which divided or partial property rights arise from "the law of legal entities." We would also resist the view of Hansmann and Mattei (n 41) 478 that the modern business trust "just clarifies the features of the trust that . . . have long constituted the most important contribution of trust law."

[93] [2018] UKPC 7. Compare the judgment of Lord Hodge, with which Lords Sumption and Carnwath agreed, with the different approach on this point of each of Lord Mance and Lord Briggs.

[94] Trusts (Jersey) Law 1984, Art. 32.

[95] Note that the majority judgment and that of Lord Mance proceed on the basis that the private international law of Guernsey is the same on this question as the private international law of England, but that assumption is challenged by Lord Briggs [2018] UKPC 7 at [239]–[242].

Hodge, with the agreement of Lord Sumption and Lord Carnwath, instead characterized the issue as one of the status of the trustee, so that it was governed by the law of the trust, as the law under which the trustee acquired that status. By insulating the personal assets of a trustee from debts incurred on behalf of the trust, the Jersey law was said to treat a trustee as having "two legally distinct capacities and two legal distinct estates,"[96] a separate "status,"[97] and thus to treat the trust as an "entity" despite its lack of legal personality.[98] Just as the status of a company is determined by the law of the company's creation, so should the status of the trustee be determined by the law of trust which, in this case, was Jersey law.

Lord Mance dissented on this point, holding instead that the mere fact that Jersey law affected the access of the creditor to the trustee's assets in enforcing the debt did not mean that the trust should be treated as an entity for the purpose of finding the relevant governing law. The provision of Jersey law simply implied a term into contracts entered into by trustees expressly acting as such:[99] that the trustee's personal assets would not be available to trust creditors in the event of default. This did not involve creating a new entity or status; Lord Briggs agreed with Lord Mance that the principles of English private international law would not regard the question as one of the status of a trustee, but differed by accepting that the rules of *Guernsey* private international law might do so.

We argue that, on the point of English private international law, the approach adopted by Lord Mance and Lord Briggs was essentially correct, and that this becomes clear once it is recognized that the law governs third party effect by a range of means. The law of corporations, trusts, and obligations provide A and B with means of binding C to different extents. The fact that Jersey law alters the third party effect of Jersey trusts on A's creditors does not automatically justify treating such trusts as entities. After all, in *Investec*, the whole Board acknowledged that an English trust is not an entity,[100] despite the fact such trusts have significant third party effect in preserving the trust assets from A's personal creditors.[101]

[96] Ibid. [61].
[97] Ibid. [85].
[98] Ibid. [83]–[84], [89].
[99] Ibid. [203]. Note though that the majority regarded Art. 32 as going beyond what a trustee can achieve by a contract with a creditor, as it can apply even where there is no contract between trustee and creditor: ibid. [61].
[100] Ibid. [59] (Lord Hodge); [202] (Lord Mance); [239] (Lord Briggs).
[101] See section II.B above.

C. Partnership

The law governing partnership provides a striking example of how different concepts, such as trusts and agency, can be combined to create a legal relationship with unique third party effects. Where A and B agree to undertake a business with a "view of profit," the law treats them as "partners"[102] and a range of rights and relations are created—two are relevant for present purposes. First, A and B become agents for one another. The terms of the actual authority of each partner to bind the others will be determined by the terms of the partnership agreement, but each acquires ostensible authority to bind the other when doing "any act for carrying on in the usual way business of the kind carried on by the firm of which he is a member."[103] After all, by trading together, each partner in a firm holds the others out as having authority to bind her in matters relating to the partnership's course of business.

Second, partners each acquire rights in respect of any joint stock of the partnership. By default partners will have equitable interests in any partnership assets, the terms of which will be governed by the partnership agreement.[104] In this regard, the partnership deed functions as equivalent to a trust deed, governing the terms on which the property will be held, the custodial duties the parties owe to one another, and when dispositions by one partner will overreach the interests of the others.[105] Partners by default have legal title to the partnership assets too, subject to general legal limitations on the vesting of legal title[106] and their express arrangements.

In addition to title to the partnership assets, partners acquire an entitlement where the firm contracts debts. Where a partnership contracts a debt the partners are personally jointly liable to repay it.[107] However, each partner has a right of indemnity in respect of such debts: this takes the form of a personal right to force her co-partners to use their shares of the partnership assets to

[102] Partnership Act 1890, s. 1.

[103] Partnership Act 1890, ss. 5–6. The formulation here is again historical and so straddles what modern lawyers regard as separate doctrines: "course of business" and "ostensible authority."

[104] The characterization of a partner's share has not been consistent, but it is generally treated as a beneficial interest, e.g., see *Re Fuller's Contract* [1933] Ch. 652, 656; *Livingston v. Commissioner of Stamp Duties* [1960] HCA 94, [14]; (1960) 107 CLR 411; *Memec v. Commissioners of the IRC* 1998 WL 1042509 (CA) (unreported); *Commissioner of State Revenue v. Rojoda* [2020] HCA 7; R.L. Banks *Lindley & Banks on Partnership* (20th ed., Sweet & Maxwell 2017) 19-01–19-08.

[105] Partnership Act 1890, s. 20(1).

[106] For instance, in English law, legal title to land can be held by no more than four persons, and so cannot be vested in more than four partners: Trustee Act 1925, s. 34(2); Law of Property Act 1925, s. 34(2).

[107] In the absence of a further undertaking, such liability in England is joint but not several during the life of a partner, but after a partner's death her estate is also severally liable for the debts of the partnership so far as they remain unsatisfied, Partnership Act 1890, s. 9.

discharge partnership debts.[108] This right of indemnity is secured by a lien over the equitable shares of the co-partners, ensuring its effectiveness upon insolvency.[109] A partner's lien and indemnity therefore helps shield her personal assets from the creditors of the business,[110] and resembles the rights of lien and indemnity a trustee has in respect of debts incurred whist acting as trustee.[111] It also explains why partnership debts on dissolution have priority over the beneficial claims of the partners: discharge of the debts is necessary to release the joint stock from the rights of indemnity and liens each partner has over it.[112] Until this happens no partners can demand that their share of the partnership assets be delivered to them, just as a trust beneficiary cannot invoke the *Saunders v. Vautier* rule and demand a transfer of the trust assets whilst the trustee retains a right of indemnity and lien over those assets.[113] So, whereas the protection afforded to C, a trust creditor, by the possibility of subrogation to a trustee's indemnity is limited by any liability of the trustee to B for breaches of trust, the protection afforded to A, a partner, by the possibility of claiming partnership assets is limited by any liability of the partners to C, a partnership creditor.

This combination of doctrines means that the effect of partnership on third parties is atypical. Simplest is the position where A sells partnership assets to C with authority under the partnership agreement. B's equitable interest in those assets is overreached by A's disposition. Where A sells partnership assets to C without authority, C is protected by the doctrine of ostensible authority. For that reason, C will acquire good title to the assets if both of the following conditions are met: (i) C is unaware of the limitations on A's authority; and (ii) A appears to be acting in the "usual way" of the partnership's business.[114]

The position with regards to creditors is more complicated. Where A, with authority under the partnership agreement, borrows money from C, both A and B are liable to repay that debt. In this scenario, B would have a right to force A to use the partnership assets to discharge the debt, and vice versa. A and B would both acquire liens over each other's equitable interests in the partnership assets to secure these rights. C would therefore be paid from the partnership assets rather than the personal estates of A or B. The position

108 Partnership Act 1890, s. 24(2).
109 Partnership Act 1890, s. 39.
110 See H. Hansmann, R. Kraakman, and R. Squire, "Law and the Rise of the Firm" (2006) 119 Harv. Law Rev. 1333.
111 See section III.B above.
112 Partnership Act 1890, s. 39.
113 *CPT Custodian Pty. Ltd. v. Commissioner of State Revenue* [2005] HCA 53, [50] and [51].
114 Partnership Act 1890, s. 5.

is the same where the partnership is insolvent. Under what is sometimes known as the "jingle rule," were A and B to be declared bankrupt, then C would be able to claim the partnership assets in priority to A and B's separate creditors,[115] by being subrogated to the liens each had over the partnership assets.[116] The mechanism is identical to the means discussed in section III.B by which trust creditors can claim trust assets.

The doctrine of ostensible authority, however, distinguishes partnership creditors from trust creditors. As noted in section III.B, a trustee who contracts a debt without authority under the trust deed has no right of indemnity, and so acquires no lien over the trust assets. However, where a partner, who appears to be acting in the course of her firm's business, contracts a debt without the authority of her co-partners, then providing the creditor was in good faith and had no notice, the debt *will* bind the partnership. The co-partners will have personal claims against the errant partner, but will also acquire rights of indemnity and liens assertable against one another, exactly as if the debt had been authorized. Likewise, the creditor of the unauthorized debt can take the benefit of the indemnity and lien exactly as if it had been authorized.

Partnership is thus a good example of how agency and trusts law rules can act together to create a new type of third party effect. Whilst the equitable interests of trust beneficiaries and partners are analytically similar, the asset-partitioning effects of each institution are differentiated by the doctrine of ostensible authority which applies to partnerships. As a result, those who in good faith deal with partners who appear to be acting in the course of business will always get the rights they expect. Partnership law thus provides A and B with the opportunity to enter into a distinct and potentially convenient type of legal relationship without needing to meet any formal requirements, but at the same time protects the autonomy of others by ensuring they are not bound by hidden aspects of that A–B relationship.

[115] Partnership Act 1890, s. 44; Insolvency Act 1986, ss. 175A. Note that the rule also provides that the separate assets of each partner are available to their separate creditors in preference to the partnership creditors, see Partnership Act 1890, s. 9; Insolvency Act 1986, s. 175B. This is harder to justify doctrinally than the priority given to partnership creditors over the partnership estate explained above. Under the Insolvency Act 1986, ss. 175A(5)–(8), where the partnership estate cannot pay its debts, the responsible insolvency practitioner can allow the partnership creditors to prove against the separate estates of the partners in direct competition with their separate creditors.

[116] *Ex p. Ruffin* (1801) 6 Ves Jun 119, 127; 31 ER 970, 974 (Ch.).

IV. The Right Kind of Simplicity?

In this area, as in many others of private law, there is no doubt that the law is complex: the answer to the apparently simple question of the impact on C of an A–B transaction will depend on the nature of the A–B relationship (e.g., agency; trust; partnership) which in turn may depend on the interaction of a number of different legal forms (e.g., legal property rights; equitable property rights; personal rights), the operation of which in turn depends on the interaction of different rules (e.g., as to the content of rights; as to the acquisition of rights; as to the enforceability of rights). Looking forward, it can be asked whether the current complexity is justified: do we need to have so many different ways of answering essentially the same question?[117]

The complexity requires justification for two main reasons. First, the complexity of the law's approach to third party effect inevitably brings with it the risk of error.[118] Even if the rules on when different third party effects arise make sense properly understood, the risk is they may be mistakenly applied, even by judges. Certainly, there is a temptation for judges or legislators to reduce complexity by confusing or merging distinct legal forms.[119] Similarly, there is a risk that if the law offers too many insufficiently differentiated options to A and B for structuring their relations, that may in fact impair their ability to make rational choices,[120] as the law will not be clear or distinct enough to guide individual action.[121] After all, how can A and B choose from the law's menu of forms, if they do not properly understand the differences between the options?

[117] W. Hohfeld, "Some Fundamental Conceptions as Applied in Judicial Reasoning" (1913–14) 23 Yale LJ 16, 19–20 states (in relation to the debate about the nature of a beneficial interest under a trust) that "the tendency—and the fallacy—has been to treat the specific problem as if it were far less complex than it really is; and this commendable effort to treat as simple that which is really complex has, it is believed, furnished a serious legal obstacle to the clear understanding, the orderly statement, and the correct solution of legal problems. In short, it is submitted that the right kind of simplicity can result only from more searching and discriminating analysis."

[118] See text at nn 69–70 above. See too, e.g., J. Penner, "An Untheory of the Law of Trusts, or Some Notes Towards Understanding the Structure of Trusts Law Doctrine" (2010) 63 CLP 653.

[119] An example, we would argue, is provided by the analysis of the Court of Appeal in *Shell UK v. Total UK Ltd.* [2011] QB 86, which mistakenly equates the position of a holder of a beneficial interest with that of an owner, stating that it would be "legalistic" ([132]) and a "triumph of form over substance" (at [143]) to give a beneficial interest a more limited third party effect than that of legal ownership. For criticism of the reasoning, see, e.g., P. Turner, "Consequential Economic Loss and the Trust Beneficiary" [2010] CLJ 445; J. Edelman, "Two Fundamental Questions for the Law of Trusts" (2013) 129 LQR 66, 67–75; W. Swadling, "In Defence of Formalism" in A. Robertson and J. Goudkamp (eds.), *Form and Substance in the Law of Obligations* (Hart 2019) 95, 103–10; B. McFarlane, "Form and Substance in Equity" in ibid. 197, 203–06.

[120] For discussion of the point that offering too many insufficiently differentiated options may in fact impair parties' autonomy see, e.g., Dagan and Heller (n 2) 97–99, 106–07, ch. 12; Dagan (n 2).

[121] Lon Fuller, *Morality of Law* (Revised ed., Yale University Press 1969); B. Zipursky, "The Inner Morality of Private Law" (2013) 58 Am. J. Juris. 27.

The risk is particularly acute in those transactions entered into without the benefit of legal advice.

The complexity can also be problematic for legislatures and regulators seeking to create rules governing certain types of behavior. The more building blocks a legal system has, the more options parties have to achieve their aims—and the harder it is to regulate behavior by targeting particular legal forms. The best example is the trust, which in England has for centuries been used to evade restrictions on other legal forms: for example to avoid the privity rule by creating contracts to benefit third parties;[122] to circumvent criminal prohibitions on private companies with transferable shares;[123] to trade without having to register (and be regulated) as a corporation under the Companies Acts;[124] to securitize transactions whilst avoiding registration requirements for company charges and anti-preferences rules;[125] and indeed to avoid tax. In the United States, trusts were put to the additional use of avoiding prohibitions on corporations acting as vehicles for real estate investment,[126] and to create monopolies—rules preventing one company owning the shares of another were avoided by creating a trust without legal personality which served as a holding device for the shares of several companies.[127] The relatively recent rise of alternatives to the corporation in the common law world, such as unit trusts and statutory business trusts, can also be seen as part of a scramble to avoid regulation and minimize taxation.[128]

In some circumstances then, it is easy to see why it might be desirable to overlook the distinct features of particular legal forms. In *Investec Trust (Guernsey) v. Glenalla Properties Ltd.*,[129] for example, it is telling that the majority judgment of the Privy Council noted (with, it seems, more than a hint of envy) the "more symmetrical" treatment, "in jurisdictions like Guernsey, Jersey and states within the USA,"[130] of creditors dealing with trustees: recourse against the trustees' personal assets, and only those assets, is available in relation to

[122] D. Ibbetson and W. Swain, "Third Party Beneficiaries in English Law: From Dutton v Poole to Tweddle v Atkinson" in Eltjo Schrage (ed.), *Ius Quasitum Tertio* (Berlin 2008).

[123] A. DuBois, *The English Business Company after the Bubble Act 1720–1800* (The Commonwealth Fund 1938); M. Freeman, R. Pearson, and J. Taylor, *Shareholder Democracies? Corporate Governance in Britain & Ireland before 1850* (University of Chicago Press 2012).

[124] *Smith v. Anderson* (1880) 15 Ch. D. 247; J. Silberstein-Loeb, "The Transatlantic Origins of the Business Trust" [2015] JLH 192.

[125] R. Stevens, "Insolvency" in W. Swadling (ed.), *The Quistclose Trust* (Hart Publishing 2004).

[126] Silberstein-Loeb (n 124).

[127] W. Forbath, "Politics, Sate Building, and the Courts 1870–1920" in M. Grossberg and C. Tomlins (eds.), *The Cambridge History of Law in America, Volume II* (CUP 2008) 658–79.

[128] See Hansmann, Kraakman, and Squire (n 91) and Sitkoff (n 90).

[129] [2018] UKPC 7. See text from n 91 to n 101 above.

[130] [2018] UKPC 7 at [99]–[101].

personal transactions of the trustees; recourse against the trust assets, and only those assets, is available in relation to trust transactions. Treating a trust, like a company, as an entity is one means to such symmetry, and may also bring with it advantages in terms of allowing trusts to be better regulated[131] and more transparent.[132]

Our view is that, despite these risks, the law's current recognition of different forms with different third party effects is justified.[133] A plurality of legal forms valuably enhances party autonomy where the range of forms tracks the diversity of ordinary transactions and makes distinctions comprehensible to the parties entering such transactions. Where transactions are genuinely different, it makes sense that the law should give effect to their distinctive features by recognizing them as such. The complexity that recognizing these different legal forms involves is justified by the value of discriminating between cases to which different considerations apply. So long as the law does this, the risk of confusion between different legal forms is also minimized. It is therefore possible to explain why the law has separate rules governing the third party effects of legal property rights (where B has a right directly in a thing); equitable interests (where A holds specific rights subject to duties owed to B, so that B has a right that relates to A's right); personal rights (where A owes a duty to B, that does not relate to a specific right of A, so that B has a right against A); agency (where A has the power to exercise powers of B); and partnership (where A and B operate together with a view to profit). Even if the language used to describe such distinctions may reflect an historical jurisdictional divide, this does not mean that there is no substance to the distinctions.[134]

[131] See, e.g., the Singaporean Business Trust Act 2004. This does not treat a trust as having legal personality, but requires the trustee to be a corporation which only carries on the business of the trust.

[132] Note, too, the move to establish registers of beneficial ownership of particular assets: see, e.g., Money Laundering, Terrorist Financing and Transfer of Funds (Information on the Payer) Regulations 2017, which has provisions for a national register of trusts. Note too Sitkoff (n 41) 436, noting that the semantic tendency in American law to regard the trust as an entity is an "embrace of substantive function over technical form."

[133] The question is in a way a form of higher order *numerus clausus* problem—not about justifying a closed list of the different rights (e.g., freehold/lease/easement etc.) that can have third party effect, but rather about justifying a closed list of the different *ways* in which a right (e.g., as a legal property right/as an equitable property right) can have third party effect. A different way to approach the problem, then, based on the analysis of Merrill and Smith (n 21), would be to see it as an economic question of optimal standardization of the different means by which a right can have third party effect.

[134] As noted, in relation to the distinction between common law and equity, by, e.g., H, Smith, "Fusing the Equitable Function in Private Law" in K. Barker et al. (eds.), *Private Law in the 21st Century* (Hart 2017) and B. McFarlane, "Equity" in A. Gold et al. (eds.), *Oxford Handbook of the New Private Law* (OUP 2020). Some care must be taken, however: whilst the different treatment of legal property rights and equitable interests reflects a relevant formal difference in the types of right, it is not obvious why the third party effect of a common law personal right arising under a contract (regulated through the tort of procuring a breach of contract) should differ from that of an equitable personal right arising in a fiduciary relationship (regulated through liability for dishonest assistance in a breach of fiduciary duty: see n 50 above): for discussion see P. S. Davies, *Accessory Liability* (Hart 2015) 283–84.

Each form of transaction poses risks to third parties, but the nature of that risk differs in each. Deciding where the risk should lie in each case raises policy issues of the type familiar to scholars of tort law.[135] However, it is not possible to evaluate the success of the law's risk allocation strategy in this area, without first understanding *how* the law allocates risk: by recognizing different transactions as giving rise to different legal forms with different third party effects. Judges do not decide in a purely policy-driven way where risk should lie between B and C; indeed it might be impossibly time-consuming to do so given the infinite contextual variety of disputes. Rather, judges make use of concepts, such as those of legal property rights and equitable interests, and outcomes are determined by focusing on the nature of A and B's relationship, the legal forms involved, and the different rules which regulate such forms.[136] As long as the different forms continue to track different ways in which parties might structure their transactions, the apparent complexity is justifiable as a means of giving effect to the diverse choices of different parties without making adjudication entirely dependent on context.

Further, we can minimize the problem that different legal forms pose to legislators and regulators, by continuing to recognize what makes each legal form distinct. As Lionel Smith writes, lawyers and their clients often seek to categorize arrangements as involving "trusts," despite their arrangements not meeting the essential elements of a trust.[137] The same point can be made about third party effect more broadly. As lawyers it is vital that we remember that the rules governing each form of A–B relationship are deeply rooted in the nature of that relationship and are not interchangeable. As has been explicitly recognized both in the context of charges[138] and leases,[139] while A and B are free to determine the incidents of their relationship, they cannot choose how that relationship ought to be categorized by the law, and what its full legal consequences

[135] For attempts to directly apply such reasoning to how the law should resolve disputes between B and C see M. Mautner, "'The Eternal Triangles of the Law': Toward a Theory of Priorities in Conflicts Involving Remote Parties" (1991) 90 Mich. L. Rev. 95; H. Dagan, "The Craft of Property" (2003) 91 Calif. L. Rev. 91; Y.C. Chang, "247 Jurisdictions in the World Get the Good-Faith Purchase Problem Wrong: A New Economic Framework" (June 23, 2019) NYU Law and Economics Research Paper No. 19-25; I. Samet and A. Nair, "What Can 'Equity's Darling' Tell Us About Equity?" in D. Klimchuk et al. (eds.), *Philosophical Foundations of the Law of Equity* (OUP 2020).

[136] The efficiency gains inherent in the use of conceptual reasoning, particularly in reducing information costs, are emphasized by, e.g., H. Smith, "Property as the Law of Things" (2012) 125 Harv. L. Rev. 1691; A. Gold and H. Smith, "Sizing Up Private Law"Univ. Toronto L.J. forthcoming: <https://www.utpjournals.press/doi/abs/10.3138/utlj.2019-0038> .

[137] L. Smith, "Mistaking the Trust" (2010) 40 HKLJ 787. See also L. Smith, "Massively Discretionary Trusts" (2017) 70 Common Legal Problems 17.

[138] See, e.g., *Re Brumark Investments Ltd.* [2001] UKPC 28 at [32] (Lord Millett); *re Spectrum Plus Ltd.* [2005] 2 AC 680 (HL).

[139] See, e.g., *Street v. Mountford* [1985] AC 809, 819 (Lord Templeman).

should be. It is thus extremely important that lawyers monitor carefully the boundaries between different forms of A–B relation, to safeguard against the system being manipulated and to ensure that like cases are treated alike. Certainly, if we are to continue to value the flexibility of private law in dealing with third party effect, we must bear the price of paying careful attention to its variety and subtleties.

6
Culpability and Negligence

*Leslie Kendrick**

How blameworthy is negligence? In recent years, this perennial question has received increased critical attention, with several scholars maintaining that acting negligently is not blameworthy.[1] On this view, actors should be judged by the information, beliefs, and reasons that they actually had, not by those that a reasonable person should have had. To hold persons blameworthy for things that were, by definition, not part of their mental calculus is incoherent, unfair, or both. As Heidi Hurd has explained it,

> The ineluctable truth that drives the conclusion that carelessness is blameless is that those who cause harm merely negligently do not choose to cause such harm, nor do such agents choose their harmful actions in light of any conscious awareness of the risks to others that attend those actions.[2]

Thus, "however 'average the man,' and however much 'ordinary intelligence and prudence' he has, he is without moral blame if the harm he causes another is a product of genuine inadvertence (however unreasonable) to the riskiness of his own behavior."[3]

Most critiques of culpability for negligence begin with the criminal law,[4] but some theorists who hold this view have argued that it applies to the civil

* I am very grateful to Kenneth Abraham, Kimberly Kessler Ferzan, John Goldberg, Paul Miller, John Oberdiek, Kenneth Simons and the other participants in the Oxford Studies in Private Law Theory for their helpful comments and to Lillian Childress and Nirajé Medley-Bacon for their excellent research assistance.

[1] See, e.g., Larry Alexander and Kimberly Kessler Ferzan, with Stephen Morse, *Crime and Culpability: A Theory of Criminal Law* (CUP 2009); Heidi Hurd, "The Innocence of Negligence" (2016) 8 Contemp. Readings in L. & Social Justice 48; Heidi Hurd, "Finding No Fault With Negligence" in John Oberdiek (ed.), *Philosophical Foundations of the Law of Torts* (OUP 2014) 387–405; Larry Alexander and Kimberly Kessler Ferzan, "Confused Culpability, Contrived Causation, and the Collapse of Tort Theory" in John Oberdiek (ed.), *Philosophical Foundations of the Law of Torts* (OUP 2014) 406–25.

[2] Hurd, "The Innocence of Negligence" (n 1) 52–53.

[3] Ibid. 51 (quoting Oliver Wendell Holmes, *The Common Law* (Little, Brown, and Co.,1881) 109).

[4] See, e.g., Alexander et al., *Crime and Culpability* (n 1); Michael Moore and Heidi Hurd, "Punishing the Awkward, the Stupid, the Weak, and the Selfish: The Culpability of Negligence" (2011) 5 Crim. L. & Phil. 147.

Leslie Kendrick, *Culpability and Negligence* In: *Oxford Studies in Private Law Theory: Volume 1*. Edited by: Paul B. Miller and John Oberdiek, Oxford University Press (2020). © The Several Contributors. DOI: 10.1093/oso/9780198851356.003.0006

context as well. For example, Heidi Hurd has contended that civil negligence is not morally blameworthy and thus tort liability for negligence is a form of strict liability.[5] According to Hurd, corrective justice proponents who believe tort liability tracks fault "have to concede that a fault-based theory of negligence is an oxymoron, and thus embarrassing *in toto*."[6] Similarly, Larry Alexander and Kimberly Kessler Ferzan criticize tort law because it holds actors liable for negligence, a state that in their view is not blameworthy.[7] Alexander and Ferzan contend that "merely not adverting to dangerous aspects of one's conduct is *not culpable*," and, "[m]erely claiming that a 'reasonable' and implicitly nonculpable person would have adverted is not itself an argument that confronts . . . that we cannot, at the time of action, directly control to what we are adverting."[8]

At the same time, another strand of criminal law argument has contended that ignorance of law is not blameworthy. If Hurd, Alexander, and Ferzan are generally concerned with the actors' ignorance of risks, or misunderstandings about the physical consequences of their actions, this strand is concerned with actors' ignorance of wrongfulness, or misunderstandings about the moral significance of their actions. Douglas Husak, for example, has offered a comprehensive account of criminal liability in which culpability is defined by a kind of akrasia—by the actor knowing that he is behaving wrongfully but nevertheless acting against his own better judgment.[9] On this view, culpability for negligence is impossible. As Husak explains, "Rational persons cannot be blamed for failing to be guided by a reason they did not believe they had, even though a reasonable person in their situation would have realized that the reason applies to them."[10] Although Husak leaves open the possibility that negligence might be culpable under some other, unspecified set of reasons, it is not culpable within the theory of culpability that he presents.[11] Husak, then, argues that ignorance of wrongfulness is as innocent as ignorance of facts.[12] After previously rejecting this view,[13] in more recent work, Alexander and Ferzan have

5 Hurd, "The Innocence of Negligence" (n 1) 48.

6 Ibid.

7 Alexander and Ferzan, "Confused Culpability" (n 1) 406–25.

8 Ibid. 409, 411.

9 Douglas Husak, *Ignorance of Law: A Philosophical Inquiry* (OUP 2016).

10 Ibid. 192.

11 Ibid.

12 Ibid. 192–93.

13 Alexander et al., *Crime and Culpability* (n 1) 411 (characterizing themselves as "deeming actors culpable for their misperceptions of reasons but not for their misperceptions of risks" and justifiying this view on the ground that "giving the interests of others too little weight—insufficient concern—just *is* the basis of culpability."). Peter Westen has made a similar distinction. See Peter Westen, "Individualizing the Reasonable Person in Criminal Law" (2008) 2 Crim. L. & Phil. 137 (arguing that people should be

come closer to embracing it.[14] Although this view has thus far addressed itself to the criminal law, the implications for civil negligence liability are obvious. If a person cannot be blamed for failing to apprehend that imposing a certain type of risk would be wrongful, then instances of negligence that are defined by such failures are not culpable. They are a form of strict liability. For instance, a driver who misperceives, not the risk that his driving imposes on others, but the fact that imposing such a risk is wrongful, would not be blameworthy on the ignorance-of-wrongfulness view. Thus this view, as much as the ignorance-of-risk view, has deep implications for civil negligence.

In both of its forms, the view that negligence is not culpable does not square with our everyday intuitions about blameworthiness. Indeed, of the idea that failure to apprehend risk is not blameworthy, Heidi Hurd has said, "If such a claim boils the blood from the outset, let me assure that that I realize its perversity. It is a claim that runs against hundreds of years of case law and scholarship, and therefore, a claim that begs for rejection. I myself have worked hard to reject it."[15] The fact that it is intuitively natural to hold actors blameworthy for failing to realize the consequences of their actions for others—and intuitively perverse to hold them blameless—is important. It suggests that perhaps, if logic argues that negligence is not blameworthy, that something has gone wrong, in either our definition of blameworthiness or our conception of the duties we have to others or our understanding of the opportunities that the average person has to avoid negligent conduct.

It matters, also, that the non-culpability view has perverse implications. It would blame those who actually apprehend and appreciate the potential consequences of their actions while holding blameless those who fail to, including those whose failures arise because they are oblivious, narcissistic, or antisocial enough not to consider the risks toward others. As Gideon Yaffe puts it in the particular context of Husak's book, "If you do not even have going for you an appreciation of what you ought to do—if you are so far gone, morally speaking, that you do not recognize the good and the right for what they are—then lucky you: you are owed the break that comes with diminished responsibility for wrongful behavior."[16] This position is at odds with much of our everyday

judged by their own individual capabilities, except that they should be held to the standard of a person with proper respect for the values reflected and incorporated into the statute at issue).

[14] Larry Alexander and Kimberly Kessler Ferzan, *Reflections on Crime and Culpability: Problems and Puzzles* (CUP 2018) ch. 6.

[15] Hurd, "The Innocence of Negligence" (n 1) 49.

[16] Gideon Yaffe, "Is Akrasia Necessary for Culpability? On Douglas Husak's *Ignorance of Law*" (2018) 12 Crim. L. & Phil. 341, 342.

sense of morality, as well as with the efforts we take to cultivate a sense of responsibility in our children and ourselves.[17] It also has perverse implications for gender, race, and cultural differences, because it privileges attitudes and behaviors that do not take others into account while penalizing those that do. Socialization occurs differently for differently situated people, and subordinated groups might face more serious social (and sometimes legal) consequences for failing to defer to others' interests or to consider the implications of their conduct for others. A system of culpability that holds blameworthy those who have had consideration inculcated in them, while holding blameless those who have the luxury of thoughtlessness, feels particularly perverse.

In what follows, I dispute the non-culpability view with both intuitions and arguments about its perverse implications. I also begin to sketch a view of what makes negligence blameworthy, one that has its foundations in the values and considerations that we attempt to inculcate in ourselves and others. This work is far from complete. I in no way expect to persuade those who already hold the non-culpability view. Their positions have taken years to work out, often against their own intuitions. I wish only to register my strong resistance to their conclusions and to identify some of the sources of that resistance. On the view I begin to sketch, tort embraces liability for negligence, at least in part, because many varieties of negligence involve a person failing to inquire into factual or moral considerations relevant to his actions. This is a failure to treat others as equals and should be recognized as such.

At the outset, a note of clarification: this piece does not argue that all instances of civil liability for negligence involve blameworthy behavior. There might be pockets of strict liability within negligence that cannot be justified on fault-based grounds. For example, Mark Grady has argued, and driving data supports, that when driving we all engage in acts of "negligence" that we are physically incapable of avoiding.[18] Grady calls this problem "compliance error" and says it is a form of strict liability: if we are physically incapable of driving any more safely, then holding us liable when we fail amounts to strict liability.[19] Similarly, scholars have considered the issue of "inattentional blindness," whereby cognitive limitations prevent us from apprehending stimuli that are right in front of us.[20] Liability in these cases, too, sounds like a form of

[17] See ibid. ("Why should a quality that all of us hope to possess, and inculcate in our children—an accurate appreciation of right and wrong—warrant greater condemnation for wrongdoing?").

[18] Mark F. Grady, "Res Ipsa Loquitur and Compliance Error" (1994) 142 U. Pa. L. Rev. 887.

[19] Grady makes this point from an economic rather than a moral standpoint, but the fact remains that if drivers lack the capacity to avoid these failures, they are examples of strict liability rather than fault.

[20] Sharon Cop, "Gorillas in the Midst of a Philosophical Debate: The Invisible Gorilla Deconstructs the Negligence Conundrum" (July 22, 2014) <https://ssrn.com/abstract=2469952> or <http://dx.doi.org/10.2139/ssrn.2469952>

strict liability. I am willing to stipulate that the negligence standard as it exists contains pockets of strict liability that are not justified on fault-based grounds. (These pockets of strict liability might exist, and might even be justified, for other reasons, such as the difficulty in the real world of distinguishing truly careless driving from truly unavoidable error.) Our term "negligence" as used in the law clearly encompasses some behavior that is not blameworthy.

Proponents of the non-culpability view, however, make a bolder claim. They argue that negligence cannot be blameworthy, full stop. As Hurd puts it, "*all* cases of negligence are cases of strict liability—not just purportedly exceptional, textbook cases like *Vaughan v. Menlove*."[21] The critics of negligence contend that all of negligence is essentially a form of strict liability, because in one way or another every act of negligence involves someone who was incapable of doing better. In responding, I do not suggest that every instance of negligence is blameworthy. I argue only that some of them are.

I. Intuitions on Negligence

To begin, we should define "negligence." Heidi Hurd defines it as "inadvertence to the unjustified risks that a defendant's conduct imposes on others."[22] This is an excellent working definition and a useful place to begin. Proponents of blameless negligence argue that negligent wrongdoing is not blameworthy. At times, they utilize examples designed to show that negligence is less blameworthy than a knowing violation, which are then further explored to reach the conclusion that negligence is not only less blameworthy, but not at all blameworthy. It is not obvious, however, that negligence is not blameworthy, nor even that it is always less blameworthy than mental states such as subjective recklessness or knowledge.[23] Some examples will illustrate this, while also serving to explicate our working definition of negligence.

A. Inadvertence to Risk

First are cases involving failures to recognize or accurately measure the risks one's conduct poses. These are the cases that approximate "mistake of fact"

[21] Hurd, "The Innocence of Negligence" (n 1) 52 (citing *Vaughan v. Menlove* [1837] 132 ER 490 (CP)).
[22] Ibid.
[23] Others have argued for the same position, in particular Seana Valentine Shiffrin, "The Moral Neglect of Negligence" (2016) 3 Oxford Studies in Political Philosophy 197.

in the criminal law context: the actor is mistaken in his understanding of or beliefs about a relevant risk. On the views of Alexander, Ferzan, and Hurd, inadvertence to risk is not blameworthy. Consider this example from Alexander and Ferzan:

> *Excellent Driver*: Mike reads a scientific article that discusses the strength of peripheral vision and becomes convinced that reading the newspaper while driving is not problematic. Mike reads the paper while driving and rear-ends a car that he failed to see had braked.[24]

The Excellent Driver has sincerely, if unreasonably, underestimated the risk his behavior poses to others. Alexander and Ferzan conclude that the Excellent Driver is not blameworthy, because he does not advert to the risk he imposes on others.

This conclusion seems wrong. Compare the Excellent Driver with:

> *The Weak-Willed Driver*: The Weak-Willed Driver is aware that reading while driving imposes unacceptable risks on others and is therefore not permissible. The Weak-Willed Driver is nevertheless tempted to glance at her phone when a text notification comes in, in order to see who has written her and to get the gist of the message. She takes her eyes off the road to read the text. She fails to see a braking car and rear-ends it.

It seems clear that the Weak-Willed Driver is culpable (and many modern drivers along with her). But whatever level of blameworthiness I assign to her, I assign as much—indeed more—to the Excellent Driver. One reason for this could be that, on the whole, the Excellent Driver appears to be much more of a menace to society. His chronic inattentive driving appears to pose a much greater risk of accident than a momentary lapse by the Weak-Willed Driver. But if we equalize that risk, does the comparison change? Suppose that the Weak-Willed Driver is sufficiently weak willed that she poses the same risk to others as the Excellent Driver. My intuition remains that the Excellent Driver is at least as culpable, indeed more so. According to the hypothetical as written, he truly believes his reading while driving either poses no risk to others or poses an acceptable level of risk. In either case, he unreasonably overestimates his own capabilities and feels confident enough that he is apparently not phased by the fact that, if he is mistaken, he is risking the life and limb of everyone around

[24] Alexander and Ferzan, "Confused Culpability" (n 1) 409.

him. This general attitude seems at least as blameworthy, if not more so, than understanding the facts and appreciating the obligations they entail but sometimes failing in them.

Perhaps some would agree but argue that this is because the Excellent Driver is actually not negligent but reckless. One issue here is that, of all possible contexts for hypotheticals, driving is a complicated one in which to stipulate that someone made a genuine mistake of this magnitude in assessing risks. Anyone who can drive legally has been licensed, which requires demonstration of at least some minimum understanding of the laws pertaining to driving and minimum possession of the skills required to operate a motor vehicle. Drivers' education generally includes the basic principle that safe driving requires keeping one's eyes on the road nearly constantly. A driver who decided that he could read while driving, or text while driving, or watch Netflix while driving, would be coming to this conclusion in spite of his knowledge of the safety rules that pertain to driving. This driver might be described as choosing to do something risky despite subjective awareness of the risks, which could mean that he might be described as reckless and therefore blameworthy.[25]

Ultimately, Hurd, Alexander, and Ferzan seem to endorse conceptions of recklessness that would place the Excellent Driver on the negligence side of the line. They would say that, if the driver sincerely believes that reading the newspaper while driving is not problematic, he is not reckless in thinking this, because he truly believes the risk of accident is much lower than it actually is. Hurd frames these situations in these terms:

> In some cases, defendants may advert to relevant risks, but they may fail to advert to factors that would give a reasonable person grounds for assigning greater value to the probability that those risks will materialize or to the gravity of the harm that will ensue, or they may over-weight the value of the burdens that would have to be shouldered in order to avert such risks.[26]

This perfectly captures the situation of the Excellent Driver: although he must be subjectively aware (from licensing requirements, etc.) that taking one's eyes off the road involves some risk, he has discounted that risk unreasonably on the

[25] Cf. Alexander and Ferzan, "Confused Culpability" (n 1) 409 (raising the possibility that the Excellent Driver's behavior could be reckless). See also Husak (n 9) 136 ("The person who is reckless—who consciously disregards a substantial and unjustifiable risk her conduct is wrongful—deserves some amount of blame for her wrongdoing, but less than that of the person who fully appreciates his conduct is wrongful.")

[26] Hurd, "The Innocence of Negligence" (n 1) 52.

basis of the scholarly article on peripheral vision. Hurd concludes that, "[w]hile some would insist that such cases should also be thought of as cases of recklessness," she is "happy to include such cases in the category of negligence cases."[27]

This seems consistent with the non-culpability view. The Excellent Driver subjectively possesses knowledge that *should* make him aware that he is taking an unreasonable risk, but clearly he has not reached that conclusion. He had the opportunity to reach a different risk assessment, but the fact is that he did not. To say that the Excellent Driver should have done otherwise is simply to reintroduce negligence—to conclude that he failed to do something that a reasonable person should have done. A reasonable person would do a better job of understanding the peripheral vision article and its limitations, or of factoring the article into his risk assessment of his own conduct, or of valuing others, perhaps by employing a precautionary principle acknowledging that, if his risk assessment is wrong, he will be unreasonably risking the physical safety of other people for the sake of his own minor indulgence. These are all varieties of negligence. Alexander and Ferzan assess the Excellent Driver in this way:

> Even if it is true that Mike could have correctly appraised the chance of an accident had he had a lower opinion of his abilities, wherein lies the fault in having a high opinion of his driving skill and perceptual abilities? Unless tort law aims to be an ad hoc redistributive system whereby when one's perceptual or intellectual mechanisms falter and cause harm, one's goods are simply redistributed to another human being, tort law must explain wherein the fault in having the faulty mechanism lies.[28]

The Excellent Driver, then, is negligent in failing to realize that his driving habits unreasonably risk harm to others. Hurd, Alexander, and Ferzan are correct in viewing this as an example of negligence, but they are incorrect in concluding that it is therefore blameless. His overconfidence in his own abilities and his concomitant unreasonable discounting of risk seem blameworthy. Indeed, as Alexander and Ferzan recognize, other theorists in the criminal law context conclude that the Excellent Driver should be considered blameworthy.[29] His conduct does bespeak culpability, but it is culpable negligence, not recklessness.

[27] Ibid.
[28] Alexander and Ferzan, "Confused Culpability" (n 1) 410.
[29] Ibid. 409 (citing Peter Westen, "Individualizing the Reasonable Person in Criminal Law" (2008) 2 Crim. L. & Phil. 137.

To the extent that intuitions are useful, they do not suggest that negligence is blameless, at least not to me. To the contrary, in some instances, failure to apprehend and appreciate a risk seems more blameworthy than knowingly engaging in impermissible conduct. Moreover, cases like that of the Excellent Driver, which are accepted by some as culpable but explained in terms of recklessness, are really negligence cases. They are indeed blameworthy, but negligent. This is not to say that all cases of negligence are more blameworthy than all cases of reckless or knowing wrongdoing: it is not necessary to make that contention in order to push back against the claim that negligence is always less blameworthy and, indeed, not blameworthy at all.[30]

B. Inadvertence to Wrongfulness

The other strand of argument supporting a non-culpability view involves actors who do not realize that their conduct is wrongful. This could describe a variety of negligence cases. Indeed, at times it might be difficult to determine whether an actor improperly judged a risk or the wrongfulness of the risk. With the Excellent Driver, for example, the hypothetical as written contemplates that he sincerely misjudges the level of risk he imposes on others. In the real world, however, we might suspect that someone who drove in that way understood the risk but did not appreciate how wrongful it was—that he improperly believed that relatively high level of risk was not wrongful. In an everyday negligence situation, it can be difficult to discern whether the actor improperly discounted the physical risk or its wrongfulness, that is, the significance of its impact on others. Does the person who improperly switches lanes and causes a collision improperly discount the risk that the other vehicle will not be able to stop or the wrongfulness of risking other people's safety in this way? The negligence standard does not inquire, because it treats both as negligent. Clearly, the idea that improper assessments of wrongfulness are not blameworthy has major implications for the blameworthiness of negligence. Here, too, intuitions suggest that ignorance can be blameworthy.

Consider one of Husak's examples. Husak imagines a weightlifter who curses at a gym without realizing that cursing is against the gym rules.[31] If he had

[30] Shiffrin (n 23) 222–23 ("The character of the reckless agent . . . may be worse than the character of the merely negligent agent . . . [T]he actions that are the product of such characters may likewise vary in their moral severity. Such distinctions are compatible with thinking that the passionate killer's episodic lapse of restraint and the negligent killer's episodic lapse of diligence, both lapses attributable to engrained defects in character, are not so different in moral significance.")

[31] Husak (n 9) 180.

read the sign posted on the wall that enumerates several gym rules, he would have known this, but he carelessly failed to do so. In Husak's view, the negligent weightlifter is less blameworthy than a knowing weightlifter who knows that cursing is forbidden but does it anyway.[32] Indeed, in the context of the criminal law, at least, Husak believes that "no respectable criminal theorist equates these two culpable states."[33]

There may be circumstances in which the Negligent Swearer seems less blameworthy than the Knowing Swearer, but there are also circumstances in which the Negligent Swearer seems, to me, more blameworthy. Imagine:

> *The Negligent Swearer*: The Negligent Swearer has been going to this gym for four years. When he registered, he signed an acknowledgment that he would follow all gym rules and policies. He has been working out in a room where the rules are posted on the wall three times a week for four years, without ever absorbing the fact that cursing is forbidden. One day, he drops a weight on his foot and curses. He is verbally reprimanded by a gym employee. He tells the gym employee that he does not deserve a reprimand, because he was unaware of the rule.
>
> *The Knowing Swearer*: The Knowing Swearer has been going to this gym for four years. When he registered, he signed an acknowledgment that he would follow all gym rules and policies. He has read the rules and knows that cursing is forbidden. One day, he drops a weight on his foot and curses. The circumstances are not such that any reasonable person would be justified or excused for swearing, but the weightlifter's foot hurts, and knowing that swearing is forbidden he decides to swear anyway. He is verbally reprimanded by a gym employee. He apologizes.

It is not obvious, at least to me, that the Knowing Swearer is more blameworthy than the Negligent Swearer. This is not to say that the Knowing Swearer is blameless. I have stipulated that he does not have a valid justification or excuse, and his conduct could reasonably be condemned by the gym employee. But the Negligent Swearer also seems blameworthy and indeed *more* blameworthy. The Knowing Swearer absorbed the rules and decided in the moment that he preferred letting off some steam to perfect compliance. Why this

[32] Ibid. 181 ("If C's degree of culpability in failing to discharge his duty of inquiry consists in mere negligence, it is hard to see how he could possibly be as culpable for Φ as A, who knows cursing to be wrong.")

[33] Husak (n 9) 152.

momentary, knowing lapse is more blameworthy than going four years without absorbing the gym rules is unclear to me.

The hypothetical also highlights a specific implication of endorsing blameless negligence: if the negligent actor's conduct is not blameworthy, then he does not deserve punishment. The gym employee should not reprimand him (though ostensibly the gym employee is also not blameworthy in doing so, because he does not know that the Negligent Swearer did not know the rules). Presumably the gym employee can tell the negligent weightlifter that his conduct is forbidden, but only to inform him of this fact. In other words, the negligent weightlifter not only gets two chances but also gets to have the rules communicated to him personally, whereas those who actually paid attention get reprimanded on the first violation.

The same holds true in other cases. Imagine a rule that most faculty members consider extremely important:

> *The Negligent Moderator*: A faculty member is moderating the faculty workshop. Despite having attended the same workshop weekly for many years, the moderator is unaware that the workshop ends at 1:00pm. When the presenter finishes answering a question, the time is 1:01pm. The moderator sees this but does not realize that it means the workshop is over. He calls on another questioner.

Contrast this with:

> *The Knowing Moderator*: A faculty member is moderating the faculty workshop. The moderator knows that the workshop ends at 1:00 pm. When the presenter finishes answering a question, the time is 1:01pm. The moderator sees this and realizes what it means, but he also sees that the next person in the queue is a faculty member who is about to retire, and this is the last workshop she will attend. The moderator calls on the faculty member to ask her question.

In each case, the faculty attending the workshop could (and likely would) be annoyed that it is going beyond its allotted time period. This may put them in the awkward position of having to walk out in order to prepare for class or meet another obligation, or it may just deeply, deeply irritate them to feel that they must sit in the workshop for a moment longer than they should have to.[34]

[34] Of course, they will be even more irritated if the faculty member who is called on asks a question, rather than seeing that time is up and yielding the floor. Here too, though, a negligent asker, who does

But if they were given the reasons for each moderator's actions, it is hard to imagine that they would find the Knowing Moderator more blameworthy than the Negligent Moderator. I imagine that many would understand the knowing moderator's reasons and forgive the imposition, but most would be outraged (in a small but deep way) that the Negligent Moderator—after all these years and after having agreed to moderate—never bothered to learn when the workshop was supposed to end.

One might be tempted to conclude that this is so because the Knowing Moderator's action was, in fact, permissible. Husak, for example, defines impermissible action in Scanlonian terms:

> Conduct ϕ is wrongful when the moral reasons against it are stronger than the reasons in favor of performing it. What these reasons are and how they are balanced does not depend on the beliefs of the defendant herself.[35]

Someone with this view might argue that, on balance, the arguments in favor of recognizing a final question by a retiring peer outweigh the arguments for observing the regular end time for the workshop. Others might think that an actor's motivations inform permissibility, and for them, the Knowing Moderator's purpose of honoring a colleague might mean that his actions are permissible. Still others might characterize holding the workshop over as a violation but one that is justified or excused. The upshot of any of these views would be that the Knowing Moderator is not blameworthy. To avoid this potential problem, let us consider:

> *The Knowing Moderator II*: A faculty member is moderating the faculty workshop. The moderator knows that the workshop ends at 1:00 pm. When the presenter finishes answering a question, the time is 1:01pm. The moderator sees this and realizes what it means, but he also sees that the next person in the queue is an expert in the subject of the paper, and he would like to hear that person's question. The moderator calls on the faculty member to ask her question.

not realize time is up, could spark as much, if not more, outrage than a knowing asker, who realizes that time is up but also recognizes that the moderator is giving her a chance to ask a final question before retirement and decides to do so.

[35] Husak (n 9) 148.

In this case, the moderator's decision to extend the workshop is not permissible or justified: the moderator is being selfish, where the first Knowing Moderator's decision was generous. The moderator had no right to detain everyone to satisfy his own curiosity; if everybody did this, the workshop would run long every week; the expert faculty member had the same chance as everyone else to get on the queue earlier; there are other opportunities to discuss scholarship besides the workshop. Nevertheless, in my view it is not obvious that this Knowing Moderator has behaved more culpably than the Negligent Moderator. It is one thing to display, in the moment, the selfishness and weakness of will to impose on one's peers deliberately: it suggests placing one's own intellectual curiosity over the interest and convenience of others. But it is another to have failed, over the course of years, to absorb a basic practice of your workplace and then to agree to a position that requires this knowledge, still without apprising oneself of it. The latter bespeaks at least equal disregard for one's colleagues, if not more.

Examples are not all that matters. Some critics of negligence readily acknowledge that their position "offends [their] strongest intuitions."[36] This is significant—it is not a point in a position's favor that it offends deeply held intuitions—but it is not the last word. The critics who endorse blameless negligence believe that it must be correct, regardless of intuitions, because blame cannot inhere in unconscious actions. That claim deserves further examination.

II. Culpability and Negligence

Critics of negligence think, as Husak has said, "Rational persons cannot be blamed for failing to be guided by a reason they did not believe they had, even though a reasonable person in their situation would have realized that the reason applies to them."[37] Because negligent actors do not choose to cause harm and do not act with awareness of the risks, or awareness of the wrongfulness of the risks, they cannot be held blameworthy.[38] This stance is the crux of the position that negligence is not culpable.

The primary responses to this position follow Hart in arguing that the culpability of negligence consists in unexercised capacity, whether unexercised

[36] Hurd, "The Innocence of Negligence" (n 1) 49.
[37] Husak (n 9) 192.
[38] Hurd, "The Innocence of Negligence" (n 1) 52–53.

capacity to advert to a risk or to the moral significance of a risk.[39] Whatever the merits of this argument in the context of criminal law, it seems a reasonable approximation of what tort law might entail, at least in some cases. Tort law permits community assessments of whether an actor should have understood a risk differently or acted upon it differently. Critics of negligence address the capability idea in various ways. I will sketch some ways that negligence might be viewed as blameworthy and then begin to address some of the arguments made by critics.

My basic claim for culpable negligence is that negligence can constitute a failure to understand the significance of one's actions for other people and that some such failures are blameworthy and should be condemned. The actor should have taken some step that she did not—for example, realizing that he or she needed to make efforts to learn or understand something, or adverting to known information, or failing to utilize capacities that could have reduced risk, or failing to value other people's interests appropriately in relation to one's own. When these failures are negligent rather than knowing or subjectively reckless, an actor may still be culpable if a reasonable person in his or her position would not have failed. This is because sometimes culpability inheres in not having sufficiently absorbed and appreciated the facts and values that make up your world.

The critics of negligence deny exactly this. They think that culpability requires consciousness of a fact or value, of a risk or a reason. They contend that someone's failing to do something that it did not occur to her to do cannot be blameworthy. But this is to focus culpability too entirely on the mental interior rather than the social exterior. Our world and the people in it constantly give us feedback about risks and about the claims and interests of others. Reasonable people absorb those signals and process them, constantly updating their understanding of their own obligations. A child learns appropriate and inappropriate action from watching and interacting with adults and peers. A young adult gains an expanding appreciation of other perspectives on the world, including radically different normative views and differing views about which behaviors are hurtful, which are risky, which are constructive, and so on. Adults have knowledge, skills, and moral values that they have developed over the course of many years, not solely by acting thoughtlessly and receiving intervention, but by watching, listening, and absorbing the social and moral cues of their society. Some do this better than others—those who do it well exhibit

[39] H. L. A. Hart, "Negligence, 'Mens Rea and Criminal Responsibility'" in Hart, *Punishment and Responsibility: Essays in the Philosophy of Law* (Oxford 1968).

a particular kind of virtue.[40] When one's unreasoned or unthoughtful action harms others, there is a generalized standard of a reasonable person that sets the minimum criteria for avoiding culpability.

I am framing culpable negligence here as missing the opportunity to apprehend or appreciate something that would prevent one from wrongfully harming others. Some, including Ferzan and Alexander, have framed that missed opportunity in fairly time-bound and subjective ways. In trying to articulate charitably what fault might be, they say that "when there is fault, it is because we can point to a prior point in time when the actor made a deliberate choice. That is, we can trace the present defect to an earlier act of recklessness—a conscious decision to take an unjustified risk."[41] This suggests that fault, if it exists, consists in (1) there being an earlier, literal moment in time when someone missed an opportunity to learn something, (2) where that opportunity involved a specific piece of relevant information, (3) which the person subjectively adverted to but at some point consciously chose to disregard.

Alexander and Ferzan find not even that account satisfactory, but I am arguing for a broader sense of responsibility than the one they outline. For people to be culpably negligent, there need not be a specific moment at which they were presented with a specific fact or reason, which they absorbed but consciously chose to disregard. The opportunities that people have to absorb facts and values are diffuse and ongoing, and one need not ever have subjectively adverted to a fact or reason to be blameworthy for not having absorbed or apprehended it. Our world and our relationships with other people present us with all sorts of information that a rational being should absorb and use to draw inferences. We take in information about the how the world works and how people ought to treat each other in specific instances, and we can extrapolate outward both factually and morally to consider what kinds of actions would be required in other contexts. People can fail to do this in a way that is culpable, because it suggests that they have not shown sufficient regard for others to make diligent efforts in learning how to act so as not to harm them.

For example, schoolchildren playing at recess absorb lessons about what types of activities and behaviors cause harm (or perhaps rather, ideally speaking, which ones their teachers intervene in before harm results). These lessons involve both specific lessons such as the physics of a swing set and the etiquette of waiting for a swing, but also more generalizable lessons about how objects move and how people are supposed to get along. Children are not held

[40] See Shiffrin (n 23) 197.
[41] Alexander and Ferzan, "Confused Culpability" (n 1) 410.

liable for negligence until they reach a certain age because the law judges that they have not had enough of an opportunity to be socialized to both facts and values. Once they are held liable, it is for what a reasonable child their own age would understand and act upon. But even before children are held legally liable, teachers reprimand them based on judgments of what the students should know at their age. Some playground behavior that is understandable from a four year old is not acceptable from an eight year old. This is not because of any particular day when eight year olds were read the rules of playground conduct, or because they can be expected to have seen and absorbed lessons about every possible iteration of playground wrongfulness. It is because they are increasingly rational beings, who are expected to pay attention to the world around them and to extrapolate lessons about how the physical world operates and how we treat each other in it. Children who do not do this are to some extent not fulfilling their capabilities, or at least they are not directing sufficient of their capabilities toward considering others.

This is not to suggest that being deemed negligent means being a bad person. Some negligent actors may have a generalized obliviousness to the workings of the world or the interests of others. But a determination of negligence is merely a determination that, in one discrete instance, one failed to access and extrapolate appropriately from the pool of knowledge and sensibility that a reasonable person should have. A person could be attuned and informed as a general matter and still have missed one thing or another. The Negligent Moderator may be a very careful driver, a diligent risk analyst, and a generally kind person. In fact, the Negligent Moderator may have managed to sit through so many years of workshops without bothering to learn when the workshop ended because he is such an engaged colleague and was not staring at the clock. His colleagues could think he is, on the whole, a good person. But they could still be exasperated by his obliviousness in this one area, and they would be right to be.

Critics of negligence require more specificity in what actors knew and generally require conscious decision-making in order to support blame. My broad response is that there is nothing unreasonable or unfair in thinking that actors have general duties to treat other people as equals and thus to consider how their actions might harm others and to inquire into that question when the answer is not clear. Here I will address a few of the specific arguments made for blameless negligence.

One argument made for blameless negligence is that the fact that an actor failed to advert to a risk shows that he was not capable of adverting to the risk.[42] Moore and Hurd refute this claim. They show that it risks undermining

[42] Discussed at Moore and Hurd (n 4) 162–63.

our understandings of recklessness and knowingly wrongful conduct, because it suggests that we should also not be held responsible for adverting when we do advert, or indeed for any of the reasons that we do or do not do anything.[43] Hurd and Moore convincingly argue, "If we have the capacity to advert when we do advert, we (sometimes at least) must have the capacity to advert when we do not advert. The possible is like a symmetrical halo around the actual—if something did happen, and it was possible that it would not have, then if something did not happen, it also must be possible that it would have."[44]

Negligence's critics also divide up the various things that negligent actors could have failed to do in various ways, along the way to concluding that none of these failures is blameworthy. For example, Alexander and Ferzan state that "an actor may fail to form a belief (or a correct belief) if he (1) lacks the requisite background beliefs, (2) lacks the intellectual ability, or (3) lacks the motivation to form the belief."[45] Moore and Hurd, meanwhile, identify the various capacity defects behind instances of negligence as motor control defects, cognitive defects, conational defects, and motivational deficiencies.[46] This approach falls in line with the analytical work of other scholars to explicate the many aspects of negligence.[47] Negligence in tort law covers many different forms of disregard, and whether or not one thinks negligence is culpable, identifying the various forms of activity covered by the term "negligence" is a useful endeavor. For those who wish to contend that negligence is not blameworthy, doing so requires identifying each variety of negligence, because each one must be analyzed and concluded to be not culpable.

However they split up the various failures that could result in negligence, the critics of negligence conclude that all these failures are not blameworthy. In contrast, I have argued that it can be blameworthy to fail to develop specific beliefs about the world (say, that gravity exists and pertains to one's actions) or to lack the motivation to develop a belief (say, the motivation to recognize that imposing large risk on others for a small benefit to oneself is wrongful). For many principles involved in negligence cases, life with other people should be enough to teach a competent adult that such principles exist, be they about the physical or the moral consequences of one's actions. In cases of lack of

[43] Ibid.
[44] Ibid.
[45] Alexander et al., *Crime and Culpability* (n 1) 83.
[46] Moore and Hurd (n 4) 165.
[47] See, e.g., Kenneth W. Simons, "Dimensions of Negligence in Criminal and Tort Law" (2002) 3 Theo. Inq. L. 283.

intellectual ability or motor control, some such deficiencies will not excuse actors from a duty to take other people's interests into account, which will include understanding how their deficiencies might risk harm to others and what steps they could take to mitigate that risk. In some cases, existing tort law fails to track this principle: for instance, it does not take account of mental disability or illness.[48] In other cases, it approximates this idea fairly well: actors are not held responsible for the sudden onset of a previously unknown physical condition or illness, but those with a known condition are held to the standard of a reasonable person with like condition.[49] Presumably the reasonable person with like condition would consider how the condition might pose risks to others and take appropriate steps to mitigate the risk.

Another way of looking at negligence considered and rejected by Hurd is that some amount of negligence could be understood as the violation of "mini-maxims," per se rules that capture well-known principles of conduct: do not run with scissors, do not leave a baby in the bath unattended, and so forth.[50] In earlier work, Moore and Hurd concluded that violations of such maxims could be blameworthy.[51] They concluded that such rules operate as epistemic rules of thumb, or well-known heuristics, and that when someone violates one "she surely has some appreciation—some awareness, some inkling, some cognizance—of the risks that doing so involves."[52] They conclude,

> One can thus use her deliberate rule violation as a "substitute" for a finding that she subjectively appreciated the risks that then materialized, for the one has a "closeness" to the other that makes such a substitution morally inoffensive. Thus the actor who knowingly violates the rule against pointing a gun at another almost knows that he is risking that other; the parent who knowingly violates the rule against leaving the child in the bathtub cannot claim inadvertence to the possibility of his death; the owner of the nightclub cannot insist that in knowingly violating the rule against no blocking the emergency exits he had no inkling of the risk that customers might be trapped in a deadly fire; and so forth.[53]

[48] See, e.g., Am. L. Inst., *Restatement (Third) of Torts: Physical & Emotional Harm* (2010) § 11 .
[49] Ibid.
[50] Hurd, The Innocence of Negligence (n 1) 57–61.
[51] Moore and Hurd (n 4) 186–91.
[52] Ibid. 191.
[53] Ibid.

In later work, Hurd has rejected this basis for blameworthiness.[54] She argues that certain examples of this kind properly resolve into instances of recklessness. Others, however, cannot be described as recklessness but also cannot be blameworthy because the mini-maxim is merely a rule of thumb rather than a deontological requirement:

> In any given circumstance, however, a precautionary rule may be bad advice, and if it is, it ought to be ignored. Inasmuch as liability becomes strict if it is imposed without regard to the context-sensitive wisdom of the mini-maxims that were arguably relevant to a defendant's decisions, negligence cannot be equated with the violation of precautionary rules, as such.[55]

In earlier work, Moore and Hurd were troubled by the notion that mini-maxims were epistemic rules of thumb, rather than deontological requirements that should not admit of any exceptions, but they concluded that this issue was not fatal.[56]

It is not clear to me why this earlier conclusion was not the right one, at least in the tort context. Once we leave the realm of the criminal law, with its prohibitions on common law crimes, why would not epistemic rules of thumb be an acceptable basis for imposing liability? Moore and Hurd's own explication of the issue seems correct: a maxim such as "don't leave the baby alone in the bath" is clear in its assertions about risk, is "well-known to all—or at least almost all," and is learned "through social osmosis."[57] A parent who violates the rule "surely has some appreciation—some awareness, some inkling, some cognizance—of the risks that doing so involves" and thus can be held blameworthy.[58]

I would go further than perhaps Moore and Hurd did to say that tort law could be understood to enable the factfinder to determine if such a rule of thumb exists; if so, the factfinder is permitted to impute knowledge of the rule to the defendant and to consider whether the actor had a good reason not to follow the rule; if he did not, the factfinder imposes liability. Imposition of

[54] Hurd, The Innocence of Negligence (n 1) 60.

[55] Ibid.

[56] Moore and Hurd (n 4) 190 ("This [recognition of the heuristic nature of mini-maxims] leaves us with the far more modest claim that some rules—and perhaps many—while not of a deontological pedigree, are nevertheless such accurate epistemic indicators of that reasonableness demands that they should be followed *as if* they had practical authority—that is, as if they displaced all reasons to act to the contrary.... In many cases of inadvertent injury, what we blame people for is not bad character or other chronic physical, connotational, or cognitive failings; it is rather for the deliberate breach of known heuristics that, if followed with unwavering loyalty, would have prevented the realization of bad results.")

[57] Ibid. 186.

[58] Ibid. 191.

liability would signal that either the actor failed to advert to the rule, which is culpable, because the jury has concluded that it was a general rule that people have the opportunity to apprehend, or that the actor knowing chose not to follow the rule without justification. The first concludes that the actor has missed something important despite sufficient opportunity to learn it. The second concludes that the actor made a conscious choice not so different from the conscious choice in a recklessness context. In either case, it does not seem unfair to hold the actor liable.

Much of tort law could be conceived of as serving this function. The role of the judge and jury in many cases could be reframed as considering whether the rule of due care violated by the defendant exists and is sufficiently widely recognized that the factfinder can reasonably conclude that the defendant had the opportunity to learn of it. Tort law does not bother to put these questions in this form, because it does not distinguish cases that are blameworthy from those that amount to strict liability. One could imagine, however, a system that did try to distinguish. Under such a system, evidence that the individual defendant truly did not have an opportunity to learn the pertinent rule of due care would be relevant to blameworthiness. In many cases, however, there would be no plausible argument of that kind. In those cases, the defendants would be blameworthy.

One could object that my conception of blameworthiness is so vague and nebulous that it illustrates exactly why the critics think culpable negligence is untenable: I am holding people responsible for not getting with the program in some unspecified way, without regard for what particular information they have ever been exposed to or adverted to. This is true, and I find it unproblematic. The issue here is similar to one anxiety that manifests in some discussions of political correctness and sexual harassment in the present era. The anxiety is that well-meaning people will be held responsible for well-meaning words or actions that other people take offense at.[59] The sense is that this would be unfair, and opprobrium would be unjust, because the actor did not subjectively know that his or her action was wrong. I offer no opinion about how credible this anxiety is in the realms of political and social culture, but I am unconcerned by its tort analogue. The potential that some people will be held blameworthy for something they could not have known was wrong does not cause me grave concern, because I see the fact-specific and community-oriented nature of the

[59] See, e.g., Byron McNutt, "I May Be Clueless, But Culpable? Van Wert Ohio Times Bulletin" (April 29, 2019) <https://timesbulletin.com/Content/News/Opinion/Article/I-may-be-clueless-but-culpable-/2/1169/219775>.

reasonable person standard as a mediating force. As a legal matter, negligence is a mixed question of fact and law, appropriate for a jury; as a moral matter, I think it is very similar. The reasonable person standard is best set through reflection by the relevant community, which should arrive collectively at a conclusion about whether, in a specific instance, a specific fact or reason is one that a member of the community should be expected to have. In the real world, juries may approximate that only very imperfectly. Conceptually, however, this process reflects the coherent and plausible imposition of blame for negligent conduct.

I have put forth a sketch of negligence in which it can be blameworthy to fail to apprehend and appreciate facts or reasons that would argue against conduct that harms others. This is because we all have ongoing opportunities to take on relevant information and to extrapolate from it. Our failure to do so suggests that we are not utilizing our capacities as rational beings or that we have not directed an adequate portion of those capacities toward recognizing other people as fellow rational beings deserving of our respect. I see no issue with blaming people for this. I do not understand a system of blame that requires the level of subjectivity and specificity that the critics of negligence require.

III. The Bonus of Blamelessness

As a final note, not only is blameless negligence normatively unattractive and conceptually puzzling, but it is also troubling in its implications for gender, race, and cultural differences. This is but one aspect of its normative unattractiveness, but it is one worth highlighting. From a normative perspective, I find it highly implausible to say that oblivious people get a free pass, that their actions are not blameworthy because they have never even done so much as mentally taken on board whatever risk they are imposing on others. Their complete mental externalization of risk becomes a shield for their physical risk externalization. I find this perverse generally. But it is particularly disturbing when we think about how subjective caution and sensitivity toward others might be disproportionally distributed.

People in more marginalized groups are likely to internalize various features of the world around them to a higher degree than those in a dominant group. This phenomenon has many aspects. People in minority religious groups are more likely to be familiar with the customs of dominant groups than vice versa. Members of a minority cultural group are more likely than majority members to be familiar with the cultures and customs of both groups and to be able to make fine-grained judgments about how to interact in both.[60] This phenomenon also has many causes. Sometimes this focus on internalizing facts and norms is a matter of belonging—of showing that you understand the culture that you are engaging with well enough to be taken seriously and valued. Women in the workplace share stories about trying to figure out how to be taken seriously, which requires understanding the system of values in place in general and how women in particular are judged within that system. Sometimes it is a matter of life and death: in a world where young African-American men are twenty-one times more likely to be shot by the police than young white men, they and their parents have every reason to attend more to questions about how to avoid conflict with police officers.[61] In a variety of contexts, and in a variety of ways, not needing to be attuned to others, to social dynamics, or to facts in the world is a privilege, and one that is not evenly distributed. Against this backdrop, to hold people accountable for being attuned, and to hold others innocent for being not attuned, feels downright perverse. The very people who are already marginalized—who have the most to lose by not paying attention—are now being blamed for paying attention. The very people who have the luxury of inattention now reap the bonus of blamelessness.

Of course, it can also be true that members of minority or marginalized groups have difficulty with decoding and internalizing standards of conduct that might have their sources in the dominant culture. The criminal law has confronted difficult questions about different conceptions of wrongfulness across cultures, and similar problems might well exist in the realm of tort liability for negligence. Ideally, such issues could be folded into and addressed by the factfinding processed discussed earlier. Juries could consider whether the individual defendant had sufficient opportunity to take on board the relevant standard of conduct. If the defendant could not have been expected to apprehend the need for or content of the standard, arguments for strict liability might be in play, but arguments for blameworthiness would not. A related issue is the possibility that standards of conduct such as the reasonable person standard might themselves be pervasively inegalitarian.[62] These problems are real and

[60] See, e.g., A. T. McWilliams, "*Sorry to Bother You*, Black Americans and the Power and Peril of Code-switching" *The Guardian* (July 25, 2018) <https://www.theguardian.com/film/2018/jul/25/sorry-to-bother-you-white-voice-code-switching>.

[61] Nikole Hannah-Jones, "Yes, Black America Fears the Police. Here's Why" *Pacific Standard* (May 8, 2018) <https://psmag.com/social-justice/why-black-america-fears-the-police>. See also "10 Rules of Survival If Stopped by the Police" <http://www.pbs.org/black-culture/connect/talk-back/10_rules_of_survival_if_stopped_by_police/> ("Be polite and respectful when stopped by the police. Keep your mouth closed. . . . Don't, under any circumstance, get into an argument with the police. . . . Do not run, even if you are afraid of the police.")

[62] See, e.g., Mayo Moran, *Rethinking the Reasonable Person: An Egalitarian Reconstruction of the Objective Standard* (OUP 2003).

significant. They are not, however, a reason to endorse a standard that turns on subjective awareness or to ignore the inegalitarian implications of such a standard. Instead, the same concerns about inequality that motivate critiques of the reasonable person standard motivate my concerns here.

Holding obliviousness to be innocent seems deeply incorrect in itself, but it also has potentially disparate impacts. These should give us pause for their own sake and for what they reflect back on the larger question of the justness of treating negligence as blameless.

IV. Conclusion

Tort law has long proceeded from the view that negligence can be blameworthy, and that is because that view is correct. Various examples of negligence seem blameworthy, even more blameworthy than knowing conduct. It seems reasonable to think of people as rational actors who can be held accountable for not having absorbed the facts and values that their environment offers up for their attention and analysis. And it seems reasonable to hold people culpable when they fail to do that, to the injury of others. Limiting culpability to a subjective state locates our responsibilities entirely within the confines of our own minds and what we have consciously chosen to take on board. It does not hold us accountable at all for failing to open our minds to the world and people around us. This seems wrong in itself. It also has disturbing implications in protecting obliviousness, a privilege often available only to the lucky few, while penalizing conscientiousness, a trait often thrust upon the marginalized. While this piece offers only a sketch of these issues, it had identified a few sources of resistance to the conclusion that negligence cannot be blameworthy.

7

Intellectual Property Law and Redressive Autonomy

Shyamkrishna Balganesh

I. Introduction

The idea that intellectual property law is a form of private law has come under serious attack over the course of the last century, at least in the United States. Much of this has to do with intellectual property's increased reliance on statutes and administrative agencies, and with it the infusion of collectivist goals and ideals into its functioning.[1] Somewhat ironically though, despite the serial addition of new normative goals and objects into its working, the basic analytical structure of intellectual property law has remained constant, over both time and context. This analytical structure, as I argue in this essay, ties intellectual property to a form of autonomy that is characteristic of much (if not all) of private law, best termed "redressive autonomy." Redressive autonomy anchors intellectual property in private law, such that any serious transformation of intellectual property into a public law subject will require a comprehensive modification of its basic analytical structure.

All of the principal forms of intellectual property law—patent, copyright, trademark, and trade secret[2]—exhibit a common basic structure, despite their myriad differences. They each grant someone a set of exclusive rights over an intangible, which simulates the functioning of property rights to varying degrees. A form of *de jure* exclusivity thus replaces the *de facto* excludability traditionally associated with tangible property. This *de jure* exclusivity is

[1] For a general account of this transformation and its causes within copyright law, see Shyamkrishna Balganesh, "Copyright as Legal Process: The Transformation of American Copyright" (2020) U. Pa. L. Rev. (forthcoming). See also Megan M. La Belle, "Patent Law as Public Law" (2012) Geo. Mason L. Rev. 41 (making an argument for treating patent infringement litigation as public law litigation). For a more direct argument along these lines, specifically from within the Australian context see Robert French, "A Public Law Perspective on Intellectual Property" (2014) 17 JWIP 61.

[2] Other areas that might be fruitfully added to this list of mainstream intellectual property rights include: rights of publicity, misappropriation, and design patent rights.

Shyamkrishna Balganesh, *Intellectual Property Law and Redressive Autonomy* In: *Oxford Studies in Private Law Theory: Volume 1*. Edited by: Paul B. Miller and John Oberdiek, Oxford University Press (2020). © The Several Contributors.
DOI: 10.1093/oso/9780198851356.003.0007

however realized in a very particular way: through the vesting of a claim right in the relevant individual, with a correlative duty that operates *in rem*.

Since the maintenance and control of exclusivity is central to the very existence of any intellectual property regime, the claim right that it relies on is critical to its functioning. Intellectual property chooses to maintain the right–duty relationship (and with it the exclusivity) by vesting in the right-holder a (secondary) private right to seek redress when the right–duty relationship is interfered with, that is, when a defendant violates the exclusivity. To be sure, there is nothing internal to the idea (or nature) of the exclusivity at issue or the primary right–duty relationship that mandates its realization through this secondary right of redress; and yet it has remained a constant feature of intellectual property since time immemorial. By steadfastly relying on a private right of redress to ensure the maintenance of the primary right–duty relationship, intellectual property law might be seen as committing itself to a particular form of autonomy, one that sees the maintenance of the exclusivity and with it the law's very need for protection as subject to the right-holder's subjective choices in constructing his or her identity through a privately initiated form of public redress.[3]

In this essay, I argue that this "redressive autonomy" is key to understanding the analytical structure of intellectual property, and its foundation as a form of private law. Redressive autonomy sheds light on a key facet of all intellectual property that has remained constant ever since the emergence of the institution centuries ago. Attempts to understand the connection between intellectual property and private law based on similarities between intellectual property and other private law areas (such as torts, property, and unjust enrichment) remain analytically incomplete without an account of redressive autonomy. Indeed, as the analysis below suggests, redressive autonomy forms an important element of all private law regimes and suggests the possibility that areas of law previously seen as outside the domain of private law might be fruitfully understood as firmly within it from this perspective.

This essay is divided into two sections following this introductory section. Section II breaks down the structure of intellectual property regimes to show how they all revolve around three central ideas: exclusivity, a primary

[3] To be clear, my use of the term "public" to describe the redress here is to contrast it to the private initiation of the mechanism and embodies three facets: (i) it is vertical, in that the final redress—as opposed to its initiation—comes from the state, (ii) as a process, it is open for all of the world to see, which has important expressive effects, and (iii) its final resolution is publicly memorialized. My continued use of the phrase "private redress" is not to be contrasted with this but is indeed synonymous and is merely a short form for "privately-initiated redress."

right–duty relationship, and the vesting of a secondary private right of redress in the primary right-holder. Section III then focuses on redressive autonomy. It first disaggregates the secondary right of redress to develop the idea of redressive autonomy and its various attributes as they manifest themselves in intellectual property, then shows how it sheds light on more than just the enforcement framework of intellectual property law, and finally shows how redressive autonomy is central to much of private law thinking, even though it assumes a special form within the context of intellectual property. A brief conclusion follows.

II. The Basic Structure of Intellectual Property Law

The term "intellectual property" today encompasses a myriad of different regimes, each of which functions by creating entitlements in intangibles. Traditionally, the areas of patent law, copyright law, and trademark law have been seen as paradigmatic of the area, even though they each focus on different intangible subject matter: patents on inventions, copyright on expression, and trademark on source identifiers. To understand the common minimum structure that these regimes embody, consider the following three hypotheticals, each of which provides a barebones picture of the regime that is analytically salient for the rest of the argument that follows.

> *N* is a novelist who writes a wholly original work of fiction. The work is lawfully printed, published, and made publicly available. *I* decides to make and sell copies of the novel without *N*'s permission. *N* considers an action for copyright infringement against *I*, but when offered a sum of money by *I*, chooses not to initiate the action.
>
> *P* is an individual inventor who develops a new, useful, and non-obvious invention. *P* applies for, and receives, a patent for the invention. After the issuance of the patent, *I* begins selling products that contain *P*'s patented invention, without *P*'s permission. *P* commences an action for patent infringement against *I* and obtains an injunction.
>
> *T* is an individual who manufactures and sells children's toys under the brand name Tizio. *T* registers the mark "Tizio" with the Trademark Office, which finds it to be sufficiently distinctive. After *T*'s entry into the market, *I* begins to sell children's toys, under the name "Teezio." *T* commences an action for trademark infringement against *I*, but midway through the action decides to abandon it realizing that *I* is not financially profitable.

Taken together, these three illustrations reveal a common analytical structure that enables us to make sense of intellectual property and its commitment to private redress.

A. Exclusivity and Excludability

A central feature of all intellectual property law is its effort to simulate the working of traditional tangible property by creating a form of exclusivity over an identified intangible.[4] In other words, each intellectual property regime seeks to ensure that the identified claimant (or owner) is the only one entitled to perform a set of actions in relation to the identified intangible, subject of course to a few important exceptions. In this crucial respect, intellectual property attempts to follow the lead of tangible property which grants owners exclusive use privileges in relation to a tangible object, except that tangible property deals with resources that are both rival (incapable of identical simultaneous use) and excludable (physically capable of excluding certain uses). Intangible resources are both non-rival and non-excludable, which makes intellectual property law's ability to rely entirely on the working of tangible property problematic.[5]

An important respect in which intellectual property takes the property baseline as a given lies in its reliance on excludability.[6] With traditional property, excludability is capable of both physical and conceptual realization. The former entails the owner's ability to perform a set of actions in relation to the protected resource (e.g., the construction of a fence, or the locking up of an object) in order to exclude others from it.[7] These exclusionary use-privileges are in turn given recognition and protection by property law, their conceptual equivalent. In intellectual property, exclusionary privileges are of limited functional utility, given the non-rival and non-excludable nature of the resource. Whereas a piece of law can be walled off or a ring can be protected by a lockbox, a novel or an invention cannot be similarly disseminated and controlled. Excludability—if it

[4] For leading theoretical work examining this connection, see Henry E. Smith, "Intellectual Property as Property: Delineating Entitlements in Information" (2007) 116 Yale LJ 1742; Richard A. Epstein, "The Disintegration of Intellectual Property? A Classical Liberal Response to a Premature Obituary" (2010) 62 Stan. L. Rev. 455.

[5] Smith (n 4) 1795.

[6] See Christopher S. Yoo, "Copyright and Public Good Economics: A Misunderstood Relationship" (2007) 155 U. Pa. L. Rev. 635, 644–45.

[7] See generally Wesley Hohfled, "Some Fundamental Legal Conceptions as Applied in Judicial Reasoning" (1913) 23 Yale LJ 16, 34–36 (discussing use privileges with the famous "shrimp salad" example).

needs to form the law's baseline in intellectual property—thus requires an alternative basis for its realization.

Intellectual property finds this alternative in its *legal* declaration of exclusivity. Each of these regimes replicates the physical attribute of excludability by declaring a set of actions relating to the intangible at issue to be "exclusive" to an identified individual—the author, inventor, or mark-holder—in the sense that the identified individual is given the sole entitlement to do something in relation to the intangible. Legally declared exclusivity thus steps in for physical excludability. The precise contours of the exclusivity may vary from one regime to another, yet it remains conceptually central.

Returning to our illustrations, *C* therefore gets a set of "exclusive rights" to copy, distribute, perform, display, and adapt the novel.[8] *P* gets the exclusive "right to exclude" others from making, selling, or using the invention that forms the subject of the patent.[9] And finally, *T* would under trademark law obtain the "exclusive right to use" the mark Tizio in commerce.[10]

B. Primary Right–Duty Correlativity

Intellectual property law however does more than just declare a set of actions to be exclusive to an individual. It further instantiates such exclusivity through a somewhat precise mechanism involving the imposition of an obligation (duty) on the world at large, and vesting a correlative right in the individual creator, inventor, or mark-holder.[11]

In this respect, intellectual property functions in almost identical terms to tangible property. Whereas property rights operationalize their excludability through *in rem* duties of "abstention" or "non-interference" the correlative of which is a right vested in the owner, intellectual property gives effect to its concept of exclusivity by obligating others to refrain from performing the acts covered by the law's declaration of exclusivity.[12] Thus, when copyright law declares that *C* is to have the exclusive right to reproduce the work in copies, it is simultaneously imposing an obligation on all others: to refrain from reproducing the work without *C*'s permission. It then vests the correlative of this right in *C*,

[8] US Copyright Act of 1976, 17 USC, § 106.
[9] US Patent Act of 1952, 35 USC, § 154(a)(1).
[10] US Lanham Act of 1946, 15 USC § 1057(b).
[11] Hohfeld (n 7) 31–32.
[12] For scholarship identifying the duty of abstention or non-interference, see J. E. Penner, *The Idea of Property in Law* (Hart 1997) 128; Thomas W. Merrill and Henry E. Smith, "What Happened to Property in Law and Economics?" (2001) 111 Yale LJ 357, 359.

commonly referred to as C's right to exclude. It is important to appreciate that as a claim-right, the right to exclude is but a correlative to the duty of abstention rather than a secondary right or power, a point to which we will return.

The right–duty correlativity may seem superfluous to the idea of exclusivity here, but it is important to understand that it is hardly so. Having committed itself to the notion of exclusivity, intellectual property law could have chosen an alternative route (or multiple alternative routes) to rendering such exclusivity functional. One obvious method would have been through a mechanism of direct state enforcement, such as criminal law.[13] In this alternative universe, the law might have chosen to operationalize exclusivity by declaring it and simultaneously rendering violations of it punishable in some form. The right to enforce the exclusivity would now be vested in the state, rendering it *public* in an important sense. The decision to root the exclusivity in a right–duty correlative, much like with property law, is therefore one of some significance. The claim right that intellectual property law vests in the creator/inventor/markholder is thus a primary right.

C. The Secondary Right of Redress

Intellectual property law's claim right that forms part of the right–duty relationship instantiating exclusivity is a *passive* right, in the sense that its existence is not contingent on the capacity of its rights-holder to do something with it, nor on the automatic existence of an avenue for its functional realization.[14] Converting it into an active component thus forms the analytical next step for intellectual property law, something that it does through the creation of a secondary right (or in strict Hohfeldian terms, a combination of a privilege and a power[15]). This secondary right of redress entitles its holder to a mechanism of civil recourse whenever the primary right is violated (through a breach of its corresponding duty).[16]

[13] To be sure, intellectual property statutes do commonly embody criminal law provisions. All the same, they are heavily dependent on private action and define the offense in terms of an "infringement," which in turn relates back to the private action. In short, criminal actions are parasitic on private redress. See Irina D. Manta, "The Puzzle of Criminal Sanctions for Intellectual Property Infringement" (2011) 24 Harv. JL & Tech. 469.

[14] See David Frydrych, "Hohfeld Vs. The Legal Realists" (2018) 24 Legal Theory 291, 295. (drawing the active/passive distinction and noting how Hohfeld's framework does not make the distinction clear).

[15] Civil recourse theory makes this point forcefully. See Benjamin Zipursky, "Rights, Wrongs, and Recourse in the Law of Torts" (1998) 51 Vand. L. Rev. 1, 5.

[16] The primary/secondary distinction was adopted by Hohfeld. See Frydrych (n 14) 299–305.

In approaching a court with a claim of infringement, *C*, *P*, and *T* is each exercising a right of redress that the law invests in each of them the moment *I* (in each case) commits the act that interferes with the law's grant of exclusivity. Again, it is crucial to appreciate that this form of private/civil recourse is hardly self-evident or necessary as an adjunct to the exclusivity or the primary right–duty relationship. It is instead intellectual property law's *deliberately chosen* model of operation, wherein it treats the interference with its original grant of exclusivity as a private wrong and offers up an avenue of recourse for its vindication and remediation. The model of civil recourse, elaborately developed and expounded by John Goldberg and Ben Zipursky, finds direct application in the working of intellectual property law.[17]

Building on what Goldberg and Zipursky say about recourse in tort law, it is crucial to recognize that the law does not automatically initiate any reparation or remediation when an infringement occurs. Nor does it indeed mandate or require such remediation. Instead, the law merely "empowers" the original holder of the primary right to initiate an action against the putative infringer in order to invoke the machinery of the state to remediate (or prevent) the infringement.[18] Straightforward and obvious as it may seem, it is within this simple reality that the area's anchoring in private law lies. For with it, intellectual property law is effectively outsourcing and delegating decisions that it analytically revolves around, to the primary right-holder.

Most obviously, these include the decisions *whether*, *when*, and *how* to commence an action for infringement, that is, to exercise the secondary right of redress. It also includes the decision whether to terminate the infringement action, once actually commenced. And intellectual property law does nothing to scrutinize the primary right-holder's reasons behind these decisions, however idiosyncratic or irrational they may be. Indeed, such is the delegation that when intellectual property law decides—as a normative matter—to attempt such scrutiny, the analytical structure of the entitlement disallows it.[19]

The creation of a secondary right of redress is of course hardly unique to intellectual property. Yet, it is of particular salience to intellectual property law

[17] See Zipursky (n 15); Benjamin Zipursky, "Civil Recourse, Not Corrective Justice" (2003) 91 Geo. LJ 695; John C. P. Goldberg and Benjamin Zipursky, "Torts as Wrongs" (2010) 88 Tex. L. Rev. 917; John C. P. Goldberg and Benjamin Zipursky, "The Moral of MacPherson" (1998) 146 U. Pa. L. Rev. 1733.

[18] Zipursky (n 15) 5.

[19] The recent controversy surrounding copyright trolls illustrates this problem. Trolls are copyright plaintiffs who have acquired no more than the right to sue and have played no role in the creation or dissemination of the work. Their business derives entirely from litigation, which courts have come to see as problematic. Yet, the law really has no firm basis on which to allow courts (and defendants) to impugn a plaintiff's reasons for initiating the infringement. See Shyamkrishna Balganesh, "The Uneasy Case Against Copyright Trolls" (2013) 86 S. Cal. L. Rev. 723.

for two interconnected reasons having to do with the centrality of exclusivity to the structure of intellectual property. First, as previously discussed exclusivity in intellectual property has no independent epistemic existence in the way in which it does in tangible property, where resources are rival. In other words, the fact that something is the subject of exclusivity is ordinarily incapable of being discerned for intellectual property, which is usually not the case with land and chattels. And second, the passive nature of the primary right makes the active secondary right functionally significant such that it introduces a good degree of normative continuity between the two rights.[20] Consequently, the discretionary exercise of the secondary right of redress (at the hands of the primary right-holder) in intellectual property poses a serious threat to the nature and form of exclusivity that the regime revolves around.

Each time the primary right-holder decides not to exercise the right of redress when an action obviously interferes with the zone of exclusivity defined by the primary right, it calls into question the existence and domain of such presumptive exclusivity. (Of course, it does so too—but to a lesser extent—when the right is not exercised because the right-holder has failed to detect the violation.) This is the continuity produced by the superimposition of an active right over a passive one. By failing to act to redress the incursion, the primary right-holder can be plausibly understood as abandoning the primary right as well—even if not in its entirety, at least in limited form. Thus, when a patent holder chooses not to pursue a competitor that is infringing its patent, or when a copyright owner decides not to act to redress non-commercial uses, the question that routinely arises is whether the original entitlement, that is, the primary right–duty relationship embodying the regime's idea exclusivity, continues to persist as well.

Several well-known intellectual property doctrines embody this dynamic, representative of the overbearing significance of the secondary right. In trademark law, a right-holder's "failure to police" the trademark can over time result in a finding that the mark has become generic or abandoned.[21] In other words, a failure to exercise the secondary (policing) right is treated as capable of vitiating the primary right. In copyright law, a willing forbearance from initiating an infringement action produces what some scholars have

[20] There is a sense in which the idea of continuity here builds on the "continuity thesis" developed and defended by John Gardner within the domain of corrective justice. According to Gardner, secondary obligations take their normative content ("rational echo") in significant part—though not entirely—from the primary obligation, making them continuous, but not identical. John Gardner, "What is Tort Law for? Part 1: The Place of Corrective Justice" (2011) 30 Law & Phil. 1, 28.

[21] J. Thomas McCarthy, *McCarthy on Trademarks & Unfair Competition* (4th ended., Thomson Reuters 2012) § 17:8; Lanham Act of 1946, 15 USC, § 1127.

termed a "tolerated use."[22] Tolerated uses do not vitiate the entire primary right; but they certainly affect its scope. Patent law has been less ready to fully incorporate this dynamic.

Interestingly, none of these doctrines treat the primary and secondary rights as perfectly contiguous in the sense that a non-enforcement is seen as automatically vitiating the underlying primary right. Instead, they recognize that it casts the primary right into something of a gray area, which then has to be unraveled contextually. And intellectual property law then goes to extraordinary lengths to unravel the two when applying each of these doctrines in practice, primarily to preserve the discretion underlying the exercise of the secondary right.[23]

Given the centrality of exclusivity to intellectual property, a more efficient (and likely more effective) mechanism of avoiding the continuity dynamic between primary and secondary right would have been easy to realize—a bright line rule disaggregating the two, a bright line rule rendering the two fully contiguous, or a mechanism of public enforcement wherein the state is allowed to step in and enforce the violation of the primary right on behalf of the primary right-holder when the latter forebears. Yet, intellectual property rejects these options and tolerates the right-holder's discretion in exercising the right of redress. And my claim here is that it does so in recognition of an important normative ideal: preserving the primary right-holder's autonomy in addressing and correcting interferences with its grant of exclusivity.

An important caveat is in order here. The analytical features identified here for the secondary right of redress are far from being unique to intellectual property. Secondary rights of redress accompany a vast range of primary entitlements; indeed, intellectual property draws on their ubiquity across other areas of law in incorporating them into its functioning. All the same, what distinguishes them here is (a) their relationship to the primary right, and (b) the disproportionate influence they exert on the analytical structure of the entitlement.

The primary right-holder's power to determine the appropriate course of action for a redressal is no simple procedural/adjectival by-product of the intellectual property system. It is instead a defining feature of the area, one which grounds it in private law, a point which the next section further unbundles.

[22] Tim Wu, "Tolerated Use" (2007) 31 Colum. JL & Arts 617.

[23] Unraveling them through a fact-intensive scrutiny of the right-holder's motives and of the systemic effects of treating the primary right as vitiated.

III. Redressive Autonomy

While intellectual property is commonly analogized to property and tort law, the basis of that analogy is often glossed over. Instead, if one understands property and tort law to embody a common structure (of a primary directive enveloped by a secondary right of redress), the analytical basis of the similarity to intellectual property starts becoming clear. The right of redress forms an essential part of intellectual property law's analytical structure, a feature that is as old as the institution itself and one that the law has never once sought to abandon over time, even when inefficient.

But why is the right of redress so essential to intellectual property law that it has continued to maintain its existence over time and context, and refused to replace it with other mechanisms? The answer, I argue, lies in the fact that the right of redress allows intellectual property law to instantiate the ideal of personal autonomy into its functioning in a very real way. Property and contract law have come to be understood as fundamentally autonomy-enhancing owing to the levels of choice and customizability that they each offer right-holders. Property law places some limits on the ability of right-holders to customize the entitlement, but offers holders an infinite set of use privileges in relation to a resource.[24] As Hanoch Dagan and Michael Heller show in new work, contract law revolves around the foundational ideal of autonomy, by enhancing the domain of choices that people have in shaping their interpersonal arrangements.[25]

Intellectual property law does something very similar, but through the right of redress. In privileging the right-holder's choices about when, whether, and how to enforce violations of the primary right as well as the possibility that a decision to not enforce might modify the primary right, the law is recognizing and prioritizing the right-holder's power to enter into and shape a relationship through the avenue of enforcement. It might well seem odd at first to describe the plaintiff–defendant (or right-holder and infringer) arrangement as a relationship, given that only one party initiates it, often times involuntarily. Yet a closer scrutiny of the secondary right of redress in intellectual property reveals this to be less problematic than it might initially seem.

[24] The infinite nature of these privileges is what Penner describes pejoratively as the "disaggregative" view of the bundle of rights conception of property, wherein each privilege is treated as a freestanding property right. See J. E. Penner, "The 'Bundle of Rights' Picture of Property" (1996) 43 UCLA L. Rev. 711, 734.

[25] Hanoch Dagan and Michael Heller, *The Choice Theory of Contracts* (CUP 2017).

In reality what the secondary right of redress grants the primary right-holder is a privilege to initiate a claim to simultaneously (i) vindicate the existence of the primary right—of exclusivity, and (ii) redress its infraction through an appropriate remedy. It is not a pure power in the sense of affording its holder the ability to unilaterally alter someone else's legal status.[26] This is important, because what it does then is to initiate a mediated bilateral negotiation with the other party, during which the other party *qua* defendant will introduce arguments to challenge the existence and scope of the primary right, its putative violation, and the form of remediation sought. The *initiation* of the lawsuit is therefore no guarantee that the right will be either vindicated or enforced. And this is hardly problematic—as it might perhaps be elsewhere[27]—once we recognize that intellectual property infringement is not a moral wrong, but instead a straightforward legal wrong. Intellectual property is entirely a creation of law, such that the infraction of the exclusivity that it creates partakes of a *malum prohibitum* (i.e., wrong because it is prohibited) rather than a *malum in se* (or wrong because it is intrinsically so).[28] Consequently, there is little that is morally constraining in the exercise of the secondary right, beyond of course the general morality of law. Once we acknowledge this reality, the idea that intellectual property's secondary right (of redress) exists to enable the primary right-holder to shape and direct relationships around the primary grant of exclusivity, begins to make both analytical and normative sense. Therein emerges the commitment to redressive autonomy, which the remainder of this section fleshes out further.

A. Redressive Autonomy and its Forms in Intellectual Property

The relationship between private law and autonomy has been the subject of previous scholarly examination, most directly in the work of Hanoch Dagan.[29]

[26] For more on Hohfeldian powers, see Andrew Halpin, "The Concept of a Legal Power" (1996) 16 OJLS 129.

[27] As scholars have pointed out, this poses a problem for corrective justice theories of private law, which focus on the realization of justice (an outcome) through the private action rather than just its initiation and invocation by the right-holder. When a court decides against the primary right-holder, or when the primary right-holder withdraws the lawsuit, the principal normative objective of the regime is never realized.

[28] For a general account of the distinction, see Susan Dimock, "The Malum prohibitum—Malum in se Distinction and the Wrongfulness Constraint on Criminalization" (2016) 55 Dialogue 9.

[29] Hanoch Dagan, "Pluralism and Perfectionism in Private Law" (2012) 112 Colum. L. Rev. 1409, 1424; Hanoch Dagan, "Autonomy, Pluralism, and Contract Law Theory" (2013) 76 Law & Contemp. Probs. 19; Hanoch Dagan, "Autonomy and Pluralism in Private Law" in Andrew Gold et al. (eds.), *Oxford Handbook of the New Private Law* (OUP 2019).

Dagan sees in all of private law an autonomy-enhancing goal, reflected most prominently in the area's creation of power-conferring (as opposed to merely duty-creating) rules. Property law, in its emphasis on alienability, and contract law in its allowance for the creation of myriad reciprocal obligations, are seen to allow actors to realize the self-determination that is critical to the concept of autonomy.

The idea of autonomy inheres in the ability of individuals to determine the normative trajectory of their lives through a series of successive decisions over which they may legitimately claim self-authorship. Private law, in helping shape individuals' interpersonal relationships, actively facilitates this self-authorship. Yet in Dagan's view, private law's autonomy-enhancing goal finds primary instantiation in its power-conferring rules, and only secondarily in its duty-creating ones.[30]

While Dagan's argument connecting private law and autonomy is persuasive, it is not clear why the claim needs to be limited in the manner in which he does. Rights of redress are power-conferring rules (even if couched as rights), but they are fundamentally different from the ones that Dagan's argument focuses. Unlike alienability (in property) and contractual freedom, the right of redress derives its analytical and normative content from a primary right, that in turn operates through a correlative duty. Turning to intellectual property, we may go one step further and say that as a purely legal institution that often deviates from common social morality, the power-conferring right of redress exists principally to maintain the substratum of primary duties relating to exclusivity that the law erects. In other words, while the power and duty are no doubt analytically distinct in intellectual property law, it is hardly the case that they are unconnected at a normative level. To the contrary, the reasons for creating the primary duty in the first instance inform the law's creation of the secondary power (right) of redressal.

A friendly extension of Dagan's core idea entails recognizing the autonomy-enhancing function of the secondary right of redress in intellectual property. In delegating a multiplicity of choices about enforcement to the primary right-holder, often at significant cost, the law is recognizing a value inherent in that right-holder's decision to operationalize and enforce the exclusivity underlying the entitlement. That value, in turn, emerges from a fundamental belief that when and how the coercive power of the state ought to be invoked (even if not actually obtained) in aid of an individual is a matter of judgement that is personal to that individual, and which implicates a variety of subjective

[30] Dagan (n 29).

considerations not all of which are capable of objective rationalization. *T*'s decision to not commence an action against *I* for infringement, even if motivated exclusively by sympathy and pity, is just as worth protecting as *N*'s decision to abandon the infringement lawsuit against *I* because of a favorable settlement.

To be clear, invoking the assistance of the state via a right of redress (*N*'s decision whether to sue *I*) is fundamentally different from invoking it in the abstract through a general directive (*N*'s decision whether to claim an exclusive right in the novel to begin with). While both entail the exercise of self-authorship, they differ in important respects that implicates the notion of autonomy. Invoking the state's power to obtain a declaration of exclusivity in an intangible no doubt generates a legal relationship in so far as it imposes a duty on all others; yet it does so in the abstract and impersonally. On the other hand, invoking the coercive power of the state to try and enforce that obligation entails identifying an individual and scrutinizing that individual's actions in a way that is far more specific and inter-personal.

Both sets of choices are autonomy-enhancing in contributing to the agent's self-determination. All the same, it is only the second one—relating to redress—that is specific to intellectual property law (as opposed to the general legal system). This is more than just about boundaries and categories. In exercising the choice of whether to obtain intellectual property protection (i.e., exclusivity) for an intangible, an actor is choosing from a variety of different options afforded to him or her by the law. The freedom to so choose is therefore hardly an artifact of the inner machinations of intellectual property but rather the working of power-conferring rules in the law more generally. By contrast, in invoking the right of redress once the intangible is indeed protected, a primary right-holder is making a choice internal to intellectual property. *Internal* not in the formal (and potentially circular) sense of being afforded by intellectual property doctrine, but internal in the sense of entailing a consideration of what enforcing intellectual property law's grant of exclusivity against a particular individual will entail.

N deciding to assert and obtain copyright protection in his original novel is thus no doubt making an important decision. Here *N* chooses among multiple options: secrecy and non-dissemination, contractual protection through confidentiality, or indeed no protection at all, among others. Similarly, when *P* chooses to patent her invention, she is choosing among options: trade secret protection, contractual idea protection, or indeed no protection at all, of different options. The basis of this choice is something that the law confers on individuals more generally. This is in contrast to *N* choosing to initiate a copyright infringement action against *I*, or *P* choosing to bring a patent infringement claim against *I*. In each of these choices, *N* and *P* have to grapple with what it means to allege a violation of the law's grant of exclusivity against *I*, knowing what they do about *I* and his motivations for the infringement. And that choice will in turn be presumptively driven by what it means to allege (and possibly obtain a finding of) copyright—or patent—infringement against a specifically identified individual. Intellectual property law wants *N* and *P* to make that choice even after its grant of exclusivity in the relevant intangible, recognizing the interpersonal element inherent in it.

The autonomy inherent in the decision to seek redress is an essential component of how intellectual property law operates, a reality that is often forgotten when the analysis stops at the creation and delineation of rights. That decision in intellectual property law is in turn multi-layered, with each reflecting a different component of redressive autonomy.

1. Cognizance

The idea of redress in intellectual property begins with the identification of an infraction, that is, an interference with the law's grant of exclusivity that it instantiates through the right–duty structure previously described. Unlike with tangible property and a variety of other infractions, the infringement of intellectual property is almost never self-evident. This prompted Justice Holmes to once retort that intellectual property:

> [R]estrains the spontaneity of men where but for it there would be nothing of any kind to hinder their doing as they saw fit. It is a prohibition of conduct remote from the persons or tangibles of the party having the right. It may be infringed a thousand miles from the owner and without his ever becoming aware of the wrong.[31]

This observation rings very true in so far as it notes the difficulty inherent in *detecting* an infraction of the law's grant of exclusivity. All the same the flowery rhetoric hides an additional layer of nuance. Even if and when an infraction is detected and identified, the primary right-holder (i.e., the intellectual property owner) has complete discretion over whether to take cognizance of it and treat it as an infraction. While this is of course true of all rights of redress, it is particularly salient with intellectual property because the very identification of the infraction is often cumbersome (and costly). In other words, an intellectual property owner may expend a significant amount of time, effort, and

[31] *White-Smith Music Publishing Co. v. Apollo Co.*, [1908] 209 US 1, 19 (SC).

resources to detect and locate infringements of the right, and then—for some or no reason—simply choose to seek redress for some, all, or none of them through the secondary right.

Put another way, intellectual property law actively delegates to the primary right-holder the decision of whether to treat an interference with its grant of exclusivity as a wrong. This is perhaps true to varying degrees of several other cause of action as well. All the same, general tort law has come to focus on what Goldberg and Zipursky call the "injury inclusive conception of wrong" wherein the injury/result sustained by a plaintiff from the defendant's conduct is critical to triggering a right of redress.[32] Intellectual property law on the other hand comes close to embodying a "pure-conduct conception of wrong"[33] wherein an actor's mere commission of an act can trigger the secondary right of redress. None of the major intellectual property regimes demand a showing of injury for a redress; to the contrary they make it available even when the defendant's conduct produces a benefit.

The point is not whether intellectual property law differs from other actions that adopt a conduct-based conception, but rather that in so doing, intellectual property law—along with these other tort actions that might adopt a similar conception—is delegating an all-important normative decision to the primary right-holder. The decision is not merely whether to commence an action for redressing a wrong, but whether to treat the defendant's conduct as legally cognizable, that is, as a wrong to begin with. When the primary right-holder decides not to seek redress for an infraction of the exclusivity (as opposed to not knowing about the infraction), that decision occupies a unique middle ground between a negation of the primary right and being a mere omission (of no normative consequence). Instead, it generates what may be best described as a *secondary immunity* in the defendant, an immunity (from liability) that is triggered by the primary right-holder's affirmative behavior. It modifies and dilutes, albeit in a very limited way, the law's directive of exclusivity (by making the right exclusive to the right-holder plus the defendant).

Another way of understanding this dynamic is through the idea of "substantive standing" drawn from the working of antitrust law and featured prominently in the work of civil recourse theorists. Substantive standing refers to the law's requirement that for conduct to be actionable it must relate to the plaintiff's injury—that is, be wrongful—in a very particular way. Most areas of law recognize that creating a mechanism of civil redress embodies a requirement

[32] Goldberg and Zipursky, "Torts as Wrongs" (n 17) 935.
[33] Ibid.

of substantive standing. Intellectual property law is singularly vague about its requirement of substantive standing. The defendant's conduct is deemed actionable the moment it violates the directive of exclusivity granted to the primary right-holder. The plaintiff need merely be the holder of the primary right, which is the closest we get to its substantive standing.[34] But if that is all there is in intellectual property law's conception of substantive standing, we can begin to appreciate the broad latitude that it affords the primary right-holder in defining the existence of a wrong that merits redress. We will return to this point later in this essay.

In short, the primary right-holder in intellectual property is vested with the unilateral power to decide whether the defendant's conduct constitutes a legal wrong, even when it meets the law's formal requirements of an infringement.

2. Initiation and Termination

Once the primary right-holder has identified an infraction of the exclusivity as a wrong and decided to pursue an avenue of redress against the putative infringer, intellectual property law does not delineate a well-defined avenue for the right-holder to pursue. Here again, the law defers quite significantly to the right-holder's choices.

To begin with, the right-holder need not commence the action right away but may choose to instead initiate a negotiation in the shadow of the potential exercise of this right. In other words, the law contemplates the right of redress being actively used as a bargaining device without a direct invocation of the state's coercive power. Then, out of deference to the right-holder's will, the law allows the right-holder to wait as long as he/she wants to initiate the action, subject of course to the statute of limitations.[35] But within that period, intellectual property law has stood relatively firm that the right-holder's reasons to delay commencing the infringement action is not open to scrutiny. The primary right-holder may thus wait until he/she is ready—a purely subjective determination—to commence the lawsuit and the court is obligated to respect

[34] One might see a similar problem with causes of action relating to tangible property as well. According to civil recourse theory, the substantive standing for such actions is the "possessory interest" that the plaintiff must establish as a precondition of the redress. Benjamin C. Zipursky, "Substantive Standing, Civil Recourse, and Corrective Justice" (2011) 39 Fla. St. L. Rev. 299, 304. This comes close to the conception suggested here, except that the possessory interest might be seen as a stand-in for an actual or likely dispossession or possessory interference, injuries that have an epistemic existence. This would not be the case for a rule of substantive standing that did nothing more than ask if the plaintiff was the right-holder—either as original grantee or a transferee of the right.

[35] The equitable defense of "laches," wherein courts examine the motives for a plaintiff's delay in commencing an action even within the formal statute of limitations, is thus taken off the table.

that decision.[36] Finally, at just about any time after commencement and for any reason, the right-holder is allowed to terminate the lawsuit and the chosen avenue of redress. When this occurs, it is treated as the equivalent of the right-holder never having exercised the right of redress and taken cognizance of the infraction.

At each of these points in the exercise of the secondary right of redress, intellectual property law enables the right-holder to commandeer the mere availability of the state's coercive power toward a desired result. It is crucial to note (again) that the law does not guarantee the deployment of its coercive power in the form desired by the right-holder. However, it is perfectly fine with the probabilistic availability of that power forming the basis of the right-holder's engagement with the defendant.

By making available to the right-holder a set of unrestricted entry and exit points related to redress, intellectual property law affords the plaintiff (right-holder) a vast amount of discretion over shaping the invocation of the state's coercive power. The non-automaticity of the state's intervention and the discretion vested in the right-holder over it, both evince a commitment to a non-dogmatic conception of redress, one where the primary right-holder is free to use the right of redress to shape and direct his or her interpersonal interactions as they relate to the intangible involved.

3. Remediation

The final and perhaps most consequential domain in the right of redress where intellectual property law affords the right-holder significant discretion lies in the choice of remedy underlying the redress. Paralleling the multiple motives and rationales that a primary right-holder might have in seeking to redress an infraction of the right, the law offers plaintiffs a fairly long menu of choices and mechanisms to remediate the infraction, if indeed that is what the right-holder seeks. These remedies range from the usual—damages and injunctive relief—to the more complex, seizure/destruction of infringing articles, obtaining attorney's fees and legal costs, and other one-off remedies that the court (in consultation with the plaintiff) sees fit.[37]

Beyond giving the plaintiff a great degree of choice during the actual proceedings, the extensive menu of remedial options that the law provides right-holders with serves the additional function of supporting and reinforcing

[36] *Petrella v. Metro-Goldwyn-Mayer, Inc.*, [2014] 134 S. Ct. 1962 (SC); *SCA Hygiene v. First Quality Baby Products*, (2017) 137 S. Ct. 954.

[37] For an overview, see Terence Ross, *Intellectual Property Law: Damages and Remedies* (Lexis Nexis 2000).

any form of connection (or lack thereof) between the parties that the plaintiff may well seek. A more limited choice would have served as a blunt edged instrument, limiting the right-holder's ability to use the redress as an avenue of negotiation.

A remedial "choice" that is routinely ignored in discussions of intellectual property is indeed the decision to not obtain a formal remedy as such. Interestingly, this is not an actual choice that intellectual property statutes delineate. Rather, it emerges through a combination of the right-holder's power to terminate the action at any stage and the procedure that courts often follow in intellectual property adjudications. In a bifurcated trial, the court commonly separates its adjudication on the existence of the right and its violation on the one hand, from its calculation of damages or award of other remedy on the other, once a violation has been found. Consequently, a right-holder/plaintiff is able to terminate the action once the first stage has ended, which would in effect do no more than vindicate the existence of the right and its infraction by the defendant's actions. Again, this produces an important dynamic for the primary right-holder to shape various relationships around the intangible at issue, and forms an important choice that the law makes available.

* * *

Redressive autonomy thus manifests itself as an important element at multiple stages in the potential exercise of the law's right of redress. The key to appreciating its significance lies in recognizing that as a *power* to initiate the state's role in affirming its primary grant, it enables the primary right-holder to make a series of important self-defining decisions relating to the intangible subject matter involved. At issue is thus the *right of* redress rather than redress as such, and it is in that difference that law embodies its commitment to autonomy by emphasizing the primacy of the right-holder's will in shaping, directing, and utilizing the *right* interpersonally.

B. Redress and Harm in Intellectual Property

An issue of significant debate in intellectual property thinking is its conception of *harm*, and the normative characteristic of the particular interest that triggers the right of redress. We have thus far characterized that interest in principally analytical terms as a violation of the law's grant of exclusivity. Yet, that incursion on the exclusivity is capable of being understood as driven by a variety of different normative considerations.

To the economically minded, the law's grant of exclusivity is a market-based grant wherein intellectual property is seen to carve out a domain of market exclusivity for the intangible, and incursions upon that exclusivity are rendered actionable because of the actual or potential market harm that is produces.[38] To Kantian thinkers (at least within copyright), violations of the exclusivity are problematic not for market reasons, but instead because it interferes with the communicative freedom of the primary right-holder, that is, the creator.[39] Both perspectives have continued to subsist within intellectual property's common law analytical structure, resulting in many scholars concluding that intellectual property has an incoherent—or at best, underdeveloped—conception of harm that it relies on.

Much of the confusion in this debate emerges from the obvious imprecision underlying the use of "harm" as an idea. On the one hand, it is used to signify the damage (or loss) that is seen as essential to trigger actionability in some forms of tort (e.g., negligence); while on the other, it is treated as equivalent to the notion of "injury," seen as a relationally constructed trigger that specifically empowers the plaintiff's right of redress. The latter has long been considered crucial to the law (*injuria sine damno*) while the former is seen as normatively irrelevant in certain contexts when unaccompanied by an injury (*damnum absque injuria*).[40]

The damage conception of harm has often been seen as irrelevant within intellectual property, with the recognition that infringement is for the most part a "strict liability" action.[41] Conceding the obvious equivocation underlying that term, the point is that infringement actions are never dependent on a plaintiff's assertion of any loss, economic or otherwise. Conduct that generates a particular result is enough to trigger the action.[42] Consequently, the incoherence is usually ascribed to copyright's conception of injury, which is described in either economic or deontic terms.

Ironically, both conceptions of intellectual property injury suffer from serious flaws. Neither adequately explains the full gamut of intellectual property law's functioning. A large swath of intellectual property infringement claims

[38] See generally William M. Landes and Richard A. Posner, *The Economic Structure of Intellectual Property Law* (2d ed. HUP 2003).
[39] See Abraham Drassinower, *What's Wrong with Copying?* (HUP 2015); Anne Barron, "Kant, Copyright, and Communicative Freedom" (2012) 31 Law & Phil. 1.
[40] See Herbert Broom, *Commentaries on the Common Law* (4th ed. 1873) 75–77 (discussing the distinction and its application in the common law).
[41] Shyamkrishna Balganesh, "The Obligatory Structure of Copyright Law" (2012) 125 Harv. L. Rev. 1664, 1682; Patrick R. Goold, "Is Copyright Infringement a Strict Liability Tort?" (2015) 30 Berkeley Tech. LJ 305.
[42] Balganesh (n 41) 1682.

are brought with absolutely no economic motivation behind them, or relating to the underlying work itself. Similarly, it is hard to identify violations of communicative freedom for intellectual property claims beyond a narrow domain of copyright infringement claims, and even within copyright the expansion of protectable subject matter (e.g., software) has resulted in this grounding becoming even more tenuous. Focusing on the role of redress (and redressive autonomy therein) within intellectual property law offers a firmer basis to make sense of these competing conceptions of injury.

As traditionally understood, the concept of "redress" stands for the setting right of a wrong, a distinctively remedial notion. Underlying this traditional understanding is therefore the intuition that a form or avenue of redress emerges once there is a wrong, which is in turn a violation of a right. Indeed this is what makes redress a "secondary" right/power, as previously discussed. The analytical scheme of right-wrong-redress (or recourse) is thus the traditional way of understanding how redress functions. All the same, it is not the only way of understanding the idea of redress.

To the late Peter Birks, the connections between right and wrong on the one hand, and wrong and redress (or "remedy" as he put it) were hardly uncontroversial.[43] As he argued, the usual sequence failed to capture the working of specific performance in contract law, but more importantly also the fundamental structure of unjust enrichment and some "proprietary rights." In these situations ("not-wrongs"), Birks argued that a set of factual circumstances generated a right that on its own enabled its holder to invoke the machinery of the state (i.e., the courts) without needing to identify a wrong, strictly speaking. The plaintiff, in Birks' words, is standing on the primary right in court—no more, no less.[44]

Birks' model does not of course carry over seamlessly to intellectual property law, where the law clearly delineates a primary right in structuring its grant of exclusivity. Yet his model identifies the possibility of a natural continuum between the primary right and redress that obviates the necessity of identifying a "wrong" under all circumstances. In other words, when an intellectual property plaintiff approaches a court (i.e., seeks redress) in an infringement action, it is plausible to analyze that situation as the plaintiff's attempt to vindicate the primary right—of exclusivity—which is functionally meaningless without the state's intervention. Just as the situation of a mistaken payment for money, the paradigmatic case for unjust enrichment, triggers an avenue of

[43] Peter Birks, "Rights, Wrongs, and Remedies" (2000) 20 OJLS 1.
[44] Ibid. 28–29.

redress independent of a wrong (but nevertheless dependent on a primary entitlement to the said money), a putative intellectual property defendant's actions can be understood as triggering an avenue of redress, wherein the plaintiff is asking the court to make good on the law's initial grant of exclusivity. In this "not-wrong" mode of analysis, the defendant's actions need not be seen as a wrong, nor as an independent basis of liability *until* the redress is triggered by the plaintiff.

The not-wrong conception of intellectual property law is not as far-fetched as it may initially seem. In all of intellectual property, the law merely makes a grant of exclusivity to an identified claimant. The law itself says nothing of correlative obligations, which have been analytically derived from the initially grant. If the exclusive right is instead understood as an "exclusive privilege," the correlative of which is merely a no-right (in that no one has a right to stop the exclusive use of the intangible), the idea of a duty recedes in importance.[45] In this scenario, an infringement claim (the redress) is little more than an attempted direct enforcement of the exclusivity underlying the privilege rather than a corrective for a wrong.

This not-wrong conception is indeed far removed from our traditional understanding of intellectual property infringement as a wrong. All the same, Birks' formulation of the problem highlights how the idea of "redress" is capable of being unmoored from a purely corrective/remedial understanding of the term that is related to a wrong, which is in turn dependent on an underlying normative rationale. It represents not just the remediation of a wrong, but also the enforcement of a right and while the two may ordinarily go together they need not always do so. Alternatively, they may go together through the mere pairing—by legal declaration or implication—of the two. It is this latter category that constitutes a purely "legal wrong," wherein something is a wrong merely because it is treated by the law as a violation of an analytically prior right, no more and no less.

The last point bears emphasis, for it suggests that the law's construction of a wrong while analytically crucial to the structure of a regime, may nevertheless be devoid of independent normative content. Or put another way, the "wrong" in the right-wrong-redress formulation when applied to intellectual property law is a mere connector of sorts.[46]

[45] Hohfeld (n 7) 34–36.

[46] A strong parallel to the idea of a "connector" is to be seen in Birks' criticism of Kit Barker's position on unjust enrichment, which refuses to accept the idea of direct enforcement. Barker instead argues that even if the set of facts that trigger a potential claim of unjust enrichment do not qualify as a wrong, they nevertheless constitute a "primary injustice," which the law then attempts to redress through a

This in turn brings us back to the conflicting normative criteria that are thought to underlie the idea of an intellectual property infringement. The legal injury underlying the wrong of an infringement—its wrongfulness or "substantive standing" so to speak—is purposely undertheorized by the law. The putative infraction of the right, that is, the defendant's conduct, automatically triggers the availability of an avenue of redress without there needing to be any direct connection to the plaintiff, beyond the latter being the grantee of the state's promise of exclusivity, or an assignee thereof. This underdeveloped conception of injury is neither a sign of the law's incoherence nor an unresolved mystery. It is instead best understood as intellectual property law's fundamental commitment to a form of normative pluralism. By refusing to specify the circumstances under which a right-holder is injured, the law allows the right-holder to examine the nature and consequences of a defendant's conduct and decide whether they merit the invocation of the redress for reasons specific and subjective to the right-holder. And those reasons might in turn be consequentialist/economic, purely moral, or indeed firmly idiosyncratic and incapable of classification.

The key is thus that intellectual property law embeds its conception of legal injury behind a firm commitment to the right-holder's autonomy. Very importantly, this is not the same as suggesting that its understanding of injury inheres in a negation of the right-holder's autonomy, as is frequently done for real property. The autonomy at issue is not the autonomy inhering in the exercise of the primary right or a set of use privileges surrounding the protected resource. It is instead an autonomy embedded within the right of redress, which empowers the right-holder to choose among potentially competing (and incommensurable) normative values, in invoking the coercive power of the state.[47]

Redressive autonomy thus goes beyond just explaining the enforcement framework surrounding intellectual property law. It additionally helps make sense of intellectual property law's concept of harm and injury, and the rather unique structure of the infringement action, which focuses almost entirely on the defendant's conduct to the exclusion of its effect on the plaintiff.

secondary right. As Birks forcefully points out, this recharacterization does little to add content to the initial set of triggering facts. Birks (n 43) 29–30.

[47] For a similar point about the value pluralism inherent in recognizing the autonomy of agents to make their own decisions, see Dagan, "Pluralism and Perfectionism in Private Law" (n 29) 1423–24.

C. Redressive Autonomy and Private Law

The idea of redress underlying intellectual property law is hardly unique to that area. To the contrary, it is a staple of almost all private law institutions with important variations, a point that has been forcefully made by civil recourse theory.[48] According to civil recourse theory, private law operates by providing actors with an avenue of private recourse—to invoke the coercive power of the state—for violations of wrongs. Each of contract law, property law, tort law, and the law of unjust enrichment operate by providing a private (as opposed to state/public) right-holder with an avenue of redress for either the remediation of a wrong, or the enforcement of a primary right.

With subtle variations, all forms of private redress embody a conception of autonomy that is in large measure identical to the one described herein as contained within the working of intellectual property law. They each afford a primary right-holder a mechanism by which to invoke the coercive power of the state to enforce a primary right or remedy a wrong. And in so doing, they allow the right-holder to make important normative decisions about deploying the mechanism that are entirely personal and originate from the individual motivations and desires of the right-holder, subjective and of questionable rationality as they may be. Underlying much—if not all—of private law is therefore a core commitment to redressive autonomy.

In important new work, Andrew Gold has attempted to show that civil recourse theory embodies a form of justice that is distinct from corrective justice, which he describes as "redressive justice."[49] The distinctiveness of redressive justice lies in its focus on the actions of the right-holder rather than the duty-holder in correcting ("allocating back") the wrong.[50] In this conception, the court is acting as the agent of the right-holder rather than on behalf of the wrongdoer. In expounding the theory behind redressive justice, Gold alludes to a crucial aspect underlying the salience of the focus on the right-holder: the importance of "authorship."[51] The reason why a focus on the right-holder rather than the duty-bearer/wrong-doer matters is because it recognizes the authorship of the right-holder in initiating the claim of redress and invoking the state's power to that end. This authorship of action is morally significant in that it shapes the individual's (i.e., right-holder's) self-identity, or put another

[48] See Benjamin C. Zipursky, "Philosophy of Private Law" in Jules Coleman and Scott Shapiro (eds.), *The Oxford Handbook of Jurisprudence and Philosophy of Law* (OUP 2002) 623.
[49] Andrew S. Gold, "A Theory of Redressive Justice" (2014) 64 UTLJ 159.
[50] Ibid. 184–86.
[51] Ibid. 192–95.

way, it recognizes the autonomy of the right-holder. Redressive autonomy is therefore a critical aspect of redressive justice, both of which emanate rather seamlessly from the civil recourse theory of private law.

In short then, redressive autonomy may be understood as a *sine qua non* of private law. To characterize or classify a body of law as private law is to recognize the centrality of a private mechanism of redress being afforded by that body to an individual right-holder, with minimal constraints on the invocation, exercise, and use of that mechanism. We now hopefully begin to see how and why intellectual property law is legitimately and firmly a body of private law, despite numerous public-regarding ideals and normative goals being ascribed to it. By rooting the idea of private law in the autonomy accompanying the private right of redress, we also are able to disengage private law from its exclusive focus on the common law (judge-made law), since private forms of redress are not the sole prerogative of the common law but may instead be developed and created by legislation as well.[52]

Once we accept the idea that private redress and redressive autonomy are indeed core features of any private law institution, we encounter the obvious problem of determining when and how an area of law is to be characterized as a body of private law. This exercise may indeed encounter the obvious preliminary question: what really turns on this classification? The answer to that question is that identifying (and characterizing) an area as a branch of private law results in its mechanism of redress being seen as non-contingent and imparting an additional set of normative ideals into the functioning of the institution. This requires further elaboration.

An emergent trend in recent public law scholarship has been the use of the idea of a "private attorney general."[53] The term refers to situations where (a) a legal regime—usually statutory—is constructed around a particular set of policy-focused goals, then (b) in order to realize those goals, the regime creates a private cause of action, wherein (c) it identifies a primary right and empowers private individuals to invoke the state's power for infractions of that right. In this construction, the private individual and the private cause of action created are treated as mere mechanisms chosen by the law from a multitude of options, to realize its ultimate policy goals.[54] In other words, they contribute nothing

[52] See Shyamkrishna Balganesh, "Private Law Statutory Interpretation" (2019) 93 S. Cal. L. Rev. 949.

[53] Trevor W. Morrison, "Private Attorneys General and the First Amendment" (2005) 103 Mich. L. Rev. 589.

[54] This approach to analysis is particularly prominent in legal literature influence by political science. For recent work in this direction, see Sean Farhang, *The Litigation State: Public Regulation and Private Lawsuits in the U.S.* (Princeton UP 2010); Robert Kagan, *Adversarial Legalism: The American Way of Law* (HUP 2003).

on their own to the normative basis of the institution involved. The state "commandeers" private individuals in furtherance of its public goals; and these individuals are private attorneys general.[55] One famous public law scholar put the point most directly, when he described them as "non-Hohfeldian plaintiffs," suggesting that they were triggering a mechanism of redress purely to vindicate/enforce a public interest rather than one in which they had a personal stake.[56]

The federal anti-discrimination statute (Title VII) is taken as a prime example of this approach.[57] The state is seen to have constructed a regime that is driven by public-regarding goals and thereafter created a set of carrots and sticks for private individuals to realize those goals via litigation. In quite literally treating private actors as pawns in this overall framework, the model altogether disregards the vast amount of control and authorship that litigants have over the claim, which is in turn driven by considerations of interpersonal morality. Redressive autonomy is the conceptual anti-thesis of the private attorney general idea.

The private attorney general model readily presumes that the statutory origin of an area of law infuses it with collectivist goals, which renders it a body of public law regardless of the substance of the rights and duties created. Yet, creating a mechanism of private redress and delegating normatively salient decisions to a right-holder introduce important private-regarding considerations into the regime, all of which emanate from the autonomous nature of the individual making decisions. The decision whether to treat an action as discriminatory *and* do so publicly through a mechanism of private redress is a deeply interpersonal one, inevitably driven by subjective considerations that the law is perfectly fine with countenancing.[58] The idea of a private attorney general eliminates this nuance.

Now, this is not to suggest that statutory regimes with private enforcement mechanisms ought to be treated as pure private law areas where public-regarding goals have no influence whatsoever. The choice need not be a purely binary one. Instead, it is sufficient if the analysis recognizes that normative role that a mechanism of private redress plays in the structuring of a regime, and the unique interpersonal values and goals that it introduces into the law.

[55] Hanoch Dagan and Avihay Dorfman, "Just Relationships" (2016) 116 Colum. L. Rev. 1395, 1430.

[56] Louis L. Jaffe, "The Citizen as Litigant in Public Actions: The Non-Hohfeldian or Ideological Plaintiff" (1968) 116 U. Pa. L. Rev. 1033.

[57] For an early example, see Robert J. Affeldt, "Title VII in the Federal Courts—Private or Public Law" (1969) 14 Villanova L. Rev. 664. See also Farhang (n 54) 85.

[58] See Sophia Moreau, "What is Discrimination?" (2010) 38 Phil. & Pub. Affs. 143; Dagan and Dorfman (n 55) 1423 n 125.

IV. Conclusion

Redressive autonomy is an integral part of private law. While private law does affirm a plurality of normative considerations, its commitment to a form of personal autonomy undergirding the mechanism of private redress has remained steadfast. In delegating to individuals the decision of *whether*, *when*, *how*, and *against whom* to invoke the state's coercive power in recognizing and enforcing a primary right, private law recognizes the connection between this power and the ability to shape one's interpersonal relationships, in turn a critical part of individual self-identity. The decision is in turn a deeply normative one, since it embodies a preliminary determination of whether a primary right exists and has indeed been violated by the defendant's conduct.

Intellectual property law is structured around the mechanism of private redress, which holds its basic framework of exclusivity together. Perhaps more so than several other areas of law, the redressive autonomy undergirding intellectual property is functionally significant to the very existence of the institution, given the oddities of the subject matter at issue. Redress and redressive autonomy are thus constitutive of the law's very construction of intellectual property, a reality that is often ignored in incomplete attempts to analogize the area to other doctrines, and in the innumerable attempts to construct grand explanatory/justificatory theories for its existence.

Recognizing the role of redressive autonomy in intellectual property should serve to emphasize its fundamental roots in private law. Modern analyses of the subject have overlooked these roots and instead treated it as little more than a regulatory mechanism, with its analytical structure coming to be seen as altogether contingent and adding nothing of normative significance. Discussions of the subject would be well advised to reconsider this myopia.

8

Good Faith in English Contract Law

A Humble "3 by 4" Approach

Mindy Chen-Wishart and Victoria Dixon

I. Introduction

Orthodox English contract law recognizes no general duty of good faith, relying instead on "piecemeal solutions in response to demonstrated problems of unfairness."[1] This was not always so. In the eighteenth century, Lord Mansfield identified good faith as a "governing principle applicable to all contracts and dealings."[2] However, ". . . Lord Mansfield's universal proposition did not survive. The commercial and mercantile law of England developed in a different direction preferring the benefits of simplicity and certainty which flow from requiring those engaging in commerce to look after their own interests."[3] More recently, the pendulum has again changed direction, with courts implying good faith duties (in fact or even in law) into particular contracts.[4] This has prompted debate over whether English law should recognize a general requirement of good faith.[5] But what do we mean by "good faith?" What difference

[1] *Interfoto Picture Library Ltd. v. Stiletto Visual Programmes Ltd.* [1989] QB 433, 439 (Bingham LJ). For variants of this orthodox position, see, e.g., Ewan McKendrick, "Good Faith: A Matter of Principle" in Angelo D. M. Forte (ed.), *Good Faith in Contract and Property Law* (Hart Publishing 1999), 39; Edward Peel, "Agreements to Negotiate in Good Faith" in Andrew Burrows and Edward Peel (eds.), *Contract Formation and Parties* (OUP 2010) 37; Michael Bridge, "Doubting Good Faith" (2005) 11 NZBLQ 430, 450: there is "no general duty of good faith and fair dealing in English contract law and there is no reason why there should be."

[2] *Carter v. Boehm* (1766) 3 Burrow 1905, 1910. See also *Mellish v. Motteux* (1792) 170 ER 113, 157: ". . . in contracts of all kinds, it is of the highest importance that courts of law should compel the observance of honesty and good faith" (Lord Kenyon).

[3] *Manifest Shipping Co Ltd. v. Uni-Polaris Ins Co Ltd. (The Star Sea)* [2001] UKHL 1, [45]. On the early reception of good faith and its subsequent rejection, see Reziya Harrison, *Good Faith in Sales* (Sweet & Maxwell 1997) 5–10; Reinhard Zimmermann and Simon Whittaker (eds.), *Good Faith in European Contract Law* (CUP, 2000), 41–44.

[4] e.g., *Yam Seng PTE Ltd. v. International Trade Corporation Ltd.* [2013] EWHC 111, [131]–[153]; *Al Nehayan v. Kent* [2018] EWHC 333 (Comm.), [174].

[5] In favor of some role for good faith, see, e.g., Mary Arden, "Coming to Terms with Good Faith" in *Common Law and Modern Society: Keeping Pace with Change* (OUP 2016) 63; Michael Levenstein, "Where Angels Fear to Tread: The Limits of Good Faith in Commercial Contracts" (2017) 9 JIBFL 569. Arguing against a general good faith principle, see David Campbell, "Good Faith and the Ubiquity of

Mindy Chen-Wishart and Victoria Dixon, *Good Faith in English Contract Law* In: *Oxford Studies in Private Law Theory: Volume 1*. Edited by: Paul B. Miller and John Oberdiek, Oxford University Press (2020). © The Several Contributors.
DOI: 10.1093/oso/9780198851356.003.0008

would it make to English law? We identify three possible roles, preferring one (humble) version of good faith, which operates via the *already existing* "piecemeal solutions in response to demonstrated problems of unfairness" in English contract law. We support an open recognition of this version, since it would:

- make explicit the implicit ethical content of English contract law;
- justify its diverse demands;
- promote the understanding and organization (taxonomizing) of the many apparently disparate rules under the rubric of good faith; and
- facilitate the incremental development of the law, consistent with common law incrementalism.

Unlike more ambitious versions of good faith, this humble version should be entirely *acceptable* to the judiciary as a familiar way to develop the English contract law.

We substantiate our thesis as follows:

- In section II, we summarize the main arguments for and against recognizing a good faith requirement.
- In section III, we examine three potential roles for such a requirement, assessed against the points of reference discussed in section II. We reject the first two versions and support a third, humble, version of good faith as an explanatory, legitimizing, and organizational principle.
- In section IV, we focus on the nature of contractual good faith as:
    - (i) constitutive of contracting as an attitude of *respect* toward the other party and the contract made, manifested in the demands of:
        - (a) honesty;
        - (b) fair dealing; and
        - (c) fidelity to the contractual purpose;
    - (ii) externally imposed but, paradoxically, also intelligible as internally assumed by the parties;
    - (iii) substantially consistent with freedom of contract and self-interested action;
    - (iv) dependent on the nature of the contract;
    - (v) colored by the social and legal culture; and
    - (vi) episodic, consistent with common law incrementalism.

the 'Relational' Contract" [2014] 77 MLR 475; Michael Bridge, "Good Faith, the Common Law and the CISG" (2017) Uniform L. Rev. 98.

- In section V, we start to sketch a taxonomy of good faith by reference to four broad types of contractual relationship. We show that:
  - even in type (1), commercial arm's length contracts, significant good faith requirements are imposed in the form of (a)–(c) above (honesty, fair dealing, and fidelity to the contractual purpose).

These requirements are variously applied with greater intensity ("topped up"):
  - in type (2) contracts that are symbiotic in nature;
  - in type (3) contracts where one party is recognized as being vulnerable to the other's exploitation; and
  - in type (4) contracts where the parties have a fiduciary relationship.

The three demands manifesting the good faith attitude—(a)–(c) above—will vary depending on where a particular contract falls along a broad spectrum between the four identified points, with arm's length at one end and fiduciary at the other.

II. Arguments against and for Good Faith

We begin by setting out the main arguments against and for recognizing a good faith requirement. To the extent that they are valid, they serve as points of reference in determining which version of good faith is best suited to the development of English law, discussed in section III.

A. Arguments against Good Faith

1. Freedom of Contract

Good faith is said to be ideologically inconsistent with English contract law, which prioritizes "freedom of contract founded upon the centrality of the individual, the creed in the creative power of his will and a restricted role for intervention for either the court or the state."[6] Moore-Bick LJ noted the "real danger" that a general good faith principle would be "invoked as often to undermine as to support the terms in which the parties have

[6] Jack Beatson and Daniel Friedman, "Introduction: From 'Classical' to Modern Contract Law" in Jack Beatson and Daniel Friedman (eds.), *Good Faith and Fault in Contract Law* (Clarendon Press 1997) 3, 7.

reached agreement." [7] The concern is that good faith, insofar as it restrains self-interest, "cuts against the essentially individualist ethic of English contract law."[8]

We believe that the dangers posed by good faith to freedom of contract are overstated. Freedom of contract cannot, is not, and never has been, absolute. English contract law has always recognized numerous procedural and even substantive restraints on self-interest. First, the need to limit freedom to preserve freedom is manifest in doctrines that vitiate a contract's validity (such as misrepresentation and duress). Further common law and legislative restrictions on freedom of contract are ubiquitous.[9] For instance, the common law restricts the enforceability of agreed damages that are too great or too small, forfeiture provisions, restraints on trade, and exemptions of liability for fraud. Numerous legislative restrictions are imposed in respect of health and safety, food safety, tenants' rights, freedom from unfair dismissal and minimum wage, and licensing requirements. These restrictions reflect an acceptance that the traditional paradigm on which contractual freedom was based (of relatively equal parties negotiating at arm's length) is outdated. The reality of modern contracting is marked by significant inequalities of bargaining power with the rise of large multinational firms that have substantial market power, the ubiquity of standard form contracts that involve no "bargain," "negotiation," or "consent" in any meaningful sense, and the evolution of increasingly complex and interdependent transactions that require parties to act cooperatively to achieve the contractual purpose.[10] These developments bring into sharp relief the tension between contractual freedom and contractual fairness. The issue is not "one or the other," but a judgment as to where the balance should lie.

2. It's Parliament's Job

The concern here is *how* good faith should be recognized. The claim is that the principle of "separation of powers" means that only Parliament can legitimately

[7] *MSC Mediterranean Shipping Co. SA v. Cottonex Anstalt* [2016] EWCA Civ. 789, [45].

[8] Roger Brownsword, *Contract Law: Themes for the Twenty-First Century* (2nd ed., OUP 2006) 114; and see Paul Davies, "Excluding Good Faith and Restricting Discretion" in Paul Davies and Magda Raczynska, *Contents of Commercial Contracts: Terms Affecting Freedoms* (Hart 2020) 89, 92.

[9] As discussed in Patrick Atiyah, *The Rise and Fall of Freedom of Contract* (OUP 1985); Michael Trebilcock, *The Limits of Freedom of Contract* (HUP 1985); Brownsword (n 8) ch. 3.

[10] On potential implications of complexity for the interpretation of contracts from a "law and economics" perspective, see Karen Eggleston, Eric Posner, and Richard Zeckhauser, "The Design and Interpretation of Contracts: Why Complexity Matters" (2000) 95 NWULR 91.

impose a good faith requirement; since it has already enacted protections for particular vulnerable groups, the courts should go no further.[11]

This ignores the well-accepted role of common law courts to restate the law and develop it incrementally.[12] As Lady Mary Arden of the UK Supreme Court commented when discussing the "role of the independent judiciary":[13]

> It is crucial for judges to seek to develop the law in line with evolving commercial and social need. It is part of their responsibility to have a vision of the law as a dynamic, not a static, set of principles and rules, to see the big picture and overall trends, and to have a sharp eye for what is coming over the horizon rather than simply that which has served us well in the past.

The details of contract law will not command the same priority on Parliamentary time as, say, terrorism, Brexit, or fiscal policy. Courts working at the coalface must fill in the gaps as they find them. As Jack Beatson observes, "there are examples of statutory regimes which express a policy from which a principle can be derived, being used analogically in developing the common law."[14] For example, Lord Bingham MR noted in the context of the Unfair Contract Terms Act 1977 (UCTA) that "the common law could, if the letter of the statute did not apply, treat the clear intention of the legislature expressed in the statute as a platform for invalidating or restricting the operation of an oppressive clause."[15]

3. Common Law Incrementalism

English law eschews broad principles in favor of cautious incrementalism; "[t]he preferred approach . . . is to avoid any commitment to overarching principles."[16] However, whether this contradicts the recognition of good faith depends on what role is assigned to good faith. Some versions may indeed be

[11] e.g., in *Alfred McAlpine Construction Ltd. v. Panatown Ltd. (No. 1)* [2001] 1 AC 518, 535, Lord Clyde considered it "inappropriate to enlarge the statutory protection" given to third parties in contract by "judicial innovation,"

[12] On the interaction of statute and common law, see Patrick Atiyah, "Common Law and Statute Law" (1985) 48 MLR 1; Jack Beatson, "The Role of Statute in the Development of Common Law Doctrine" (2001) 117 LQR 247; Andrew Burrows, "The Relationship between Common Law and Statute in the Law of Obligations" (2012) LQR 232.

[13] Arden (n 5) 63.

[14] Beatson (n 12) 299.

[15] *Timeload Ltd. v. British Telecommunications plc* [1995] EMLR 459, 468.

[16] *R (on the application of European Roma Rights Centre) v. Immigration Officer, Prague Airport* [2004] UKHL 55, [59] (Lord Hope). And see Paul Davies, "The Basis of Contractual Duties of Good Faith" (2019) J. Commonwealth L. 1, 32: "... [G]ood faith is too novel and potentially disruptive to become a default rule (at least in one big leap, and at least in the commercial context)."

incompatible with the common law approach; but others may not be. An instance of the latter is the familiar neighbor principle in negligence law. Prior to *Donoghue v. Stevenson*,[17] "most eminent lawyers thought that there were a number of separate torts involving negligence, each with its own rules, and they were most unwilling to add more."[18] Lord Atkin's famous articulation of the underlying principle resonates with the good faith principle:[19]

> You must take reasonable care to avoid acts or omissions which you can reasonably foresee would be likely to injure your neighbour. Who then in law is my neighbour? The answer seems to be persons who are so closely and directly affected by my act that I ought reasonably to have them in contemplation as being so affected when I am directing my mind to the acts or omissions which are called into question.

Note that the neighbor principle does not operate as a direct cause of action, nor does it apply directly to all cases that may fall within its description. Rather, it has facilitated cautious incremental development through reasoning by analogy with existing authorities.[20] An analogous good faith requirement would thus not be foreign to the *modus operandi* of the common law.

4. Uncertainty

The standard objection to good faith is that it would introduce excessive uncertainty into English contract law;[21] it is a "nice idea" but its precise content is "resistant to structured formulation."[22]

Again, the force of this objection depends on what version of good faith is adopted. Moreover, certainty concerns are something of a "red herring." First, the importance and achievability of legal certainty is often overstated. It cannot be an end in itself; a rule that invalidates the contracts of people below a certain height would be relatively certain, but not fair or indeed useful. Second, important qualitative standards that are quantitatively uncertain (such as "reasonableness," "proximity," and "foreseeability") are indispensable in many areas of

[17] [1932] AC 562.
[18] *Home Office v. Dorset Yacht Co Ltd.* [1970] AC 1004, 1026 (Lord Reid).
[19] *Donoghue v. Stevenson* [1932] AC 562, 580.
[20] See, in particular, *Caparo Industries pic v. Dickman* [1990] 2 AC 605, 617–18; *Michael v. The Chief Constable of South Wales Police* [2015] AC 1732, [102]: "[T]he development of the law of negligence has been an incremental process rather than giant leaps."
[21] See, e.g., Michael Bridge, "Limits on Contractual Freedom" (2019) 7 Chinese J. Comp. L. 387, 412; Paul Davies, "Excluding Good Faith and Restricting Discretion" in Paul Davies and Magda Raczynska (eds), *Contents of Commercial Contracts: Terms Affecting Freedoms* (Hart 2020) 89, 100.
[22] Jane Stapleton, "Good Faith in Private Law" 1991 (52) CLP 1, 1.

English contract law without fatally destabilizing them. For example, Priestly JA explains in the Australian context that:[23]

> . . . the ideas of unconscionability, unfairness and lack of good faith have a great deal in common. The result is that people generally, including judges and other lawyers . . . have grown used to the courts applying standards of fairness to contract which are wholly consistent with the existence in all contracts of a duty upon the parties of good faith and fair dealing in its performance.

Third, even commercial parties, who are ostensibly the most concerned about legal certainty, recognize the necessity of expressly deploying quantitatively uncertain terms[24] such as obligations to "cooperate," use "best endeavours," or "reasonable endeavours" or, even, "act in good faith."[25] In *Yam Seng*,[26] Leggatt J. observed that good faith involves "no more uncertainty than is inherent in the process of contractual interpretation."[27] Fourth, explicit recognition that good faith underlies the "piecemeal rules" in response to problems of unfairness can only enhance our understanding of these rules, assist in taxonomizing them (as we seek to do in section V), and facilitate their orderly development.

5. Undermining English Contract Law's "Exportability"

English legal services contribute significantly to the UK economy.[28] English contract law is often selected as the law of choice even when neither party has any significant connection to the United Kingdom. Anecdotally, it is often suggested that a key reason lies in the absence of an express and general principle of good faith, thus minimizing uncertainty and judicial discretion. Hence, the importation of a general good faith requirement would undermine the attractiveness and "exportability" of English law.

This is simply a different expression of the concern about restricting freedom of contract. But, whether recognition of good faith will undermine

[23] *Renard Construction (ME) Pty Ltd. v. Minister for Public Works* (1992) 26 NSWLR 234, 268.

[24] See Hugh Beale, *Chitty on Contracts* (33rd ed., Sweet & Maxwell, 2018) paras. 1-053-54A, 2-123, 2-146, and references therein, for a detailed discussion of such terms. Also, Arden (n 5), 29.

[25] Recent examples of such express provisions include: *Astor Management AG v. Atalaya Mining plc* [2017] EWHC 425 (Comm.) ("all reasonable endeavours" clause enforceable); *Gold Group Properties Ltd. v. BDW Trading Ltd.* [2010] EWHC 1632 (TCC) (good faith obligation included in property development agreement); *Berkeley Community Villages v. Pullen* [2007] EWHC 1330 (Ch.) ("utmost good faith" obligation).

[26] *Yam Seng* (n 4).

[27] Ibid. [152].

[28] Constituting 1.6 percent of total value added in 2015; see The Law Society, 'Economic Value of The Legal Services Sector' (March 2016) <https://www.lawsociety.org.uk/support-services/research-trends/a-25-billion-legal-sector-supports-a-healthy-economy> (accessed November 2019).

English contract law's attractiveness depends, again, on the version of good faith in play. Some versions may indeed unduly restrict contractual freedom, but others less so, as we show in section III below. Second, civil justice is not primarily a commodity that should be designed to appeal to its "consumers."[29] It should not be determinative that the party with stronger bargaining power (who can dictate the choice of law) would prefer a governing law that is devoid of good faith obligations. Rather, law is a public and social good which should reflect, as far as possible, the values to which society aspires.

Third, recognizing good faith need not undermine English law's attractiveness. If good faith is intrinsic to the rules of the contract game (as we argue in section IV), and if its ethical stance is already through and through English contract law (as we show in section V), then it is misleading not to acknowledge its influence on English law. Indeed, Lady Arden suggests that recognition of good faith might make English law more attractive in the global market.[30]

B. Arguments Supporting Good Faith

1. Wide Recognition in other Jurisdictions

Good faith in some form is accepted in most civil law jurisdictions (including Germany,[31] France,[32] Italy,[33] China,[34] and Japan[35]) and some common law jurisdictions (e.g., the United States,[36] Australia,[37] and Canada[38]).

[29] For discussion on the commodification and privatization of civil justice and its effect on the rule of law, see Hazel Genn, *Judging Civil Justice* (CUP 2010); Robert Dingwall and Emilie Cloatre, "Vanishing Trials: An English Perspective" (2006) 1 J. Dispute Resolution 51; see also *R. (on the application of Unison) v. Lord Chancellor* [2007] UKSC 51, [66] (Lord Neuberger).

[30] Arden (n 5), 63.

[31] German Civil Code (Bürgerliches Gesetzbuch, BGB), s. 242. Under s. 157, contracts should be interpreted in the light of good faith and, under s. 138, "any legal act contrary to accepted standards of good behavior" is void. See also Werner Ebke and Bettina Steinhauser, "The Doctrine of Good Faith in German Contract Law" in Jack Beatson and Daniel Friedman (eds.), *Good Faith and Fault in Contract Law* (Clarendon Press 1997) 171.

[32] French Civil Code, arts. 1134 and 1135.

[33] Italian Civil Code, arts. 1337 (conduct of negotiations and formation of contract) and 1375 (performance). Art. 1366 requires contracts to be interpreted in accordance with good faith.

[34] Wang Liming and Xu Chuanxi, "Fundamental Principles of China's Contract Law" (1999) 13 Colum. J. Asian L. 1, 15–19.

[35] Japanese Civil Code, art. 1(2).

[36] US Uniform Commercial Code, § 1-304; *US Restatement (Second) Contracts*, § 205. They recognize obligations of good faith in the performance and enforcement of contracts.

[37] *Paciocco v. Australia and New Zealand Banking Group Ltd.* [2015] FCAFC 50, [287]: good faith is "an implication or feature of Australian contract law attending the performance of the bargain and its construction and implied content" (Allsop CJ).

[38] *Bhasin v. Hyrnew* [2014] 3 SCR 495, [33]. The Supreme Court recognized it as a "general organizing principle of the common law of contract."

Internationally, it is recognized by the United Nations Convention on Contracts for the International Sale of Goods (CISG),[39] the UNIDROIT Principles of International Commercial Contracts (PICC),[40] the Principles of European Contract Law (PECL),[41] the European Draft Common Frame of Reference (DCFR),[42] and the Common European Sales Law (CESL).[43]

Indeed, good faith has even been expressly incorporated into English law via the EU Directive on Unfair Terms in Consumer Contracts.[44] Its impact will continue after Brexit; Part 2 of the Consumer Rights Act (CRA) 2015 invalidates non-core terms in consumer contracts that are unfair in the sense that, "contrary to the requirement of good faith," they ". . . cause a significant imbalance in the parties' rights and obligations arising under the contract."[45]

The need for extreme caution when relying on jurisdictional comparisons to support the importation of a new legal requirement is readily acknowledged.[46] Nevertheless, in refusing openly to recognize good faith in any form, English law is "swimming against the tide."[47]

2. We Already Have it

It is impossible to overstate the extent to which English contract law already practices good faith (as we show in section V). The "piecemeal solutions in response to demonstrated problems of unfairness"[48] operate at every stage of a contract's life. As Jane Stapleton observes,[49] once these are recognized as motivated by good faith, it is evident that good faith plays a "widespread and profoundly important role" in our private law. English contract law has been "speaking prose" all along without knowing it. As such, its open recognition as the justifying principle behind many rules and doctrines only makes explicit what is implicit.

[39] CISG, art. 7(1), requiring contracts to be interpreted and applied in a way that promotes "the observance of good faith in international trade."

[40] PICC, art. 1.7(1), provides that the parties must "act in accordance with good faith and fair dealing in international trade." Art. 1.7(2) provides that this duty may not be excluded or limited.

[41] PECL, arts. 1.06(1) and 1.201.

[42] DCFR, art. I.-I:103(2).

[43] CESL, art. 2.

[44] Council Directive (EC) 13/1993 of 5 April 1993 on unfair terms in consumer contracts, implemented into UK law via the European Communities Act 1972, s. 2(2).

[45] CRA 2015, s. 62.

[46] Michael Bridge, "Does Anglo-Canadian Law Need a Doctrine of Good Faith?" (1984) 9 CBLJ 412, 414

[47] *Yam Seng* (n 4) [125] (Leggatt J.).

[48] *Interfoto Picture Library Ltd. v. Stiletto Visual Programmes Ltd.* [1989] QB 433, 439 (Bingham LJ).

[49] Stapleton (n 22) 6; and see Magda Raczynska, "Good Faith and Contract Terms" in Paul Davies and Magda Raczynska, *Contents of Commercial Contracts: Terms Affecting Freedoms* (Hart 2020) 68.

3. Good Faith Protects the Autonomy-Enhancing Institution of Contract

We naturally make deals (cooperate and coordinate) with family and friends within the private domain because we trust them and our relationships give us leverage over them. Beyond that domain, the institution of contract enhances the reliability of voluntary exchanges and bridges the gaps in trust and sanctions by guaranteeing redress for breach, backed up by the coercive power of the state. While bargains would still be struck without legal enforcement, parties would tend to regard each other with suspicion, like parties in a hostage swap with a "you first!" stance. They would have to devise alternative enforcement schemes (think of the Mafia), or bias exchanges toward those that take place instantly or persons with a reputation for promise-keeping. Thus, ". . . the supportive role of the law helps to make contracts outside the framework of ongoing relations much more common"[50] and allows individuals to project their intentions into the future and plan actions that require concrete pre-commitments.[51]

However, in supporting contracts by deploying the power of Leviathan at a party's request, contract law must set appropriate standards for how the contract game should be played and what can be obtained from playing it. These have two aims. First, they spell out what it means for participants to treat others on the basis of equal respect for the other's autonomy, consistent with the Kantian injunction that persons are ends in themselves with an absolute dignity which must be respected; they must be treated not only as a means of attaining one's own ends, but also as ends which one should simultaneously serve.[52] Second, the rules must uphold the integrity of the institution (the game) of contract by protecting it from abuse; the parties can change some of these rules by agreement, but other rules are mandatory—contract law prescribes some irreducible minimums. Accordingly, the parties' ability to exclude (contract out of) contract law's constitutive rules—on formation (e.g., the objective test of intention and the requirement of agreement and consideration), on vitiation of contract (e.g., rescission for fraud or duress), or on default remedies for breach[53]—are non-existent in most cases, and severely restricted in others. Many of these rules are rooted in good faith, as civil law jurisdictions make

[50] Joseph Raz, "Promises in Morality and Law" (1982) Harv. L. Rev. 916, 934.

[51] Mindy Chen-Wishart, "Regulating Unfair Terms" in Louise Gullifer and Stefan Vogenaur (eds.), *English and European Perspectives on Contract and Commercial Law* (Hart Publishing 2015) 105, 118–19.

[52] Ibid. See Immanuel Kant's moral theory as set out in Immanuel Kant, *Foundations of the Metaphysics of Morals* (1785).

[53] See Daniel Friedmann, "Good Faith and Remedies for Breach of Contracts" in Jack Beatson and Daniel Friedmann (eds.), *Good Faith and Fault in Contract* (Clarendon Press 1997) 399.

explicit, and adherence to these minimum standards of contractual behavior is a condition of entitlement to play the contract game and to pray the aid of the law. Otherwise, the contract relation risks becoming the locus of exploitation or manipulation. Contract law then risks colluding with such exploitation and thus permitting the erosion of the institution of contract itself.

It is also possible to justify good faith as something that parties would choose behind John Rawls' "veil of ignorance."[54] As mere mortals who lack omniscience, are driven by changing passions and desires, have limited processing capacity, and cannot plan for every conceivable contingency that may occur in the life of the contract, pragmatic and self-interested parties would agree that participants in the contract game should act in good faith even when they are disinclined to do so. Restraining the freedom to engage in opportunistic and exploitative conduct protects the institution of contract and makes contracting parties more secure and so more willing to enter contracts:[55]

> [T]rickery and sharp practice impede commerce by decreasing trust and increasing risk. Good faith and fair dealing promote commerce by supporting the central conception and basic foundation of commerce: a requisite degree of trust. Business people understand these things.

III. The Role of Good Faith

Good faith is an elusive concept. Even jurisdictions that explicitly recognize it share "no common concept."[56] In arguing for[57] or against[58] its recognition, commentators and judges have often talked at cross purposes. The aim of this section is to disentangle three distinct roles that a good faith requirement might play in English contract law and to assess them against the criteria discussed in section II above.

[54] See John Rawls, *A Theory of Justice* (Belknap Press of Harvard University Press 1971).

[55] *Paciocco v. Australia and New Zealand Banking Group Ltd.* [2015] FCAFC 50, [293].

[56] *Director General of Fair-Trading v. First National Bank* [2001] UKHL 52, [17] (Lord Bingham).

[57] See Johan Steyn, "The Role of Good Faith and Fair Dealing in Contract Law: A Hair-Shirt Philosophy?" (1991) Denning LJ 131; Roger Brownsword, "Two Concepts of Good Faith" (1994) 7 JCL 197; "'Good Faith in Contract" Revisited" (1996) 49 CLP 111; Daniel Markovits, "Good Faith as Contract's Core Value" in Gregory Klass, George Letsas, and Prince Saprai (eds.), *Philosophical Foundations of Contract Law* (OUP 2014) 272; Michael Levenstein, "Where Angels Fear to Tread: The Limits of Good Faith in Commercial Contracts" (2017) 9 JIBFL 569; Arden (n 5) 63.

[58] See, e.g., Bridge (n 1), (n 5), and (n 46); Roy Goode, "The Concept of 'Good Faith' in English Law" (1992) Centro di studi e ricerche di diritto comparato e straniero, Roma, 3; David Campbell, "Good Faith and the Ubiquity of the 'Relational' Contract" [2014] 77 MLR 475.

A. Good Faith as an Independent Cause of Action: *The "Charging Bull"*

The most radical version is to introduce good faith into English contract law as an independent and direct cause of action. This version of good faith is often assumed by good faith naysayers when they cast good faith as a "contagious disease of alien origin,"[59] or the proverbial "bull in the China shop," marauding unrestrained through the carefully curated china shop of English contract law.[60] This approach would be analogous to bringing a negligence action directly on the basis of the neighbor principle. That is, the basic requirement to "do unto your neighbour as you would that he should do to you" is converted into a legal requirement to take reasonable care to avoid acts and omissions which it is reasonably foreseeable will injure your neighbor. In our context, this would take the form of an unmediated legal requirement to act in good faith toward the counterparty.

Morality and law are not coterminous and attempts to treat the neighbour principle as laying down a general rule for negligence liability have been rightly criticized; it "would be difficult to follow as a moral precept. It becomes intolerable . . . when imposed in law."[61] The neighbor principle was "not intended to be, and cannot properly be treated as being, a general formula which will explain all conceivable cases of negligence."[62] Instead, ". . . even at a fairly high level of abstraction [the neighbour principle] needs considerable qualifications and reservations before it can be accepted."[63] It is after all, ". . . reaching for the moon . . . to expect to accommodate every circumstance which may arise within a single short abstract formulation."[64] All of this applies equally to the notion of good faith in contracting.

The potential difficulties of treating good faith as an independent and unmediated cause of action are evident from the experience of those jurisdictions that come closest to doing so. Israeli contract law requires parties to "act in . . . good faith"[65] in negotiating a contract, and "an obligation or a right arising out of a contract must be fulfilled or exercised . . . in good faith."[66] Israeli

[59] Gunther Teubner, "Legal Irritants: Good Faith in British Law or How Unifying Law Ends up in New Divergences" (1998) MLR 11, 11.
[60] Bridge (n 1) 448.
[61] Joseph C. Smith and Peter Burns, "*Donoghue v. Stevenson*—The Not so Golden Anniversary" (1983) 2 MLR 147, 147–48.
[62] Robert Heuston, "*Donoghue v. Stevenson* in Retrospect" (1957) 20 MLR 1, 23.
[63] Ibid. 23.
[64] *Merrett v. Babb* [2001] QB 1174, 1193.
[65] Israeli Contracts (General Part) Law 1973, s. 12(a).
[66] Israeli Contracts (General Part) Law 1973, s. 39.

courts have applied this good faith duty extensively, responding directly to its contravention.[67] This has "totally changed the contractual map" by replacing "rigid, rational and clear" laws expressive of an "individualistic-capitalist outlook" with "flexible and less clear-cut" rules which express "an altruistic-moral view."[68] Israeli courts have refrained from setting the boundaries of good faith, instead taking the view that it should develop casuistically,[69] thus making contract a "dynamic, fluid creature." The Israeli experience "demonstrates that a price must be paid for the desire to enhance the standard of moral behaviour in the contractual area,"[70] that of uncertainty. In the context of pre-contractual liability, Cohen observes:[71]

> To the uncertainty as to the question whether a contract has been created at all, another uncertainty has now been added, namely whether even in the absence of a contract the negotiations involve a breach of the duty of good faith, and, if so, what is the proper remedy. It follows that almost any negotiation is susceptible to future litigation, the results of which are hardly predictable.

This version of good faith is unsuitable for English law. It runs into the objections raised in section II.A by posing a significant threat to freedom of contract and contradicting English law's extreme reluctance to recognize general principles, preferring instead cautious incrementalism.[72] This iteration of good faith is also unacceptably amorphous and unpredictable, and so unduly uncertain. It amounts to saying that the law is what is "just." The charging bull thus marauds under the palm tree of "justice." If law is to be a purposive enterprise intended to subject human conduct to the governance of rules, it is necessary, as Fuller identifies, for it to meet various "principles of legality," including clarity, coherence, constancy, and the absence of impediments to compliance with the rules by those subject to them.[73] Good faith as a direct cause of action undermines

[67] e.g., in *Atia v. Ararat Insurance Co.* (1977) 31(ii) PD 780 (the Supreme Court held that an insurance company had breached the duty of pre-contractual good faith by failing to draw the insured's attention to the scope of the insurance policy) and *Rot v. Yashpe* (1979) 33(i) PD 617 (a contractor was unable to rely on an exemption clause after delivering an apartment six months late because the exercise of its contractual rights contravened good faith).

[68] Gabriela Shalev, "Forty Years of Contract Law" (1990) 24 Israel L. Rev. 657, 662.

[69] *Kot v. Organization of Tenants, Commercial Centre, Ramat Yosef* (1976) 30(iii) P.D. 813, discussed in Shalev, ibid. 667.

[70] Nili Cohen, "From the Common Law to the Civil Law: The Experience of Israel" in John Cartwright and Martijn Hesselink (eds.), *Precontractual Liability in European Private Law* (CUP 2009) 398, 428.

[71] Ibid..

[72] On this, see McKendrick (n 1), 44–48; Bridge (n 46), 415.

[73] Lon Fuller, *The Morality of Law* (YUP 1969) and the eight principles of legality identified therein.

these principles and poses undue risks to the attractiveness and exportability of English contract law.

B. Expanding Existing and Generating New Obligations: *The "Relentless Woodpecker"*

A less radical version of good faith casts it not as an independent source of obligations itself, but as the creative inspiration behind other obligations and defenses to which the parties may appeal. Good faith, on this model, is not a charging bull cutting a swathe through contract law, but a "relentless woodpecker" that assertively pecks away at non-conforming parts of the law, rapidly transforming it.

German law offers a good example of this approach, with good faith being mediated through the development of more specific rules and doctrines. This model differs from the "charging bull" in that ". . . it is not the general clause but the case law of the courts which produces the rules."[74] Thus, while Article 242 of the German Civil Code requires parties to perform their contractual obligations "in such a manner as good faith (*Treu und Glauben*) requires," good faith is not an autonomous cause of action in itself. Instead, the courts have actively relied upon the fundamental good faith obligation in Article 242 actively to develop the law. Ebke and Steinhauser identify three roles for good faith in German law; (i) it has been used to create new causes of action (e.g., the granting of contractual remedies to some third parties and the imposition of secondary contractual obligations in various circumstances, including pre-contractual duties of good faith);[75] (ii) it may be relied upon as a defense where the basic assumptions underlying the contractual relationship have changed fundamentally (e.g., the doctrines of impracticability and impossibility of purpose);[76] and (iii) it allows the reallocation of risks to avoid perceived undesirable results [77] (e.g., the doctrine of "contractual basis" allows the adjustment of the contract where the assumptions underlying it subsequently become incorrect).[78] In these ways, the good faith obligation is given concrete form by more specific doctrines developed by the courts.

[74] Basil Markesinis, "The Legacy of History on German Contract Law" in *Foreign Law and Comparative Methodology: A Subject and a Thesis* (Hart Publishing 1997), 90.

[75] Ibid. 173–79.

[76] Ibid. 180–82.

[77] Werner Ebke and Bettina Steinhauser, "The Doctrine of Good Faith in German Contract Law" in Jack Beatson and Daniel Friedmann (eds.), *Good Faith and Fault in Contract Law* (Clarendon Press, 1995) 171, 171–72.

[78] Ibid. 182–89.

This approach, whilst more moderate than the "charging bull," still involves good faith actively and forcefully *adding* to the substantive content of the parties' obligations, most obviously in via an implied-in-*law* duty of good faith during the formation, performance, and enforcement of a contract. This is one interpretation of the tenor of Leggatt J.'s judgment in *Yam Seng*,[79] although not said in so many words.[80] He took that step in a later case, observing that "[t]he legitimate expectations which the law should protect in relationships of this kind are embodied in the normative standard of good faith"; thus, he would have been prepared to imply a good faith requirement in *law* as well as implying one in *fact* "on the basis that the nature of the contract . . .implicitly requires (in the absence of a contrary indication) treating it as involving an obligation of good faith.".[81] Other changes would include the imposition of greater obligations of disclosure during negotiations or the performance of a contract, and greater restrictions on the exercise of contractual rights relating to the performance or enforcement of the contract (such as the exercise of discretionary powers or the election to terminate or affirm a contract on breach).

The advantage of this version of good faith is its ability to "contribute to a greater consistency in the law by exerting pressure upon rules which are incompatible with the idea of good faith."[82] Analogous to a mandate to interpret legislation in a way that is compatible with human rights,[83] the "relentless woodpecker" of good faith would require the courts actively to bring into line the many rules that do not currently conform to its requirements[84] and create new ones that do. In doing so, legal change would be accelerated.

This less radical version of good faith still goes several steps too far for English law. Continental lawyers have dealt with good faith requirements in a way that is "abstract, open-ended, principle-oriented, but at the same time strongly systematised and dogmatised"; this is "at odds with the more rule-oriented,

[79] Simon Whittaker, "Good Faith, Implied Terms and Commercial Contracts" (2013) 129 LQR 463, 467.

[80] Indeed, in *Yam Seng* (n 4) [131], Leggatt J. was doubtful whether ". . . English law has reached the stage . . . where it is ready to recognize a requirement of good faith as a duty implied by law, even as a default rule, into all commercial contracts".

[81] *Al Nehayan v. Kent* [2018] EWHC 333 (Comm.), [167], [174].

[82] Friedmann (n 53) 399–40

[83] The Human Rights Act 1998, s. 3, requires legislation to be interpreted as far as possible compatibly with rights protected by the European Convention on Human Rights.

[84] Possible "targets" are *Arcos Ltd. v. EE Ronaasen & Son* [1933] AC 470 (exercise of a right to reject non-conforming goods even though they were fit for purpose and "merchantable"); *Union Eagle Ltd. v. Golden Achievement Ltd.* [1997] AC 514 (exercise of a right to terminate for failure to complete on time when completion was ten minutes late and resulted in forfeiture of the buyer's deposit); and *CTN Cash & Carry Ltd. v. Gallaher Ltd.* [1994] 4 All ER 714 (payment of sum not owed could not be recovered from a supplier who bona fide believed it was owing).

technical, concrete but loosely systematised British style of legal reasoning."[85] As Teubner reminds us, a legal principle cannot simply be transferred from one system to another but requires "careful implantation and cultivation in the environment." Otherwise, it "works as a fundamental irritation which triggers a whole series of new and unexpected events" and, most deleteriously, "irritates law's 'binding arrangements'."[86] Thus, implementation of this version of good faith may lead to the demotion or neglect of other policies or principles that are currently weighed in the balance by English courts (although sometimes *sub silentio*). It would also run into many of the objections to good faith mentioned in section II.A, such as undermining common law incrementalism and creating uncertainty as to how existing principles and policies will be balanced. Moreover, English appeal courts have already expressly rejected this version of good faith.[87]

C. Good Faith as an Explanatory, Organizational and Legitimizing Principle: *The "Measured Tortoise"*

Humble good faith does not aspire to play an overtly creative role in English contract law. Rather, it merely reveals how many existing and apparently disparate rules of English contract law can be explained, organized, and justified as manifestations of the good faith requirement. Consistently, Leggatt J. said that there is "nothing novel or foreign to English law in recognising an implied duty of good faith in the performance of contracts,"[88] citing other manifestations of this duty in: an implied-in-*fact* duty to cooperate, the implied limits on the exercise of discretionary powers and the requirement of reasonable notice to incorporate onerous or unusual terms in unsigned documents. This humble view of good faith does not necessitate any immediate additions to the parties' obligations or defences; the courts need not actively seek to change the law, but simply make transparent the standards of contractual

[85] Teubner (n 59) 19.

[86] Ibid. 12. For more on the difficulties involved with "legal transplant," see Pierre Legrand, "The Impossibility of 'Legal Transplants'" (1997) 4 Maastricht J. Eur. & Comp. L. 111.

[87] See, e.g., *Interfoto Picture Library Ltd. v. Stiletto Visual Programmes Ltd.* [1989] QB 433, 439; *Walford v. Miles* [1992] AC 128, 138; *Mid Essex Hospital Services NHS Trust v. Compass Group UK & Ireland Ltd.* [2013] EWCA Civ. 200, [105]; *R. (on the application of European Roma Rights Centre) v. Immigration Officer, Prague Airport* [2004] UKHL 55, [59]; *UTB LLC v. Sheffield United Ltd.* [2019] EWHC 2322 (Ch.), [201]–[204]; *TAQA Bratani Ltd. v. RockRose UKSC 8 LLC* [2020] EWHC 58 (Comm.) [56]; *Russell v. Cartwright* [2020] EWHC 41 (Ch.) [87].

[88] *Yam Seng* (n 4) [146].

dealing which are generally accepted in the marketplace and *already* recognized by the law.

We favor this humble version of good faith. First, it finds widespread support in othercommon law jurisdictions such as Canada[89] and Australia.[90] Moreover, Lord Hope noted that, "... [g]ood faith in Scottish law, as in South African law, is generally an underlying principle of an explanatory and legitimating rather than an active or creative nature ... It is not a source of obligation in itself."[91] In contrast, the US Uniform Commercial Code rejects the "charging bull" but appears to embrace the "relentless woodpecker"; § 1-304, which imposes a mandatory duty of good faith in performance for "every contract" within its scope, is elaborated in the *Official Comment* as follows: "... the doctrine of good faith merely directs a court towards interpreting contracts within the commercial context in which they are created, performed, and enforced, and does not create a separate duty of fairness and reasonableness which can be independently breached."

Second, it provides a framework within which to illuminate and taxonomize the character of the piecemeal and apparently disparate contract law rules. This decreases rather than increases uncertainty. Third, it necessitates no further restrictions on freedom of contract. Thus, fourth, it will not unduly detract from English contract law's attractiveness. Fifth, it is entirely consistent with the common law's incremental approach.[92] Sixth, in explaining and justifying significant parts of English contract law, it reveals the ethical content of that law.

Unlike the "charging bull" or "relentless woodpecker," the "measured tortoise" of good faith is not designed to usher in significant or immediate change to the law, being merely a restatement of the existing law. Nevertheless, its creative potential cannot be ignored. Open recognition of good faith as an organizing principle will facilitate incremental developments *over time*, in line with the common law method.[93] On this view, Leggatt J.'s support for the good faith requirement simply represents:[94]

89 *Bhasin v. Hrynew* [2014] 3 SCR 495, [93]. The Supreme Court treats good faith as a "general organizing principle" underpinning many facets of contract law.

90 *Paciocco v. Australia and New Zealand Banking Group Ltd.* [2015] FCAFC 50, [287] (Allsop CJ).

91 *R. (on the application of European Roma Rights Centre) v. Immigration Officer, Prague Airport* [2004] UKHL 55, [59]]–[60].

92 *Yam Seng* (n 4) [148].

93 In *Bhasin v. Hrynew* (2014) 3 SCR 494, [33] and [83], the Canadian Supreme Court's recognition of good faith as a "general organizing principle" gave rise to a more specific, enforceable, duty of honesty.

94 Ewan McKendrick, "Doctrine and Discretion in the Law of Contract Revisited" (2019) Chinese J. Comp. L. 1, 14–15.

> . . . a fascinating example of the incremental development of the law . . . as a judge in a particular case seeks to draw together a number of different threads running through the case law and derive . . . a principle, cautiously expressed, but capable in time, of developing into a principle of broader application.

The difference between the "relentless woodpecker" and the "measured tortoise" is a matter of degree; they differ in the pace of change precipitated. They may overlap, insofar as incrementalism may facilitate the evolution of new obligations. For example, as Gerard McMeel reminds us:[95]

> . . . it is likely that all today's implied terms in law commenced as incidents of particular transactions, and then migrated to the sub-category of terms implied in law (once the existence of that classification was made explicit). Today, similar journeys are being made.

IV. What Is Good Faith?

We will argue that good faith:

(i) is not a "duty" in the Hohfeldian sense of generating a "right"; rather, it is intrinsic to the definition of contracting as an *attitude* that is respectful of the other contract party and of the contract;
(ii) is mediated through existing doctrines[96] whose application varies with the type of contract in question;
(iii) is externally imposed but also intelligible as internally assumed;
(iv) leaves ample scope for freedom and self-interest;
(v) is colored by the social and legal culture; and
(vi) is episodic and consistent with common law incrementalism.

A. The Attitude of Good Faith

"Humble" good faith does not create new causes of action, add to the parties' existing rights or obligations, or change the agreed substantive terms of the

[95] Gerard McMeel, *The Construction of Contracts* (3rd ed., OUP 2017) para. 9.14.
[96] e.g., the courts may impose liability, refuse enforcement (if the contract is voidable or a term unenforceable), imply a term, interpret a clause in a particular way, grant or refuse remedies, or calculate remedies in a specific way; see section V.

contract. Rather, good faith is an *attitude* (a stance or mindset) that contract parties are required to assume when they participate in the activity of contracting.[97] The relevant attitude is threefold. It requires:

— respect for the legitimate interests[98] of one's counterparty as an equal, expressed as:
  (a) honesty; and
  (b) fair dealing; and

— respect for the contract itself, expressed as:
  (c) fidelity to the contractual purpose.

Indeed, Leggatt J. identified (a), (b), and (c) under the rubric of good faith in *Yam Seng*.[99] This good faith attitude expresses a commitment to the particular normative and legal relation that is *required* of those playing the contract game, irrespective of a party's actual attitude. The analogy is to the objective interpretation of a party's intentions; the result is treated as her *voluntary* intention even if it deviates from her actual intention. As John Finnis explains, the law is "for the sake of persons" and its rules "are fundamentally relationships between persons."[100] Thus, Finnis defends a "conversational" model of interpretation that is objective, with a notable good faith rider:[101]

> [A] properly juridical interpretation will not be as ready to consider authoritative an unjust as it will a just meaning. Thus, it differs from sensible conversationalists, who like good historians are quick to detect, and not too ready to overlook, interlocutors' perhaps vicious purposes and deficiencies of personal character.

[97] Markovits (n 57) 272.

[98] Supporting this as central to good faith, see Paul Finn, "The Fiduciary Principle" in Timothy Youdan (ed.), *Equity, Fiduciaries and Trusts* (Carswell 1989) 4 (while "permitting a party to act self-interestedly," good faith "qualifies this by positively requiring that party, in his decision and action, to have regard to the legitimate interests . . . of the other"). The Canadian Supreme Court has also referred to good faith as appropriate regard for the other party's legitimate interests; *Bhasin v. Hrynew* [2014] 3 SCR 495, [69]. The New South Wales Court of Appeal described the duty as one to "recognise and to have due regard to the legitimate interests of both of the parties in the enjoyment of the fruits of the contract as delineated by its terms"; *Overlook v. Foxtel* [2002] NSWSC 17, [67]. The European Directive on Unfair Terms in Consumer Contracts 1993, now implemented in English law via the CRA 2015, requires the consumer's "legitimate interests" to be taken into account to satisfy the test of good faith.

[99] *Yam Seng* (n 4) [136], [151], and [141] respectively. At [141] Leggatt J. refers to the "fidelity to the parties' bargain."

[100] John Finnis, "The Priority of Persons" in Jeremy Horder (ed.), *Oxford Essays in Jurisprudence*, 4th series (OUP 2000) 1, 32.

[101] Ibid. 33.

Likewise, the good faith attitude (of respect toward the counterparty and the contract made) is intrinsic to, or constitutive of, the activity of contracting. Like objective interpretation, it is part of the rules of the contract game that bind all who play. It is not a duty in the Hohfeldian sense of necessarily generating a "right"[102] that yields liability for breach. Rather, the effects of contravention will depend on the doctrines through which the good faith attitude is mediated, as discussed in section V.

B. Mediated through Existing Rules but Demands Vary with the Nature of the Contract

Good faith is not only an attitude, it is also a standard. Its constituents (of honesty, fair dealing, and fidelity to the contractual purpose), which are expressed through existing rules, are not susceptible to quantitative precision in the abstract. Its specific demands will depend on the context.[103] This is the starting point for our taxonomy in section V. Broadly speaking, it will be no surprise that the good faith attitude applies with increasing intensity along a spectrum of: (1) arm's length contracts, (2) symbiotic contracts, (3) contracts involving one recognized vulnerable party, and (4) contracts involving parties in a fiduciary relationship (explained further in section V below).

C. Externally Imposed

The good faith attitude is externally imposed; being constitutive of contracting, it is mandatory or non-excludable. It attaches whether the parties agree to it or not. But that does not make the parties' agreement irrelevant since any express inclusion or exclusion of good faith is evidence (along with other indications) of the nature of the contract and so the intensity of the appropriate good faith attitude, as explained in section V.

Paradoxically, the good faith attitude is also intelligible as being internally assumed by the contract parties. The analogy is again to the objective test of the parties' intentions. The mandatory nature of this rule, even if its result deviates from the parties' actual intentions, does not deprive a contract of its

[102] See Wesley N. Hohfeld, *Fundamental Legal Conceptions as Applied in Judicial Reasoning* (Ashgate 2001).

[103] *Yam Seng* (n 4) [147].

"voluntary" character. Objective interpretation, like the good faith attitude, is simply part of what it means to enter into a voluntary agreement. To make a contract with another *just is* to "voluntarily" adopt the attitudes of honesty, fair dealing, and fidelity to the contractual purpose, objectively interpreted.

The internal view of good faith is supported by much of the recent case law and academic literature. On this view, when courts recognize good faith, they are giving effect to the parties' intentions or "reasonable expectations,"[104] rather than imposing standards external to the parties' intentions. Thus, in *Yam Seng*, Leggatt J. said that "the basis of the duty of good faith is the presumed intentions of the parties" and that "the relevant background against which contracts are made includes not only matters of fact known to the parties but also shared values and norms of behaviour."[105] On this approach, there is no need to "abandon [the common law's] characteristic methods,"[106] such as implied-in-fact terms.

Nevertheless, the ubiquitous appeal to the parties' implied intentions in English contract law should be treated with a degree of suspicion. The crux is the scope of the "background context" to which the parties are taken to have impliedly consented. It clearly includes the specifics of the particular transaction (past dealings, commercial practices, purpose, and background legal rules), but how much more? Once it includes shared normative understandings of general moral considerations such as fairness and good faith,[107] the language of private intentions merely obscures the public nature of these values. That is, normative considerations are "smuggled in" behind a façade of implied or hypothetical agreement.[108] This is associated with the (virtually)

[104] Johan Steyn, "The Role of Good Faith and Fair Dealing in Contract: A Hair-Shirt Philosophy" [1991] Denning LJ 131, 133; Johan Steyn, "Contract Law: Fulfilling the Reasonable Expectations of Honest Men" (1997) 113 LQR 433; *First Energy (UK) Ltd. v. Hungarian International Bank Ltd.* [1993] 2 Lloyd's Law Reports 194, 196; *Associated Japanese Bank (International) Ltd. v. Credit du Nord SA* [1988] 3 All ER 902, 903; David Campbell, "Good Faith and the Ubiquity of the 'Relational' Contract" [2014] 77 MLR 475; Ewan McKendrick "Good Faith in the Performance of a Contract in English Law" in Larry DiMatteo and Martin Hogg (eds.), *Comparative Contract Law: British and American Perspectives* (OUP 2016) 196; McKendrick (n 94) 13–15; Hugh Collins, "Implied Terms: The Foundation in Good Faith and Fair Dealing" (2014) CLP 297; John Enman-Beech "The Good Faith Challenge" (2019) 1 J. Commonwealth L. 35.

[105] *Yam Seng* (n 4) [149], [134].

[106] Ibid. [148].

[107] e.g., Stephen Smith, *Contract Theory* (OUP 2004) 300–03; Raz (n 50) 932.

[108] Ronald Dworkin, *Taking Rights Seriously* (HUP 1977) 151: "Suppose that you and I are playing poker and we find, in the middle of a hand, that the deck is one card short. You suggest that we throw the hand in, but I refuse because I know I am going to win and I want the money in the pot. You might say that I would certainly have agreed to that procedure had the possibility of the deck being short been raised in advance. But your point is not that I am somehow committed to throwing the hand in by an agreement I never made. Rather you use the device of a hypothetical agreement to make a point that might have been made without that device, which is that the solution is so obviously fair and sensible . . . the fact that I would have chosen it myself adds nothing of substance to that argument."

"no gaps in contracts" school,[109] according to which, if enough background context is taken into account, it is *always* possible to tell what the parties (impliedly) intended in the circumstances. Indeed, on an extreme version of this argument, almost *all* of contract law can be viewed as impliedly agreed by the parties. However, as Charles Fried accepts: "... as we move further from actual intention, the standard of presumed intention tends to merge into the other substantive standards used to solve the problems caused by a failure in the agreement."[110]

The justifications for the good faith requirement[111] mean that the parties should not be able to exclude it.[112] Attempts to limit or exclude good faith may still evidence the particular type of contract entered (such as an arm's length relationship) and so *may* reduce the intensity of the good faith attitude required,[113] but they cannot be determinative. Analogously, the parties cannot exclude rescission for fraud or duress; any agreed "no reliance" clause cannot exclude liability for misrepresentation if it is unreasonable;[114] employers may not exclude the implied term of mutual trust and confidence in employment contracts, which obliges them to exercise their discretion toward their employees in a just and fair way, in good faith and not capriciously,[115] even if the contract confers discretionary powers on employers in unlimited terms.

D. Ample Scope for Freedom of Contract and Self-Interest

Humble good faith is, prima facie, an attitude toward *whatever*[116] contractual content (price or main subject matter) is agreed by the parties, however

[109] Brian Leiter, "Legal Realism and Legal Positivism Reconsidered" in *Naturalising Jurisprudence: Essays on American Legal Realism and Naturalism in Legal Philosophy* (OUP 2007) 60, 62–63.

[110] Charles Fried, *Contract as Promise: A Theory of Contractual Obligation* (HUP 1981) 61; Stephen Smith, *Atiyah's Introduction to the Law of Contract* (Clarendon Law Series 2006) 177.

[111] Discussed in section II.B.

[112] Thus, we prefer the view put forward by Cromwell J. in *Bhasin v. Hyrnew* [2014] 3 SCR 495, [74]–[75] that the parties would not be free to exclude the duty of honesty, which we have suggested is a requirement of the attitude of good faith, since it is a "general doctrine of contract law that imposes as a contractual duty a minimum standard of honest performance", to that of Leggatt J. in *Yam Seng* (n 4) [150] that duties of good faith may be expressly excluded.

[113] As Cromwell J. acknowledges in *Bhasin*, ibid. [77]; "the precise context of honest performance will vary with context and the parties should be free in some contexts to relax the requirements of the doctrine...".

[114] *First Tower Trustees Ltd. v. CDS (Superstores International) Ltd* [2018] EWCA Civ. 1396.

[115] *Cantor Fitzgerald Intl v. Horkulak* [2004] IRLR 942; *Manor House Healthcare v. Hayes* EAT/1196/99.

[116] Barring contracts that are illegal or against public policy.

unevenly or unfairly balanced.[117] The good faith attitude does not permit the law to make that substance fairer or more even; it "does not require either party to give up a freely negotiated financial advantage embedded in the contract."[118] Thus, good faith is reconcilable with freedom of contract and the parties' self-interested stance, *except* that parties must honor the proper (objective and good faith) interpretation of their agreement, and treat each other with respect in its performance (with honesty and fair dealing).

E. Varies with the Social and Legal Culture

The attitudes of honesty, fair dealing, and fidelity to the contractual purpose will vary with the social culture in which the jurisdiction is situated. For examples, in upholding an express duty to negotiate a rent review in good faith, the Singapore Court of Appeal stated: [119]

> [W]e think that such "negotiate in good faith" clauses are in the public interest as they promote the consensual disposition of any potential disputes. We note, for instance, that it is fairly common practice for Asian businesses to include similar clauses in their commercial contracts . . . We think that the "friendly negotiations" and "confer in good faith" clauses . . . are consistent with our cultural value of promoting consensus whenever possible. Clearly, it is in the wider public interest in Singapore as well to promote such an approach towards resolving differences.

Further, in contrast to English law, which recognizes no general duty to disclose information, the Korean Supreme Court has found actionable non-disclosures in sales of condominiums where the seller failed to disclose the existence of a nearby waste disposal facility[120] or public cemetery.[121] Likewise in Taiwan, where there is extreme reluctance to live in properties where unnatural deaths

[117] This is defeasible by the courts or Parliament enacting special protection for groups identified as requiring protection, e.g., the penalty rule, relief for forfeitures, and statutory invalidity for unreasonableness or unfairness under UCTA 1977 and CRA 2015. See section V below.

[118] *Gold Group Properties v. BDW Trading Ltd. (formerly Barratt Homes Ltd.)* [2010] EWHC 1632 (TCC), [91].

[119] *HSBC Institutional Trust Services (Singapore) Ltd. (Trustee of Starhill Global Real Estate Investment Trust) v. Toshin Development Singapore Pte Ltd.* [2012] 4 SLR 738, [40].

[120] Supreme Court Decision 2004Da48515 dated October 12, 2006.

[121] Supreme Court Decision 2005Da5812, 5829, 5836 dated June 1, 2007.

have occurred, a seller of property must disclose the fact that someone was killed or committed suicide in the property.[122]

The good faith attitude is also colored by the legal culture through which it is interpreted. As Jane Stapleton explains:[123]

> [T]raditionally English courts have "read" our commercial culture as based on arm's-length dealing so that parties are not taken to have undertaken to act in support of the interests of their contractual partners. Rightly or wrongly, the judicial view has been that business people agree and accept that the arm's-length model is a cornerstone of general economic prosperity, at least of the City. So long as this judicial perspective remains in England, certain deliberate self-interested uncooperative behaviour will not be judged dishonest or unconscionably contradictory in England, whereas it might well be on the Continent . . . It is not necessarily that the elements of good faith, such as honesty, undertaking, and conscience, are different on the Continent, but that the socio-legal interpretation of whether they apply to a fact situation may well be different.

F. Good Faith Is Episodic and Consistent with Common Law Incrementalism

The precise application of the good faith attitude is "episodic."[124] Not all instances of dishonesty, unfair dealing, or infidelity to the contractual purpose are sanctioned. That is precisely the difference between good faith as the "relentless woodpecker" and the "measured tortoise"; the former would demand such consistency, but the latter does not. Analogously, the neighbor principle has not imposed negligence liability *whenever* carelessness results in foreseeable harm. As Holmes famously said, "[T]he life of the law has not been logic; it has been experience."[125] The courts' *modus operandi* is the careful examination of the facts and the weighing of relevant policy considerations. Courts reach their conclusions by carefully selecting the applicable rules, determining

[122] Wu Ying-Chieh, "Contract Formation in Taiwan" in Mindy Chen-Wishart, Stefan Vogenauer, and Alexander Loke (eds.), *Studies in the Contract Laws of Asia II: Formation of Contract and Parties* (OUP 2018) 310, 325. In practice, a real estate agent will require the seller to fill out a form disclosing whether anyone has committed suicide or was killed on the property. Such property will usually be sold at a significant discount.

[123] Stapleton (n 22) 13.

[124] Ibid. 29.

[125] Oliver Wendell Holmes, *The Common Law* (Little, Brown and Company 1881) 1.

the applicable standard, and fashioning the appropriate remedial response. Common law courts will generally go no further than is necessary to decide the case before them. A notable example is *Royal Bank of Scotland v. Etridge* which allows a party to avoid a transaction induced by a vitiating factor attributable to a third party only in very narrow circumstances;[126] namely, (i) where a non-commercial party (typically a wife) is induced to guarantee the debts of the primary debtor (typically her husband or his company) by the latter's undue influence, misrepresentation, or duress, (ii) the lender knows that the guarantor acts in a non-commercial capacity and that the loan is for the debtor rather than the guarantor, and (iii) the lender has failed to take simple administrative steps (mainly insisting that the guarantor obtain independent legal advice). This is the result of the court's careful balancing of the policies involved. Against upholding the guarantee are the scope for abuse that the marriage relationship provides (where a husband who, desperate for finance, may unfairly induce his wife to act as his guarantor); and the avoidance of homelessness, with its attendant social problems especially for children. In favor of upholding the guarantee are concerns that the lender may not have behaved reprehensibly, that the wife may stand to benefit from any loan to her husband, and that such lending is socially and economically useful by unlocking the wealth tied up in the family home for commercial purposes; lenders will be *reluctant to lend* if they lack confidence in the enforceability of their security and such lending is vital to the economy.[127] Good faith is necessary, but it is not all that matters. English courts will proceed cautiously. This is the incrementalism of the common law; the "measured tortoise" marches in synch with its "characteristic methods."[128]

V. Good Faith: A Taxonomy

Humble good faith explains and legitimizes many disparate rules and doctrines of English contract law. A more detailed exposition of this claim will begin to address a key objection to good faith—its uncertainty. Our starting point is that the good faith attitude already manifests in existing rules, the application of which vary with the nature of the contractual relationship and the

[126] [2001] UKHL 44.

[127] Lord Nicholls points out that 95 percent of all businesses in the United Kingdom are small businesses responsible for about one-third of all employment and their most important source of finance is bank loans raised by second mortgages on the family home; ibid., [34].

[128] *Yam Seng* (n 4) [148].

interests of the parties. Consequently, "the legal norm should not be confused with the factual question of its satisfaction" in the particular circumstances.[129] As Steven Burton explains, ". . . [a]ll language, except some proper names, is abstract; we do not have separate words for each of the shapes that a snowflake may take."[130] It is through the aggregation of particular scenarios, and the consequent development of rules, that the abstract becomes concrete.

In sum, our proposed "humble good faith 3 x 4" requires contract parties to display an attitude of respect for:

(i) the legitimate interests of their contractual partners, expressed in requirements of (a) honesty and (b) fair dealing; and
(ii) the contract itself, expressed in a requirement of (c) fidelity to the contractual purpose.

The nature of the contractual relationship calibrates the *intensity* of the good faith attitude manifest in the requirements of (a), (b), and (c). We identify in Figure 8.1 four points along the spectrum of contractual relationships, namely:

(1) arm's length;
(2) symbiotic;
(3) entailing a recognized vulnerable party; or
(4) entailing a fiduciary relationship.

(1) Arm's length	"We each look after ourselves."
(2) Symbiotic	"The contract requires me to rely on you."
(3) Vulnerability	(i) "I have trust and confidence in you," or (ii) "Our bargaining power is markedly unequal."
(4) Fiduciary relationship	"You must look after my interests."

Figure 8.1 Types of contractual relationships

Broadly speaking, arm's length contracts (class (1)) attract a "base-level" or "core" of good faith requirements; this is nevertheless quite substantial, as we will see. Figure 8.2 below shows how this base-level is "topped up" with

[129] *Paciocco v. Australia and New Zealand Banking Group Ltd.* [2015] FCAFC 50, [290].
[130] Steven Burton, "Reply to Ewan McKendrick, 'Good Faith in the Performance of a Contract in English Law'" in Larry DiMatteo and Martin Hogg (eds.), *Comparative Contract Law: British and American Perspectives* (OUP 2016) 220, 222.

additional requirements calibrated to the nature of the relationship for the other three classes ((2), (3), and (4)).

An important caveat: our proposed taxonomy can only be a starting point; it is relatively coarse-grained; it provides no algorithmic certainty. Broad standards inevitably vest significant latitude in the courts to concretize their demands in quantitative terms depending on the particular facts; this is a matter of judgment and fine balancing of relevant considerations. Nevertheless, humble good faith is usefully understood along the lines of our proposed taxonomy below, although, inevitably, much further work can and shouldmbe done.

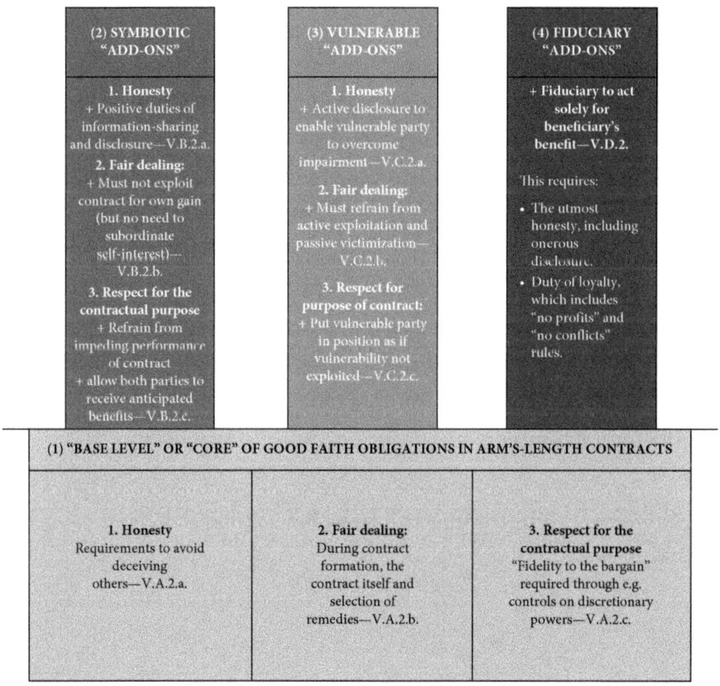

Figure 8.2 Taxonomizing good faith

A. Arm's Length Contracts

1. The Nature of the Relationship- "We each Look after Ourselves"

The paradigmatic arm's length contract is one which is: (i) individually negotiated, (ii) between commercial parties, (iii) discrete in the manner of a "hit-and-run" exchange where each party's performance is relatively instantaneous and independent of the other's, and (iv) "presentiated," in that all eventualities can be provided for.

Each of these factors is a matter of degree, with none being necessary or determinative, but the closer a contract comes to the paradigmatic case, the less intense is the good faith attitude required. Examples of arm's length contracts include commercial sales contracts,[131] commercial banking relationships,[132] the relationship between a company and its noteholders,[133] equipment leases,[134] and non-exclusive agency agreements.[135]

2. The Demands of Good Faith in Arm's Length Contracts

The body of rules that demonstrate respect for the other party and the contractual purpose, which manifest the good faith attitude, is substantial even for arm's length contracts. This is the basis of our claim that good faith is already implemented through and through English contract law. These demands may attach at contract formation, in determining the presence of vitiating factors, the contents and performance of contacts, or the available remedies for breach. They may be procedural or substantive in nature.

a. Honesty

Honesty has been described as the "core value"[136] and "minimum content" of good faith;[137] ". . . underlying the contractual arrangements of the parties there will be a common assumption that the persons involved will behave honestly."[138] Thus, for example:

- **Fraud** in negotiations renders a contract voidable, and liability for fraud cannot be exempted.[139]

[131] In *Yam Seng* (n 4) [143] Leggatt J. appeared to consider "simple exchanges" the antithesis of relational contracts.
[132] *Property Alliance Group Ltd. v. The Royal Bank of Scotland plc* [2016] EWHC 3342, (Ch.), [250] "sophisticated commercial parties" were negotiating standard banking documentation.
[133] *Myers v. Kestrel Acquisitions Ltd.* [2015] EWHC 916 (Ch.), [62].
[134] *National Private Air Transport Services Co v. Windrose Aviation Co Ltd.* [2016] EWHC 2144 (Comm.), aircraft lease not a relational contract.
[135] *Acer Investment Management Ltd. v. The Mansion Group Ltd.* [2014] EWHC 3011 (QB).
[136] *Yam Seng* (n 4), [141].
[137] See, e.g., Ewan McKendrick, "Good Faith in the Performance of the Contract in English Law" in Larry DiMatteo and Martin Hogg, *Comparative Contract Law: British and American Perspectives* (OUP 2016) 196, 203.
[138] *HIH Casualty and General Insurance Ltd. v. Chase Manhattan Bank* [2003] UKHL 6, [68] (Lord Hoffmann).
[139] *S Pearson & Son Ltd. v. Dublin Corp* [1907] AC 351.

- A party (*X*) is prevented from enforcing a contract that she enters **knowing the counterparty (*Y*) did not intend to contract on the ostensible terms (i.e.** was "mistaken as to its terms").[140] Further, if the mistake results in benefit to *X* or detriment to *Y* and *X* failed to draw *Y*'s attention to it, or made "false and misleading statements" to prevent *Y* from discovering the mistake, the contract may be rectified to *Y*'s intention.[141]
- Where the parties' common intention, up to contract execution, was mistakenly recorded in the contract, **rectification** is available.[142]

However, duties of disclosure are not generally imposed at formation or performance; the parties must look after themselves. No duty of disclosure during performance is likely to be implied into a simple exchange.[143]

b. Fair dealing

The good faith attitude of respect for the counterparty requires each party to deal fairly with the other. This is expressed through numerous rules in English law. For example, at formation:

- Contracts induced by ***non*-fraudulent misrepresentations** are voidable, and damages are available for qualifying misrepresentations.[144] There is a **duty to correct** statements that are subsequently falsified.[145]
- Contracts induced by illegitimate pressure (under the rubric of **duress**) are voidable.
- Fair dealing is one explanation for the **objective test of intentions**, which protects contract parties' reasonable reliance and the institution of contract.[146]
- A party's inertia cannot be exploited to bind her to a contract; hence **silence** generally cannot amount to acceptance of an offer.[147]
- Courts lean heavily toward curing contractual **uncertainty and incompleteness** once parties have commenced performance.[148]

140 *Smith v. Hughes* (1870-71) LR 6 QB 597; *Hartog v. Colin & Shields* [1939] 3 All ER 566.

141 *Commission for the New Towns v. Cooper* [1995] Ch. 259; *Thomas Bates & Sons Ltd. v. Wyndham's (Lingerie) Ltd.* [1981] 1 WLR 505.

142 *Chartbrook Ltd. v. Persimmon Homes* [2009] UKHL 38; *FSHC Group Holdings Ltd. v. GLAS Trust Corporation Ltd.* [2019] EWCA Civ. 1361, [142] Leggatt LJ recognized this as being "based on an equitable principle of good faith."

143 *Yam Seng* (n 4) [143].

144 Misrepresentation Act 1969.

145 *With v. O'Flanagan* [1936] Ch. 575; *Spice Girls Ltd. v. Aprilia World Services BV* [2002] EWCA Civ. 15.

146 Raz (n 50) 936.

147 *Felthouse v. Bindley* (1862) 6 LT 157.

148 *WN Hillas & Co. Ltd. v. Arcos Ltd.* (1932) 43 Ll. L. Rep. 359.

- Reasonable notice is required to incorporate terms in unsigned documents that purport to be part of the contract; the more **onerous or unusual the terms**, the greater the notice required.[149]

Fair dealing is required even when no contract eventuates. Thus, where one party has made promises, engendered reasonable expectations or reliance, or has been unjustly enriched at the other party's expense, the court may impose various forms of **estoppel** (promissory, proprietary, and estoppel by convention), find a constructive **trust**, or order restitution for **unjust enrichment**.[150]

In the **interpretation** of contracts, ambiguous terms are construed against the party who introduced them (*contra proferentem*). Lord Hoffmann conceded that, ". . . [W]hen judges say that 'in the absence of clear words' they would be unwilling to construe a document to mean something, they generally mean . . . that the effect of the document is unfair."[151]

Fair dealing is also manifest after contract formation, most obviously when significant changes in circumstances **frustrate** the contract or when the doctrine of **promissory estoppel** prevents a party from resiling from its promise to relieve the counterparty of some contractual obligation.

Fair dealing is clearly evident in the restrictions on the availability of certain remedies for breach, for example:

- the **bars to specific enforcement** where:
  - the claimant lacks "clean hands,"[152] gave inadequate or no consideration,[153] or delayed unduly in making the claim;[154] or
  - performance would be impossible for,[155] unduly harsh to,[156] or require the personal services of the contract-breaker;[157]
- the bar on **affirmation** of the contract where the aggrieved party requires the contract-breaker's cooperation or has no "legitimate interest";[158]

149 The "red hand rule" in *J. Spurling Ltd. v. Bradshaw* [1956] EWCA Civ. 3.

150 *Chitty* (n 24) paras. 2-211–14, 4-109 et seq., 5-042–44.

151 *BCCI v. Ali* [2001] UKHL 8, [61].

152 e.g., *Shell UK Ltd. v. Lostock Garage Ltd.* [1976] 1 WLR 1187; *Quadrant Visual Communications Ltd. v. Hutchinson Telephone (UK) Ltd.* [1993] BCLC 442.

153 Although generally not sufficient unless accompanied by some other inequitable behavior (which does not, however, have to amount to fraud); Chitty (n 24) para. 27-051.

154 *Mills v. Haywood* (1877) 6 Ch. D. 196; *P&O Nedlloyd BV v. Arab Metals Co., The UB Tiger* [2006] EWCA Civ. 1717.

155 *Forrer v. Nash (1865) 35 Beav.* 167, 171; "the court does not compel a person to do what is impossible".

156 *Patel v. Ali* [1984] Ch. 238.

157 *Cooperative Insurance Society Ltd. v. Argyll Stores Holdings Ltd.* [1997] UKHL 17; *De Francesco v. Barnum* (1890) 45 Ch. D. 430.

158 *White and Carter (Councils) Ltd. v. McGregor* [1962] UKHL 5.

- the bar on claiming the **cost of cure** if it disproportionately exceeds the claimant's loss;[159]
- the bar on **termination** of the contract unless the breach is of a condition in the legal sense,[160] or the breach of an innominate (intermediate) term substantially deprives the aggrieved party of substantially the whole of the expected benefit;[161]
- the requirement that the claimant **mitigate** her loss[162] and the bar on claiming loss that is unforeseeable and so too **remote**[163] or to which she has **negligently contributed**,[164] the restrictions on **agreed remedies clauses**, such as the unenforceability of agreed specific performance clauses,[165] the reading down of agreed termination clauses,[166] the prohibition of penalties,[167] and the restrictions on limitations or exclusions of liability.[168]

c. Fidelity to the contractual purpose

The good faith attitude requires "fidelity to the parties' bargain"[169] or "faithfulness to the agreed common purpose."[170] Even in arm's length contracts, this imposes numerous demands. For example:

- A **discretionary power** conferred by the contract to make decisions affecting the counterparty is limited by "concepts of honesty, good faith and genuineness, and the need for the absence of arbitrariness, capriciousness, perversity and irrationality."[171]
- The court may impose liability for **collateral terms** where one party relies on the other's assurances during negotiations: ". . . the oral promise or representation has a decisive influence on the transaction—it is the very

[159] *Ruxley Electronics and Construction Ltd. v. Forsyth* [1995] UKHL 8

[160] *L Schuler AG v. Wickman Machine Tool Sales Ltd.* [1973] UKHL 2.

[161] *Hong Kong Fir Shipping Co Ltd. v. Kawasaki Kisen Kaisha Ltd.* [1962] 2 QB 26.

[162] Chitty (n 24) paras. 26-087 et seq.

[163] *Hadley v. Baxendale* [1854] 9 Exch. 341; *Victoria Laundry (Windsor) Ltd. v. Newman Industries Ltd.* [1949] 2 KB 528; *Czarnikow Ltd. v. Koufous (The Heron II)* [1967] UKHL 4.

[164] If there is a concurrent tortious duty of care and damages are reducible under the Law Reform (Contributory Negligence) Act 1945 or the contributory negligence may break the chain of causation.

[165] Since it is an equitable remedy and at the discretion of the courts.

[166] *Rice v. Great Yarmouth Borough Council* [2003] TCLR 1.

[167] *Dunlop Pneumatic Tyre Co. Ltd. v. New Garage & Motor Co. Ltd.* [1914] UKHL 1, as reconsidered in *Cavendish Square Holdings BV v. Talal El Makdessi* [2015] UKSC 67.

[168] UCTA 1977, ss. 2, 3, 6, 7.

[169] *Yam Seng* (n 4) [139]; *New Balance Athletics v. Liverpool Football Club and Athletics Ground* [2019] EWHC 2837 (Comm.), [44].

[170] *Berkeley Community Villages Ltd. v. Pullen* 2007] EWHC 1330, [110].

[171] *Socimer International Bank v. Standard Bank London* [2008] EWCA Civ. 116, [66]; *Watson, Hersov and Moore v. Watchfinder.co.uk Ltd.* [2017] EWHC 1275 (Comm.).

thing which induces the other to contract—and it would be most unjust to allow the maker to go back on it."[172]

- Terms will be **implied-in-fact** if *necessary,* to give business efficacy to the contract[173] or if so obvious they go without saying.[174] Thus, "there will generally be an implied term not to do anything to frustrate the purpose of the contract."[175]
- terms **implied-in-law** specify the "minimum kit" for certain types of contracts; ". . . the existence and scope of standardised implied terms raise questions of reasonableness, fairness and the balancing of competing policy considerations."[176]
- **UCTA 1977** protects commercial parties who contract on the counterparty's standard terms from exclusions or limitations of liability (widely cast to include terms that give the counterparty the discretion to give no, partial, or substantially different performance from that reasonably expected by the protected party)[177] unless such exemptions are fair and reasonable.
- The **frustration** doctrine will discharge a contract when its purpose is impossible to achieve due to change of circumstances.[178]

All of the above make concrete the base-line obligations of good faith; they apply to *every* contract, including arm's length contracts. The following three categories of contracts attract a greater intensity of the good faith attitude manifest in distinct rules.

B. Symbiotic Contracts

1. The Nature of the Contract—"The Contract Requires me to Rely on you"

In contrast to the relative independence of parties to arm's length contracts, "symbiotic" contracts are characterized by the parties' *interdependence in achieving the contractual purpose.* Such contracts have been described as

[172] *Mendelssohn v. Normand Ltd.* [1970] 1 QB 177, 184.
[173] *The Moorcock* (1889) 14 PD 64.
[174] *Shirlaw v. Southern Foundries (1926) Ltd.* [1940] AC 701.
[175] *Hamsard 3147 Ltd. v. Boots UK Ltd.* [2013] EWHC 3251, [86].
[176] *Crossley v. Faithful & Gould Holdings* [2004] EWCA Civ. 293, [36] (Dyson LJ). e.g., Sale of Goods Act 1979, ss. 12–15 and UCTA 1977, s. 6, imply certain terms relating to title, description, and quality into all contracts for the sale of goods, including arm's length contracts, to protect the buyers' reasonable expectation.
[177] UCTA 1977, s. 3(2)(b).
[178] *Krell v. Henry* [1903] 2 KB 740.

"relational,"[179] since they are said to involve "not merely an exchange, but also a relationship between the contracting parties."[180] This terminology has been heavily and rightly criticized. Since all contracts establish relationships,[181] denoting a sub-category as "relational" does not explain why the good faith attitude is intensified. Recent cases have downplayed the importance of the concept of a "relational" contract. [182] We prefer the terminology of "symbiotic" to describe the paradigmatic contract that:

(i) is interdependent, in that it *necessitates* trust and confidence by one party in the other (if not by each in the other) in order to achieve the joint contractual purpose and so generates a justified expectation of "loyalty," "integrity," ongoing communication,[183] and cooperation[184] from the trusted party;[185] and
(ii) is not or cannot be "fully presentiated,"[186] so that adjustments may be required to accommodate ongoing changes in circumstances.

[179] This term was first used by Professor Ian Macneil in developing "Relational Contract Theory", a norms-based approach to contract law; see Ian Macneil, "Contracts: Adjustment of Long-Term Economic Relations under Classical, Neoclassical and Relational Contract Law" (1977–1978) 72 NWULR 854; Ian Macneil, "Relational Contract Theory as Sociology: A Reply to Professors Lindenberg and de Vos" (1987) 143 J. Institutional and Theoretical Economics 272, 276–77, where he calls them "intertwined" contracts.

[180] Melvin Eisenberg, "Relational Contracts" in Jack Beatson and Daniel Friedmann (eds.), *Good Faith and Fault in Contract Law* (OUP 1995) 291, 296.

[181] In the Australian case of *Barker v. Commonwealth Bank* [2014] HCA Trans. 73, the concept was criticized since it "advances the analysis not at all, not merely only a little way, but not at all. All contracts create a relation between the parties to it."

[182] See e.g. *UTB LLC v. Sheffield United Ltd.* [2019] EWHC 2322 (Ch.), [201]–[204]; *TAQA Bratani Ltd. and Others v. RockRose UKCS 8 LLC* [2020] EWHC 58 (Comm.), [56]; *Russell v. Cartwright* [2020] EWHC 41 (Ch.), [87], *Cathay Pacific Airlines Ltd v. Lufthansa Technik AG* [2020] EWHC 1789 (Ch.), [218]–[219]; and see David Campbell, "*Arcos v Ronaasen* as a Relational Contract" in David Campbell, Linda Mulcahy, and Sally Wheeler (eds.), *Changing Concepts of Contract: Essays in Honour of Ian Macneil* (Palgrave Macmillan 2013) 138, 138–41.

[183] *Yam Seng* (n 4) [142].

[184] Ibid.; *Bates v. Post Office (No. 3: Common Issues)* [2019] EWHC 606 (QB), [725] (the parties will be "committed to collaborating with one another"). Practically no cooperation being required militated against a relational contract in *National Private Air Transport Services Co v. Windrose Aviation Co* [2016] EWHC 2144 (Comm.).

[185] *Yam Seng* (n 4) [142]; *Al Nehayan v. Kent* [2018] EWHC 333 (Comm.), [167] relational contracts "involve trust and confidence . . . that the other party will act with integrity and in a spirit of cooperation"; *Bates v. Post Office (No. 3: Common Issues)* [2019] EWHC 606 (QB), [725] the parties must intend contractual performance "with integrity, and with fidelity to their bargain."

[186] *Al Nehayan v. Kent* [2018] EWHC 333 (Comm.). At [167], Leggatt LJ described the parties as being committed to collaborating with each other "in ways which respect the spirit and objectives of their venture but which they have not tried to specify, and which it may be impossible to specify, exhaustively in a written contract"; at [143] referencing contracts where the parties' relationship is not "legislated for in the express terms of the contract". In *Bates v. Post Office (No. 3: Common Issues)* [2019] EWHC 606 (QB), [725], referencing cases where "the 'spirits and objectives' of their venture may not be capable of being expressed exhaustively in a written contract"; *Cathay Pacific Airlines Ltd. v. Lufthansa Technik AG* [2020] EWHC 1789 (Ch.), [201]: referring to contracts where "they have not specified (or have been unable to specify) in detail the terms governing their relationship."

Such contracts are often said to be of longer duration[187] and to require "substantial commitment" from the parties.[188] However, these terms may equally describe arm's length contracts and are not especially distinctive of symbiotic contracts. Moreover, the type of contract or "label" given by the parties to the contract is not determinative. It was suggested in *Yam Seng* that joint venture agreements, franchise agreements, and long-term distributorship agreements might be examples of such contracts.[189] However, whether a contract is symbiotic depends on the extent to which it necessitates cooperation to achieve the joint contractual purpose, so that a more intensive good faith attitude is necessary to give the contract "business efficacy."[190] Symbiotic contracts simply would not make sense if the parties could treat each other as if they were at arm's length. Collins notes that the "key variable" of such contracts is their "incentive structure."[191] They are not a "zero sum game" where both parties seek to maximize their advantage at the cost of the other. Rather, the parties must repose trust in each other to *maximize* the intended benefits for *both* parties. In *Yam Seng*, Leggatt J. located this category between "fiduciary relationships containing onerous disclosure obligations, and other contractual relationships where there was supposedly no duty of disclosure."[192] The concept is illustrated by the following cases:

- In *Yam Seng* itself, the claimant invested significant resources, incurred significant costs, and put its reputation on the line in reliance on the defendant to perform its part of their distributorship arrangements. In

[187] *Yam Seng* (n 4) [143]; also *Al Nehayan v. Kent*, [2018] EWHC 333 (Comm.), [173], where Leggatt LJ found a "relational" contract in a "long-term collaboration". Fraser J. identified length (or at least intended length) as a factor in his list of "indicators" in *Bates v. Post Office (No. 3: Common Issues)* [2019] EWHC 606 (QB), [725]. In *Amey Birmingham Highways Ltd. v. Birmingham City Council* [2018] EWCA Civ. 264, [92], Jackson LJ suggested a contract length of 25 years rendered a contract "relational". Likewise a private finance initiative contract of the same length was described as the "paradigm example of a relational contract" in *Essex County Council v. UBB Waste (Essex) Ltd.* [2020] EWHC 1581 (TCC), [113]. However, contracts are not "relational" just because long-term; the following were not relational contracts: *National Private Air Transport Services Co. v. Windrose Aviation Co.* [2016] EWHC 2144 (Comm.) (aircraft lease); *Carewatch Care Services Ltd. v. Focus Caring Services Ltd. and Grace* [2014] EWHC 2313 (Ch.) (long-term non-exclusive agency agreement); *Cathay Pacific Airlines Ltd. v. Lufthansa Technik AG* [2020] EWHC 1789 (Ch.) (long-term aircraft maintenance contract).

[188] *Yam Seng* (n 4) [143]; *Bates v. Post Office (No. 3: Common Issues)* [2019] EWHC 606 (QB), [725]: There may be a "substantial financial commitment" by one party (or both) or "exclusivity of the relationship." Contra *Hamsard 3147 v. Boots UK Ltd.* [2013] EWHC 3251 (Pat.), a supply contract where arrangements were short-term and interim with no obligation to order stock; *Acer Investment Management Ltd. v. Mansion Group Ltd.* [2014] EWHC 3011 (QB), [109], where neither party saw the contract as exclusive or was "required to spend significant sums".

[189] *Yam Seng* (n 4) [142].

[190] Ibid.

[191] Collins (n 104) 326–27, calling them "quasi-integrated production networks."

[192] *Yam Seng* (n 4) [143].

return, it was entitled to honesty, effective communication, and cooperation from the defendant.[193]

- In *Bristol Groundschool Ltd. v. Intelligent Data Capture Ltd.*,[194] the parties' collaboration required the defendant to give the claimant access to its IT systems. This imposed an implied duty on the claimant not to abuse it by using its access to obtain confidential information for its own purposes.
- In *Al Nehayan v. Kent*,[195] the parties' business interests were interlinked, they saw themselves commercially if not legally as partners and their business relationship was "formed and conducted on the basis of a personal friendship and involved much greater mutual trust than is inherent in an ordinary contractual bargain between shareholders."[196] These factors precluded covert negotiations by one party to dispose of its interest or exploitation of its shareholder position to obtain a financial benefit for itself at the other's expense.[197]

Since good faith is an attitude that is constitutive of the contract itself, any suggestion that the parties can expressly exclude a good faith duty is misconceived.[198] The better view is that an express exclusion of good faith (which would seem an extraordinary thing to agree) *may*, in combination with other factors, point to the true nature of the contract and so indicate the appropriate intensity of the good faith attitude required. For example, in a distributorship agreement where the degree of the parties' necessary reliance on, and commitment toward, each other is limited,[199] an express exclusion of good faith may "tip" the contract into the arm's length category attracting a lesser intensity of good faith. However, where a contract *necessitates* the reposing of trust and confidence by the parties in each other, without which the contract is incapable of proper performance, excluding good faith or specifying that a contract is not "relational" cannot change its essential nature as symbiotic in nature. Just as the additional protection offered to certain parties recognized as vulnerable (category (3) discussed below) cannot be excluded by re-categorizing the relationship,[200] neither should it be possible to exclude the "add-on" obligations

[193] *Yam Seng* (n 4) [142], [143].
[194] [2014] EWHC 2145 (Ch.).
[195] [2018] EWHC 333 (Comm.).
[196] Ibid. [173].
[197] Ibid. [176].
[198] e.g., *Bates v. Post Office Ltd. (No. 3: Common Issues)* [2019] EWHC 606 (QB), [725].
[199] e.g., in *Acer Investment Management Ltd. v. Mansion Group Ltd.* [2014] EWHC 3011 (QB), the distributorship agreement in question was arm's length due to a lack of exclusivity and required commitment.
[200] See section V.C below; e.g. "Employees" and "workers," receive far greater legal protection than independent contractors. What is critical in determining an individual's status is the substance of the

appropriate to symbiotic contracts. If the parties must rely on each other in order to achieve the contractual purpose, then the resultant obligations which express the good faith attitude should not be capable of exclusion.

2. The Demands of Good Faith in Symbiotic Contracts

a. *Honesty*

The honesty requirement in symbiotic contracts may go beyond refraining from outright lies or misinformation.[201] An affirmative obligation of information sharing and disclosure may be implied as necessary for the proper performance of the contract.[202] Had it been argued, Leggatt J. said in *Yam Seng* that he would have been prepared to find some "positive obligations of disclosure" in the distributorship agreement, as the distributor was entitled to expect to be kept informed of when products were likely to be available and told of material changes "without having to ask."[203] In *Bates v. Post Office*, Fraser J. refers to the requirement of "transparency."[204]

b. *Fair dealing*

For symbiotic contracts, the fair dealing requirements are intensified. The parties must observe "standards of commercial dealing . . . so generally accepted that the contracting parties would reasonably be understood to take them as read without explicitly stating them . . ."[205] This requires "integrity,"[206] precludes "commercially unacceptable" conduct[207] and obliges the parties to "observe reasonable commercial standards of fair dealing."[208] A party who exploits the contractual relationship in a way that would be regarded as "commercially unacceptable by reasonable and honest people"[209] would breach her obligations.

An example is secretly downloading confidential information belonging to the other party for one's own purposes when access had been granted

relationship or "true agreement," not the parties' label, (cf. *Autoclenz v. Belcher* [2011] UKSC 41, [29]). The same applies to the label "consumer" for the purposes of consumer protection legislation.

201 *Yam Seng* (n 4) [142].
202 Ibid. [143]. Also *Horn v. Commercial Acceptances Ltd.* [2011] EWHC 1757, [67], where an express good faith clause imported an obligation to disclose of "all material facts".
203 *Yam Seng* (n 4) [144].
204 *Bates v. Post Office (No. 3: Common Issues)* [2019] EWHC 606 (QB), [738].
205 *Yam Seng* (n 4) [138].
206 *D&G Cars v. Essex Police Authority* [2015] EWHC 226 (QB), [175].
207 *Bristol Groundschool Ltd. v. Intelligent Data Capture Ltd.* [2014] EWHC 2145 (Ch.), [196]; *Essex County Council v. UBB Waste (Essex) Ltd.* [2020] EWHC 1581 (TCC), [116].
208 *Berkeley Community Villages Ltd. v. Pullen* [2007] EWHC 1330 (Ch.), [88].
209 *Bristol Groundschool Ltd. v. Intelligent Data Capture Ltd.* [2014] EWHC 2145 (Ch.), [196]; *New Balance Athletics v. Liverpool Football Club and Athletics Ground* [2019] EWHC 2837 (Comm.), [44].

specifically to facilitate contractual performance.[210] It may also be a breach for either party to a joint venture to "use his position as a shareholder of the companies to obtain a financing benefit for himself at the expense of the other."[211] In *Al Nehayan v. Kent*,[212] the court considered the conduct of one party in a joint venture in agreeing or entering into negotiations to sell her interest to a third party covertly and without informing the other party as "furtive or opportunistic conduct" inconsistent with good faith.

Beyond the requirement of fair dealing, parties need not prefer their counterparties' interests over their own;[213] "no party is fixed with the duty to subordinate self-interest which is the lot of the fiduciary"[214] and good faith "does not require either party to give up a freely negotiated financial advantage embedded in the contract."[215] Unlike fiduciary relationships (discussed at V.D below), which require the fiduciary loyally to subordinate her own interests, the trust in symbiotic contracts "is trust that the other party will act with integrity and in a spirit of cooperation."[216]

c. Fidelity to the contractual purpose

Fidelity to the contractual purpose in symbiotic contracts requires the parties to "act in a way that will allow both parties to enjoy the anticipated benefits of the contract."[217] Much will depend on the precise facts. Thus, in a distributorship agreement for products to be sold at an airport duty free shop, a term was implied in fact that the defendant would not prejudice the claimant's sales by offering the same products for sale within the same territories at a lower price than the claimant was allowed to offer.[218] A contract between a property developer and landowner to maximize the development potential of certain land was held to prevent the landowner from selling or disposing of it so as to prevent the developer from performing its obligations.[219]

210 As occurred in *Bristol Groundschool*, ibid.

211 *Yam Seng* (n 4) [176].

212 [2018] EWHC 333 (Comm.), [176].

213 *Hamsard 3147 Ltd. v. Boots UK Ltd.* [2013] EWHC 3251. Norris J. was skeptical, [86] that "there is to be routinely implied some positive obligation upon a contracting party to subordinate its own commercial interests to those of the other contracting party".

214 *CPC Group Ltd. v. Qatari Diar Real Estate* [2010] EWHC 1535 (Ch.), [67].

215 *Gold Group Properties v. BDW Trading Ltd. (formerly Barratt Homes Ltd.)* [2010] EWHC 1632 (TCC), [91]; *Essex County Council v. UBB Waste (Essex) Ltd.* [2020] EWHC 1581 (TCC), [194]; *Russell v. Cartwright* [2020] EWHC 41 (Ch.), [98].

216 *Al Nehayan v.* Kent [2018] EWHC 333 (Comm.), [167] (Leggatt LJ).

217 *Gold Group Properties Ltd. v. BDW Trading Ltd.* [2010] EWHC 1632 (TCC), [91].

218 *Yam Seng* (n 4) [161]–[165].

219 *Berkeley Community Villages Ltd. v. Pullen* [2007] EWHC 1330 (Ch.), where an express good faith clause was included. It should make no difference absent such a clause.

C. Recognized Vulnerability of One Party

1. The Nature of the Contract "I Have Trust and Confidence in you" or "I Have Markedly Inferior Bargaining Power to you"

In this category, one party is recognized in law as being particularly vulnerable to the other's advantage-taking (albeit by lawful conduct). Her vulnerability may stem from her:

(i) *relationship with the counterparty*—Where one party (*X*) vests trust, confidence, reliance, affection, or commitment in the counterparty (*Y*), *X* is likely to have her guard down and so be vulnerable to *Y*'s exploitation.[220] Thus, ". . . where someone relies on the guidance or advice of another, where the other is aware of that reliance and where the person upon whom reliance is placed obtains, or may well obtain, a benefit from the transaction or has some other interest in it being concluded,"[221] the doctrine of **undue influence** can avoid the contract. Parties in some sorts of relationships attract heightened protection.[222]

(ii) *recognized unequal bargaining power*—This may arise from a party's:
  (a) *membership of a protected class*—for example, **consumers**, **employees**, **tenants**, and **non-commercial guarantors** attract special protection to counter their inferior bargaining power vis-à-vis traders, employers, landlords, and commercial lenders respectively; or
  (b) *mental impairment*—such as **infancy**, **mental incapacity**, **drink**, or **drugs** or other personal bargaining impairment required to establish an **unconscionable bargain.**[223]

In symbiotic contracts, it is the nature of the contract that necessitates a party's reliance on the counterparty to achieve the contractual purpose. Here, vulnerable parties in category (i) rely because of their relationship of trust and confidence with the counterparty. This relationship entitles them to expect a degree of care, rather than exploitation, from the counterparty. The good faith attitude

[220] e.g., between husband and wife (*BCCI v. Aboody* [1990] 1 QB 923), great-uncle and great-nephew (*Cheese v. Thomas* [1994] 1 WLR 129), an elderly man and his housekeeper (*Re Craig* [1971] Ch. 95), a pop singer and his manager (*O'Sullivan v. Management Agency and Music Ltd.* [1985] QB 428), and a junior employee and her employer (*Credit Lyonnais Bank Nederland NV* v. *Burch* [1997] 1 All ER 144).

[221] *Lloyds Bank Ltd. v. Bundy* [1975] QB 326, 341 (Sir Eric Sachs).

[222] E.g., between doctor and patient, parent and child, guardian and ward, and religious adviser and follower; "[T]he law has adopted a sternly protective attitude towards certain types of relationship"; *Royal Bank of Scotland v. Etridge (No. 2)* [2002] UKHL 44, [18].

[223] e.g., *Evans v. Llewellin* (1787) 1 Cox's Chancery Cases 333, 340; *Fry v. Lane* (1888) 40 Ch. D. 312, 323; *Credit Lyonnais Bank Nederland NV v. Burch* [1997] 1 All ER 144.

is calibrated accordingly. In category (ii) contracts, good faith requirements are imposed as a result of policy choices by Parliament or the courts. There is no investigation of the parties' actual bargaining power; membership of the relevant vulnerable class is enough. Finally, the unconscionable bargains doctrine will not permit the activity of contracting to be used to exploit those suffering cognitive impairments short of incapacity in order to obtain a contractual advantage that "shocks the conscience of the court."[224]

2. The Demands of Good Faith where one Party has a Recognized Vulnerability

a. Honesty

Here, the requirement of honesty may go beyond refraining from dishonesty to require *affirmative disclosures* at formation. For example:

- Part of the case for an **unconscionable bargain** is that the benefitting counterparty failed to inform the protected party of the disadvantageous nature of the contract for the protected party.[225]
- In the **consumer** context, a very long list of information[226] must be provided to the consumer (which is then treated as terms of the contract) to bind the consumer to the contract. Consumers can also seek redress where misleading[227] or aggressive practices by businesses have caused them to enter the contract or pay for goods, services, or digital content. The scope of "misleading actions" is broad,[228] including: any presentation that in any way deceives or is likely to deceive the average consumer, even if the information is factually correct; any marketing of a product which creates confusion with any products, trademarks, trade names, or other distinguishing marks of a competitor; and any failure by a trader to comply with a commitment contained in a code of conduct with which the trader has undertaken to comply.
- In **employment** contracts, employers may in some circumstances have a duty to inform employees of their rights.[229]

[224] e.g., *The Libyan Investment Authority v. Goldman Sachs International* [2016] EWHC 2530 (Ch.), [161].

[225] e.g., *Evans v. Llewellin* (1787) 1 Cox's Chancery Cases 333, 340; *Fry v. Lane* (1888) 40 Ch. D. 312, 323; *Credit Lyonnais Bank Nederland NV v. Burch* [1997] 1 All ER 144.

[226] Consumer Contracts (Information, Cancellation and Additional Charges) Regulations 2013, ch. 1 and Sch. 1 for on-premises contracts, 2 for distance and off-premises contracts, and 3 for information on exercising the right to cancel.

[227] See the Consumer Protection from Unfair Trading Regulations 2008, Part 4A. But there is no claim for a misleading omission.

[228] Consumer Protection from Unfair Trading Regulations 2008, Reg. 5.

[229] e.g., *Scally v. Southern Health Board* [1992] 1 AC 294.

- Insurance contracts are traditionally classed as a **contracts *uberrimae fidei*** (of the utmost good faith) because knowledge of material facts lies with one party, who must therefore make full disclosure to the other party.[230]

b. Fair dealing

Here, a party must refrain from active exploitation of the vulnerable party to obtain a contractual advantage, even if the conduct is lawful per se. Examples include cases of **actual undue influence,**[231] **unconscionable bargains** involving active unconscionable conduct,[232] and the Consumer Protection from Unfair Trading Regulations 2008, which protect consumers from **aggressive commercial practices,** defined broadly.[233]

Fair dealing may also require a party to refrain from "passive victimisation";[234] this may translate into a requirement to take positive steps to ensure that someone "up to the job" protects the vulnerable party (hence the preoccupation with independent advice in the doctrines of **undue influence, unconscionable bargains,** and in respect of **non-commercial guarantees**). In some circumstances, it may not be enough simply to advise the vulnerable party to obtain independent advice. The counterparty may have to ensure that advice is *sought*, *received*, *adequate* in a demanding sense,[235] and, perhaps, even have in fact *saved* the vulnerable party from the catastrophic contract.[236]

Fair dealing in the case of **infancy** translates into protection from substantive unfairness. Thus, infants need only pay a reasonable price for necessaries received.[237] Contracts that are generally beneficial to the infant are presumptively valid unless set aside by the infant.[238] All other contracts are unenforceable against the infant unless she ratifies them on reaching adulthood.[239]

[230] *Carter v. Boehm* (1766) 3 Burr 1905, although the duty has been softened to take account of the consumer-insured's weaker bargaining power, see the Consumer (Disclosure and Representations) Act 2012, s. 2(4) (for consumer insurance contracts), and the Insurance Act 2015, ss. 3(1) and 14(1) (for non-consumer insurance contracts).

[231] e.g., *Langton v. Langton* [1995] 3 FCR 521; *Drew v. Daniel* [2005] EWCA Civ. 507.

[232] e.g., taking the initiative in the transaction, haste in concluding it, contributing to a misapprehension without creating it, and low-level pressure on the complainant to agree.

[233] See Consumer Protection from Unfair Trading Regulations 2008, Reg. 7 in particular.

[234] *Cresswell v. Potter* [1975] 1 WLR 255.

[235] *Inche Noriah v. Shaik Allie Bin Amar* (1929) AC 127.

[236] e.g., *Credit Lyonnais Bank Nederland NV v. Burch* [1997] 1 All ER 144. See Mindy Chen-Wishart, "The *O'Brien* Principle and Substantive Unfairness" (1997) 56 Cambridge Law Journal 60.

[237] Mental Capacity Act 2005, s. 7 (adults); *Peters v. Fleming* (1840) 151 ER 314 (infants).

[238] These are contracts that enable the infant to earn a living or to obtain an education or training, and where the infant is acquiring an interest in the subject matter of a permanent nature to which continuing obligations are attached, so that it would be unjust to allow her to retain the interest without fulfilling the corresponding obligations.

[239] Chitty (n 24) paras. 9-007, 9-036 et seq.

c. Fidelity to the contract

Where there is a relationship of vulnerability, fidelity to the contractual purpose translates into requirements aimed at ensuring that the vulnerable party's reasonable expectations are protected.

For example:

In **consumer** contracts:

- certain non-excludable[240] statutory rights are conferred on consumers in respect of the sale or supply of goods, services, or digital content;[241]
- unfair terms other than price or main subject matter can be set aside by reference to their fairness.[242] The court is under a duty to consider the issue of fairness, even if neither party raises it.[243] Schedule 2, Part 1 of the CRA sets out a list of 20 indicatively unfair terms that broadly red-light: (i) terms that defeat the consumer's reasonable expectations,[244] (ii) terms that reduce the consumer's redress on the trader's breach,[245] and (iii) terms that impose unreasonable burdens on the consumer in performance or on breach;[246]
- the court implies a term in consumer credit contracts that the lender's contractual power to vary the interest rate in its absolute discretion cannot be exercised dishonestly, for an improper purpose, capriciously, arbitrarily, or in a way in which no reasonable lender, acting reasonably, would do.[247]

In **employment** contracts:

- certain statutory rights are conferred on employees, including rights to guaranteed payment,[248] protection against unlawful deduction of wages,[249] paid time off for antenatal care,[250] a minimum notice period,[251] and not to be unfairly dismissed.[252] The parties cannot exclude these rights by agreement;[253]

[240] CRA 2015, ss. 47 and 57.
[241] CRA 2015, Part I, s. 31(1).
[242] CRA 2015, Part II, s. 62(4).
[243] CRA 2015, s. 71, but only "if the court considers that it has before it sufficient legal and factual material to enable it to consider the fairness of the term."
[244] e.g., paras. 7, 10–13, and 16.
[245] Paras. 1, 2, 18, and 19.
[246] Paras. 4–6, 9, 14, and 15.
[247] *Paragon Finance plc v. Nash* [2001] EWCA Civ. 1466.
[248] Employment Rights Act (ERA) 1996, Part III.
[249] ERA 1996, Part II
[250] ERA 1996, ss. 55–56
[251] ERA 1996, s. 86.
[252] ERA 1996, ss. 94, 98.
[253] ERA 1996, s. 203(1). See also the National Minimum Wage Act 1998, s. 1, the Working Time Regulations 1998, Regs. 4, 12, and 13.

- a higher standard of rationality is required of an employer in exercising a discretionary contractual power since the employer must comply with the implied obligation of trust and confidence toward the employee.[254]

In **tenancy** contracts, legislation imposes various obligations on landlords,[255] including maintenance obligations,[256] and protects tenants from illegal eviction.[257]

D. Fiduciary Relationships

1. The Nature of the Contract—"You Must Look after my Interest."

Fiduciary relationships exist where one party ". . . has undertaken to act for or on behalf of another in a particular matter in circumstances which give rise to a relationship of trust and confidence."[258] Usually this will be in relation to another's "property or affairs."[259] Broadly, the courts have recognized two categories of fiduciary relationships; status-based and fact-based. The former are fairly well established.[260] The latter, a fact-based fiduciary relationship, requires the assumption of the obligation of loyalty by one party toward the other, or by the parties toward each other, on the specific facts of the case, and in particular, that the fiduciary acts on behalf of the other party in some way.[261]

Prior to the recognition of symbiotic contracts as a distinct category (discussed in section V.B above), there was sometimes a temptation to shoehorn such contracts into the fiduciary category. For example, in *Button v. Phelps*,[262] where the judge contemplated whether to treat the parties' relationship as fiduciary since "all parties were agreeing to work together for a common aim" and they "cannot have envisaged that any one of them would be free to undermine the whole purpose of the venture," in this case, by promoting a rival bid.[263]

[254] *Braganza v. BP Shipping Ltd.* [2015] UKSC 17.
[255] e.g., Landlord and Tenant Acts 1985 and 1987.
[256] Landlord and Tenant Act 1985, s. 11.
[257] Protection from Eviction Act 1977.
[258] *Bristol & West Building Society v. Mothew* [1998] Ch. 1, 18.
[259] *White v. Jones* [1995] 2 WLR 187, 209.
[260] And include, e.g., the relationship between principal and agent, partner and co-partner, solicitor and client, mortgagee and mortgagor, and, of course, the paradigm example of trustee and beneficiary; see John McGhee, *Snell's Equity* (33rd ed., Sweet & Maxwell 2015) para. 7-004, on the settled categories of fiduciary relationship.
[261] In *Ross River v. Waveley Commercial* [2013] EWCA Civ. 910, a fiduciary relationship was found where one joint venture party relied on the other to manage a property development; see also *Sintra Homes Ltd. v. Beard* [2007] EWHC 3071 (Ch.) and *Murad v. Al Saraj* [2004] EWHC 1235 (Ch.), [332].
[262] [2006] EWHC 53 (Ch.).
[263] Ibid. [59].

Ultimately, the judge correctly identified the case as not fiduciary in nature since one party was not undertaking to act "for or on behalf of" the others.[264] Such contracts would now fit more easily within the intermediate symbiotic category with its own good faith requirements, thus reducing the temptation or need to "shoehorn" them into the fiduciary category.

2. The Requirements of Good Faith in Fiduciary Relationships

The law imposes stringent duties on fiduciaries. While these are often viewed as being distinct from good faith, we argue that they are simply further along the spectrum, demanding a higher standard or intensity of honesty, fair dealing, and fidelity to the contractual purpose. Broadly speaking, the fiduciary must act solely for the benefit of the beneficiary and disregard her personal advantage entirely: [265]

> . . . [t]he essential idea is that a person in such a position is not permitted to use their position for their own private advantage but is required to act unselfishly in what they perceive to be the best interests of their principal.[266]
>
> The various obligations of a fiduciary merely reflect different aspects of his core duties of loyalty and fidelity. Breach of fiduciary obligation, therefore, connotes disloyalty or infidelity.[267]

The fiduciary's obligation to act with the utmost honesty entails "onerous obligations of disclosure."[268] The precise disclosure required depends on the precise nature of the relationship.[269]

The "no profit" rule prevents the fiduciary from making any personal profits from her position to the extent not expressly authorized by the beneficiary. She must account to the beneficiary for any such profit, irrespective of whether

264 Ibid. [60].

265 e.g., directors have a duty to promote the success of their company; Companies Act 2006, s. 172. The Companies Act 2006 codifies certain directors' duties in Ch. 2.

266 *Al Nehayan v. Kent* [2018] EWHC 333 (Comm.), [159].

267 *Bristol and West Building Society v. Mothew* [1998] Ch. 1, 18 (Millett LJ).

268 *Yam Seng* (n 4), [143].

269 e.g., solicitors are required to act with complete honesty toward their clients, which includes making full disclosure of all relevant facts when entering into financial transactions with clients (*Nocton v. Lord Ashburton* [1914] AC 932) and informing their clients of any errors, mistakes, or misconduct on their part and advising the client to obtain independent legal advice where appropriate. Company directors have a duty to act honestly and make full disclosure of relevant matters, which includes declaring any interests and disclosing their own breaches of duty or the breaches of fellow directors if in the best interests of the company (Companies Act 2006, s. 177).

there has been any active wrongdoing by the fiduciary.[270] The "no conflict" rule means that a fiduciary must not, without the beneficiary's consent, place herself in a position where her interests or duties to another party conflict, or potentially may conflict, with her duty to the beneficiary. Further, fiduciaries may not delegate their powers in order to advance their own or a third party's interests. These duties cannot be excluded by agreement.

VI. Further Questions for Consideration

The topic of good faith is a protean one. The scope of this chapter is necessarily limited, to justifying the required good faith attitude, supporting a "humble" role for good faith in English law, and beginning to map out the contours of its taxonomy.

Many questions remain for future consideration. These include:

- How should we classify particular types of contracts, such as supply contracts and partnerships, for the purpose of calibrating the requisite intensity and the concrete demands of the good faith attitude?
- How does the good faith attitude operate at the different stages of the life of a contract: formation, vitiation, performance, and remedies for breach?
- What are the remedial implications of failing to observe good faith?
- How might recognizing good faith facilitate incremental development of contract law on formation, vitiation, performance, and remedies for breach?

VII. Conclusion

We conclude with a summary of our claims:

(1) Contrary to the conventional wisdom, good faith is no stranger to English law; it has been hiding in plain sight. The arguments against expressly recognizing good faith are answerable, while there are compelling justifications in favor of its recognition, primarily because its

[270] e.g., *Keech v. Sandford* (1726) Select Cas Temp King 61; *Regal (Hastings) Ltd. v. Gulliver* [1942] UKHL 1; *Boardman v. Phipps* [1967] 2 AC 46; the Partnership Act 1890, s. 29.

ethical content protects the autonomy-enhancing institution of contract from abuse.

(2) The real question is: what role should a good faith requirement play in the development of English contract law? We reject the "charging bull" model of good faith that would confer a new independent cause of action. We also reject the "relentless woodpecker" model of good faith that would aggressively realign the current law with its perceived demands at the expense of other important policies. Rather, we advocate a humble version of good faith as the "measured tortoise" that explains, organizes, and legitimizes the *current* law, with the potential for cautious incremental development.

(3) Good faith, understood in this way is characterized by six features:
   (i) it is intrinsic to the definition of contracting as an attitude that requires respect for the counterparty and for the contract itself, expressed as demands for: honesty, fair dealing, and fidelity to the contractual purpose;
   (ii) the intensity of the good faith attitude depends on the nature of the contractual relationship; it increases along the identified points along the spectrum of contracts of (1) arm's length, (2) symbiotic, (3) entailing recognized vulnerability and (4) fiduciary;
   (iii) the good faith attitude is externally imposed, and non-excludable, but may also be understood as internally assumed since the parties choose to participate in the activity of contracting to which the good faith attitude (like the objectivity of intentions) is intrinsic;
   (iv) the good faith attitude is consistent with ample scope for freedom of contract and self-interested action;
   (v) it is colored by the social and legal culture through which it is interpreted; and
   (vi) it is episodic, consistent with the cautious incrementalism characteristic of the common law.

(4) We take the first steps[271] toward achieving a better understanding of this "well hidden"[272] principle by mapping the three demands of the good faith attitude (honesty, fair dealing, and fidelity to the contractual purpose) against the four types of contractual relationships (arm's length, symbiotic, entailing recognized vulnerability and fiduciary). The pattern is of a substantial base-level of good faith requirements that apply

[271] More categories and more detailed demands can be identified that map onto our basic taxonomy.
[272] *Abbey Developments Ltd. v. PP Brickwork Ltd.* [2003] EWHC 1987, [148] (Humphrey Lloyd QC).

to all contracts, including arm's length contracts. In the other three categories, the intensification of the good faith attitude is manifested in further requirements calibrated to the nature of the relationship.

It is undeniable that the good faith attitude permeates English contract law; it is time to openly recognize this. While this claim may seem radical, our thesis is in fact deeply conservative. English law should adopt the "measured tortoise" model of good faith which is marked by its continuity with the orthodox case-by-case incrementalism of the common law. The pace of the inevitable incremental developments will depend on political, cultural, and even commercial considerations.[273] We have seen that the good faith "lite" that currently flavors English contract law is so familiar that we are no longer conscious of its presence. It already imposes substantial demands on contract parties. If English law were ready to go further—"half-fat" or even "full-fat"—it will not want for inspiration on the substance from civil law, European law, and international instruments. The humble "measured tortoise" can go far. But it need not do so, and certainly it will be in no hurry.

[273] e.g., when UCTA was passed, many international sales contracts, and contracts to which English law applies only because that is the law chosen by the parties, were specifically exempted; ss. 26, 27.